W9-CAG-579

Geri is a natural at whatever she does. It was a joy to work with her. It's a joy to read this book.

— Ian McShane
(Al Swearengen, *Deadwood*)

Funny, provocative, daring, and yet incredibly inspiring, *I'm Walking As Straight As I Can* took me by surprise — a good surprise. Geri Jewell shows us that all dreams are available to the one who never gives up. What a wonderful ride. This book should be read by everyone!

— Rev. James J. Mellon,
author, *Mental Muscle*

Geri is an amazingly courageous, talented actor. Her view of life is inspirational.

— Lily Tomlin,
comedian and actress

I have known, admired, and adored Geri Jewell since the beginning of her comedy career. She is not only brilliant and funny, she has overcome an impossible obstacle in Hollywood: she's brunette.

— Elayne Boosler, comedian,
writer, and founder of Tails of Joy

Geri Jewell not only is a fabulous comedienne, actress, and motivational speaker, but advocating for people with disabilities has made a difference in the lives of millions. Lord knows she's had an impact on my life! Granted if she could just sit still, I could read her lips once in a while!

— Kathy Buckley,
comedian and actress

I laughed, cried, and then stood up and applauded when I finished reading Geri's book. It's much more than a great read; it's a salute to the human spirit and an inspiration for everyone with a dream.

— Anson Williams,
actor/director (Potsie, *Happy Days*)

I'M WALKING AS STRAIGHT AS I CAN

Transcending Disability in Hollywood and Beyond

GERI JEWELL
with TED NICHELSON

ECW Press

Published by ECW Press, 2120 Queen Street East, Suite 200,
Toronto, Ontario, Canada M4E 1E2
416.694.3348 / info@ecwpress.com

LIBRARY AND ARCHIVES CANADA CATALOGUING IN PUBLICATION

Jewell, Geri, 1956–
I'm walking as straight as I can : transcending disability
in Hollywood and beyond / Geri Jewell ; with Ted Nichelson.

ISBN 978-1-55022-883-0
ALSO ISSUED AS:
978-1-55490-908-7 (PDF); 978-1-55490-975-9 (EPUB)

1. Jewell, Geri, 1956–. 2. Actors with disabilities–United
States–Biography. 3. Comedians with disabilities–United
States–Biography. 4. Cerebral palsied–United States–Biography.
I. Nichelson, Ted II. Title.

PN2287.J55A3 2011   791.4502'8092   C2011-900433-X

Cover image: © Sunny Bak
Editor: Jennifer Hale
Cover and text design: Tania Craan
Typesetting: Mary Bowness
Printing: Edwards Brothers   2   3   4   5

This book is set in Garamond and Electra.

To the best of her ability, the author has recreated experiences, places, people, and organizations
from her memories of them. In order to protect the privacy of others she has, in some instances,
changed the names of certain people and details of events and places.

PRINTED AND BOUND IN THE UNITED STATES

ECW PRESS
ecwpress.com

I dedicate this book to my sister Gloria, who has been there for me time and again. She is not only my sister, but an angel in my path and the wind beneath my wings.

I also dedicate this book to my parents. Without them, I would not have been given the gift of life. Through the lessons and love that they gave me, they will always be in my heart.

CONTENTS

PREFACE

I have wanted to write my autobiography for many years, but it was difficult getting started. For a while, I thought it might be easier to write it as fiction, and so I wrote it as a novel called *The Remarkable Journey of Jenny Gem*. It was going to be a story based on my life. I was about a third of the way along with *Jenny Gem* when I met Ted Nichelson.

Ted and I became acquainted through my friend, Susan Olsen. After discovering that Ted had collaborated on Susan's book, *Love to Love You Bradys*, I asked Ted if he would be interested in helping me with my book. Ted and I had wonderful chemistry, and he had the ability to guide and direct me in a way that brought my real-life story onto the page. I came to trust him completely, telling him what *really happened* in the life of Jenny Gem. I explained to Ted how painful certain things were, and that it was easier to write my story in the third person.

Ted contacted his publisher, ECW Press, and everyone agreed that my book would have a greater impact if it was a first-person memoir. So, the first thing we had to do was dissect my novel, removing everything that was fictional and writing the truth about Geri Jewell.

Ted was a godsend as my writing partner. Although I was confident in my writing skills, I knew nothing about putting together a book proposal. I learned that even the best book in the world is not going to get through the door of a publisher without a good proposal first. Together, Ted and I wrote the proposal for this book. As exciting as it was when Ted's publisher accepted the proposal, it was only the beginning. In the next year, I wrote almost daily, often for six to ten hours at a time.

Working with Ted couldn't have been more perfect. He never once, in all the months that I wrote with him, took my words and made them his. He allowed me to tell my story in my own words, only pointing out the times when he felt I was not clear, or too wordy, or when I needed to write more. The period of false starts was over, and Ted helped me to keep moving forward even when I felt there were some things that were just too painful to write about. Ted believed in me, and reminded me that the most important thing was that I believed in myself and was not afraid to tell the truth.

Because of my spirituality, it was *very* important that I was always aware of my intent. I did not want my book to be a trashy tell-all that could potentially hurt other people, but I had to find a way to write about what some people did that ended up shaping my life. I chose not use everyone's real name because I did not want to hurt family members and friends who are in their lives today.

I believe forgiveness is so important, and what was done to hurt me, whether intentional or not, does not matter. What matters is that all of us learn from our experiences so we can forgive ourselves and move forward. Writing this book healed me in many ways. I have no anger or regrets about the choices I made or anyone else made. If we grow and evolve through our many missteps in life, I believe the pain and suffering are worth it.

I also believe that in order to survive hardship and adversity, we must have a healthy sense of humor about oneself and the world around us. I have incorporated my sense of humor throughout my book, and I hope that the readers enjoy the lightheartedness I use to tell some stories that were quite painful at the time. I could not have written this book without my sense of humor — I would have given up years ago, and the stories that I held in my heart and mind would have never made it to print.

I truly hope you enjoy reading about the journey that I have taken in life. I was born with cerebral palsy, but I can only be a victim of it if I choose to be. I have been very blessed in life, and I don't take anything for granted, including having this opportunity to tell my own story through my own words.

— Geri Jewell, January 2011

FOREWORD

Dear Reader,

I beg your indulgence as I send a long overdue valentine to Geri Jewell:

Geri, who'd have thought our connection would be so profound? When we met more than 30 years ago, all we had in common was our fear of performing live on Norman Lear's television special, *I Love Liberty.* We were good celebrities inviting our fellow citizens to fully participate in our beloved democracy. As is our way, we cheered each other on.

How could we ever have guessed that in the ensuing years, we'd be living damn near parallel lives? Besides striving to keep our careers afloat, we've shadow boxed with our respective disabilities, your cerebral palsy and my bipolar disorder. We're a pair, all right. In reading *I'm Walking as Straight as I Can*, I couldn't help but shake my head again and again as I came to know how many demons we had in common and above all, that any other human being could rival me in the insecurity department. Oh my dear!

But let me not dwell on painful histories, for we don't live there anymore. Let us, together, invite your readers to share in the bounty borne of endurance and cock-eyed optimism. Your willingness — indeed, your eagerness — to share your road "less traveled," demonstrates the generosity of your spirit, your sense of humor, that is just irreverent and divine. The following pages of this book are less about disability and more about learning to identify and accept the good fortune that is yours.

Congratulations, dear friend. Thank you for the insights and, of course, for the healing laughter you bring to your fellow travelers.

Thank you, too, dear Reader. Enjoy!

— Anna Patty Duke

CHAPTER ONE

Buffalo, Wings, and a Prayer

It was a warm day on September 12, 1956. My mom was relaxing on the front porch, reading, when a car lost control, going too fast around the corner. The car hit the maple tree on our lawn, smashed into the front porch, and threw Mom into the air. She landed on the front lawn, bleeding and in pain. Our neighbor had seen the whole thing from her bay window. She was horrified, knowing that Mom was six months pregnant with me.

In 1956, my parents, Jack and Olga Jewell, had been married for 12 years and had two sons, David and Fred. Mom and Dad came from large families, and when they found out my mother was expecting another child, the whole family was excited. My brothers were hoping for another brother, but Mom knew instinctively that the next child would be a girl. Dad was employed by DuPont in Cheektowaga, New York, where they lived, and worked hard to put food on the table. He was a little worried about finances, but Mom had tremendous faith in God and believed that where there's a will, there's a way. She had no idea that this would be no ordinary pregnancy.

The story of my birth has been told by family members over and over again, and, to be honest, I have become bored with the retelling of it. Not that it was a boring event in itself, only that I have told it so many times that I sound like a broken record. (For those of you who are too young to know what a broken record sounds like, consider that a small blessing.)

My mother was rushed to the Sisters Hospital in Buffalo, where doctors frantically tried to save her life. She was hemorrhaging, and my parents were sadly informed that Mom had lost her baby. Mom was screaming that they were wrong — she knew that I was alive even though the doctors didn't. They explained to her that there was no indication of a heartbeat, and that they would have to do a Caesarean section. "We must remove the baby in order to save your own life at this point."

Mom had lost a lot of blood and suffered great trauma. They explained to my dad that it could be a very long night, as they had to stabilize my mom before they could perform surgery to remove me. My dad's sister, my Aunt Gerry, was in the waiting room with him, and she reassured him that it wasn't over yet — she told him not to give up. The following morning, after a tremendous effort in stabilizing Mom, the doctors were finally ready to perform surgery. However, the only thing that ended up being aborted was the surgery itself. In the process of prepping for surgery, a tiny miracle was born! On the morning of September 13 at 8:34 a.m., I came into the world with a faint heartbeat, weighing just less than three pounds.

Mom was crying, saying through her tears, "I told you she was alive!" Doctors immediately informed Dad that his wife was going to make it, and that he was the father of a baby girl. He hugged Aunt Gerry, realizing that she had been right. I was placed in an incubator, going from a womb without a view to a room with nothing but windows! My parents couldn't think of a name for me, so for the time being, I was only known as "Precious Jewell." In 1956 babies that tiny rarely lived, so the moniker was fitting and soon caught on with everyone. "Precious Jewell in the Glass Case" made the morning paper, announcing that at that time, I was the tiniest baby who survived at that hospital. That was my very first press release.

When most babies come into the world, they find the reassuring comfort of being held in their mother's arms, being fed and cared for. I always wondered what it must have felt like for me living within a heated glass enclosure for the first three months of my life. I have seen pictures of me inside the incubator with one leg propped up on the thermometer. Perhaps I was content; after all, what did I have to compare it to? It was all I knew.

One morning at 4 a.m. my parents were awakened by the shrill ring of the phone. They immediately went into a panic, knowing intuitively that something was wrong, and expected the worst. Somehow I had managed to get pneumonia, and I was not expected to survive the night. A nurse told my parents it was imperative that I be baptized immediately. "We have contacted the parish priest," she said, "and he will be waiting for your arrival." Mom notified my godparents, Aunt Gerry and Uncle Russell, so they could be present for my baptism. Soon everyone was gathered around me, praying for my life but knowing that I might not live to see daybreak.

I obviously lived but was unable to keep any formula down until a doctor decided to give me some mashed banana, mainly for the potassium and weight gain. It could have been a combination of everything that gave me the strength needed to survive: between the Jewish doctor who had donated his blood for my transfusion, the Hindu nurse who watched over me, and the Catholic priest who performed my baptism, it seemed I had many faiths rooting for me! I was finally named Geraldine Ann Jewell, but "Precious Jewell" remained on my incubator. Aunt Gerry always thought I was named after her, but Mom had named me after Saint Gerard, the sacred saint of life, because I fought for my life coming into the world. "Geraldine" was as close to "Gerard" as Mom could get without it sounding butch. Aunt Gerry couldn't have been more pleased that I was named after her, and my parents were not about to spoil that pleasure for her. My name was always spelled Gerry until I personally changed the spelling in the ninth grade to Geri.

At three months, I finally weighed in at seven pounds, and my parents were notified. "Come get her quickly, before she loses any weight!" When my parents brought me home, it was a huge celebration. I was the size of a doll, and my brothers were amazed that they could hold me with one hand! Our German shepherd, Kim, intuitively took her post as my protector, standing guard over the bassinet and watching me intently. This made Dad nervous.

"Get Kim away from the baby!" he said.

"Dad, Kim's not going to hurt her!" David protested. Nevertheless, Dad ordered Kim to come over to him, but she refused. She just gave Dad a doggy dirty look and lay down under my bassinet. Everyone agreed, Kim was *very* protective of this precious jewel.

Once, when Aunt Gerry babysat me, Kim wouldn't let her near me. My family backed down the driveway in their dark green 1955 Chevrolet station wagon, leaving the three of us alone. When Aunt Gerry went to pick me up, to her surprise and frustration, Kim wouldn't budge and actually growled at her! There was no way Kim was going to leave her post. My aunt was wily, though: she threw a bone down the basement stairs and locked Kim down there. As much as Kim loved me, dogs will be dogs. She ran after it and felt duped. When she was finally let back in, she ran faster than Rin Tin Tin, right back to my side. Kim adored me, and at night she was always curled up on the floor, watching over me like a guardian angel.

The entire first year of my life was jotted down in a steno pad. Every movement, mood, and *bowel movement* was painstakingly kept in a journal by Mom. I was being monitored closely, just in case my health took a turn for the worse. Mom didn't mind doing this at all. In fact, by observing me so closely, she became aware that something wasn't right with me. Dad sometimes became impatient with her very detailed account of everything and felt at times that she was *looking* for problems that didn't exist. "My God, Olga, you're so bent on every single detail, you'd think this steno pad belonged to a detective working on an unsolved murder!" Mom just ignored him most of the time, but it did create some tension between the two of them.

As much as Mom wanted to believe that everything was all right, she couldn't shake the feeling that I was different. As the months went by, Mom became more and more convinced that something wasn't right. She kept comparing me to what my brothers had done at the same age, and even though her pediatrician kept assuring her that I was normal, that not every baby does everything at the same time, Mom was not convinced. She took me to two other doctors, seeking second and third opinions. One sleepless night, she woke up my dad, telling him that she believed that I had cerebral palsy. Dad didn't think he had heard her correctly, but she repeated the same words with equal conviction in her voice.

The following morning, Mom brought up the subject again. "Jack, we need to talk about Geri. She is not progressing normally."

"Olga . . . the doctors say she is fine, just a little slower."

"Jack, I don't care what the doctors say. They don't see her day in and day out. They see her once a month for about thirty minutes!"

He cut her off, waving his arms. "And they are the *doctors*! Did *you* go to Harvard?"

"Jack, I know Geri has cerebral palsy. David started crawling at six and a half months, and Fred was crawling by eight months. Geri hasn't even tried to crawl yet, and she's almost a year old!"

"What makes you believe that she has cerebral palsy? I mean, there are other conditions that it could be as well."

"Do you remember when I took that job in Maine for the summer, as a nanny?"

"Well, yes, but what does that . . . ?"

"Jack, they had a twelve-year-old daughter with cerebral palsy. Her mother, Anna, gave me a crash course on cerebral palsy. She wanted me to fully understand Ann's condition, so that I could be more able to care for her properly."

Dad was stunned, not least because the girl's name was Ann and that is my middle name. "Did you name Geri after this other child?" Mom admitted that, in fact, she had. She loved the Turner family and wanted to pay tribute to Ann. Dad had always assumed I was named after his mother, Anna Jewell.

Naming me was one thing, but Dad was beginning to understand that Mom's intuition wasn't something to be ignored, so they promptly made an appointment with a specialist in downtown Buffalo. The doctor there was the first to agree with Mom. After examining me, he believed that there was definitely something not right developmentally. In fact, he even suggested that they give me up before they become too attached. "What?!" Mom was stunned, to say the least. "She will be a year old next month! It's a little late to not get attached, don't you think?"

"Listen, I know you think I am being cruel to suggest giving her up, but believe me, it is the best thing for you and the child." The doctor had been through this routine time and again and was used to this reaction; he felt with absolute conviction that it was the right thing to do, to spare families of any further grief down the road.

Mom was furious. "Well, does she or does she not have cerebral palsy?"

"We will have to run some tests to find out conclusively. However, I have seen babies like this before, and I can tell you that most likely she will never be able to walk, and she probably has mental retardation. It is my professional opinion that these babies are much better cared for in state institutions. They have qualified staff who give the absolute best care possible to these unfortunate children. I assure you that the pain of giving up your daughter at this point is nothing compared to the future heartache and financial burdens these babies ultimately come into the world with."

Dad was beside himself. "The only financial burden we have right now is paying your astronomically high specialist fee! What is your specialty, doctor? Is your degree in Insensitive, Stupid, and Assholiness training?"

"I understand your anger, Mr. Jewell, but I know what I'm talking about."

As far as my parents were concerned, regardless of what diagnosis I was given, they would absolutely never hand me over to the state. Mom believed that I was put into their lives for a reason, and it was their responsibility to care for me. She understood that it might not be the option for everyone, but in her heart of hearts she knew she couldn't live with herself if she did anything other than provide a loving home for me. "No one's going to rip this family apart. If anyone should try, they're going to have to get past Kim first!" Not another word was ever said about giving me away. End of story.

My parents were so frustrated and overwhelmed. They went to at least six doctors over the following year, seeking second, third, and fourth opinions and getting nowhere, or so it seemed. She decided to call Anna Turner. The Turners knew Mom now had a daughter, but Mom didn't want to worry them with her own concerns. Now it finally occurred to her what a valuable resource they might be. After all, they had been through this whole ordeal with their daughter. Mom had a lot of anxiety about calling them but didn't know where else to turn. She felt better simply by hearing the lovely calm voice of Anna Turner on the other end of the line. "Hello?"

"Anna, it's Olga."

"Oh, how wonderful to hear from you! I haven't gotten a letter from you in quite some time. Is everything all right, dear?"

"Well, truthfully, I'm calling because I need some advice."

"Oh? About what?"

"It's about Geri. Anna, I don't mean to upset you, but I think Geri has cerebral palsy just like Ann." There was a deep silence. "Anna, did you hear what I just said?"

"Yes, of course I did, child. I have been waiting for this call."

Mom's eyes welled up with tears. "What do you mean?"

"Ever since we heard about Geri's traumatic birth, her lack of oxygen, we believed that there might be further consequences down the road, but it wasn't our place to raise these concerns. If everything had turned out okay, then we would have worried you needlessly. You had to be the one to mention it first."

"Oh, Anna, it has been a nightmare. She is almost a year old, and she can't even sit up on her own yet! And the doctors! Last week we were told it was best to give Geri to the state, to have her institutionalized!" Anna wasn't the least bit surprised, as she was told the same thing 22 years earlier. She asked Mom how my dad felt about the situation. Mom explained that, although he became short-tempered at times, he was not about to give me up. However, they didn't know where to turn or where the best-qualified help was. "She hasn't even been officially diagnosed yet," Mom explained. Anna was a no-nonsense type of person and didn't waste any time pointing Mom in the right direction.

She suggested that she call the March of Dimes Foundation. Mom was surprised, as she had always thought that their cause was the fight against polio. At one time, that is what the March of Dimes represented. In fact, it was Eddie Cantor who coined the phrase "March of Dimes" as a campaign in theaters to raise money to help the fight against polio. But by 1956, the March of Dimes had expanded its scope to the prevention and treatment of all birth defects. Mom couldn't thank her friend enough, and Anna told her that she could call her anytime.

Mom called the March of Dimes Foundation in New York City. The woman she spoke with was supportive and didn't once suggest giving me to the state. She explained how crucial it was for me to be diagnosed as quickly as possible so early intervention and therapy could begin immediately. She gave Mom the names of two very good doctors in New York City and said an appointment was well worth the train or plane ride. When Mom hung up, she realized there was some truth in what the first specialist had said: a trip to NYC wasn't in their budget.

When Mom told Dad about her call to the March of Dimes Foundation and how she was directed to these two wonderful doctors in the city, he seemed a bit overwhelmed. His concern was the same as hers. How were they ever going to afford such a trip? The next day, before Mom could even dial one of the New York numbers, the phone rang. It was Anna, who told Mom that she'd just become aware of a fabulous organization called the United Cerebral Palsy Foundation, UCP for short. Some of the best doctors on the forefront of cerebral palsy research were in southern California, making groundbreaking progress with children. Dr. Margaret Jones and Dr. Kenneth Jacques were the forerunners in the field at UCLA. "You must take Geri to California!" exclaimed Anna. Mom could only laugh. "What is so funny, Olga?"

"Oh Anna, Jack is going to lose his mind!"

"Well, let him lose his mind, dear. You take that baby to California, I tell you!"

"But . . ."

"No buts about it!" Mom knew Anna was right, and whatever the cost, they would find the money somehow.

The time came to tell the boys about the trip to California and that their baby sister might have cerebral palsy. The whole family sat down for dinner, which always began with a prayer, and thanked the Lord for their meals, which tonight was Hungarian goulash and Buffalo wings. Dad told the boys that their mother and sister were going to take a trip to California to see some doctors there who would help their little sister. Fred didn't quite understand. "Is she sick, Daddy?" David punched his younger brother in the arm.

"No, she is not sick," my dad calmly explained, "but she has some kind of a disability." Although David and Fred had already heard the term cerebral palsy" one night when they were lying awake, this was one meal of

Hungarian goulash and Buffalo wings the boys would remember for a long time to come.

As much as Mom wanted to get on a plane the next morning, she knew it was next to impossible. There was so much to do to prepare for such a huge trip. The first thing she had to do was call Dr. Jacques to schedule an appointment for me. To her surprise, Dr. Jacques did not have an opening until February 14th, several months away! "You must be joking. My daughter may have cerebral palsy!" Dr. Jacques' assistant understood Mom's frustration, but unless there was a cancellation, there was really nothing she could do. Mom tried to explain that they were coming all the way from Buffalo, New York.

"Mrs. Jewell, the doctor is seeing children from as far away as Peru. Try not to view this as a delay, but rather as a needed time for preparation." How could this woman possibly know what it felt like for the parent of a baby with a disability? To be told that the doctor couldn't see them for at least six months felt like an eternity.

Then she was hit with another thought. "Are there that many babies with cerebral palsy?"

"I'm afraid there are, Mrs. Jewell, as well as a host of many other disabling conditions."

"What about Dr. Margaret Jones? I was given her name as well."

"Dr. Jones and Dr. Jacques both have about the same length waiting list. Trust me when I say this: there is so much you must accomplish to make this trip as comfortable as you possibly can, for yourself and your child. You must consider where you'll stay, how much to budget for meals, and, after your baby is diagnosed, what therapy programs to begin. Please take this time as a blessing, so that you can plan this trip very carefully, minimizing any surprises." As much as Mom wanted to scream, this woman's logic actually did make sense. She thanked my mom for her patience and scheduled my appointment for Valentine's Day.

The assistant in Los Angeles couldn't have been more correct; there was so much to do. In fact, in the process, Mom convinced Dad that they should actually *move* the entire family to California! So now they were preparing for not one trip, but two. Dad and the boys were going to drive out to California at the end of June, so David and Fred could finish the school year. Fred couldn't have been happier; he was still young enough to welcome the excitement of change. David, on the other hand, wasn't quite as thrilled with the idea. He had been looking forward to starting school in the fall with all his friends. He didn't want to leave his relatives either. Fred tried to convince him how much fun California would be, but there was little that would change this boy's mind. In a way, David left a part of his heart in Buffalo (buried under six feet of snow). This move to California was definitely a sacrifice for his baby sister, but he loved me with all of his heart.

In any case, everyone was going to California, just like Lucy and Ricky. Everything was falling into place, and, as fate would have it, Mom's niece, Diana, had just moved out to California with her newlywed husband, Charlie. Mom asked Diana if she could stay with her for about three months. Diana was thrilled! She missed her relatives after leaving Buffalo. Charlie was in the air force, stationed at Edwards Air Force Base in Lancaster, California. "Aunt Olga, we live in the desert! It is the complete opposite of Buffalo. I'm talking tumbleweeds, cacti, and sand!" Even though Lancaster seemed like another world altogether, it is actually only about 40 miles north of Los Angeles.

It worked out perfectly for everyone, and my parents couldn't express their gratitude enough for Charlie and Diana's willingness to open their home to them. It relieved a lot of stress, knowing that we had a place to stay temporarily. Mom still kept up her steno pad entries that she'd been recording since I came home from the hospital, although now she also kept adding to a checklist of things that needed to be done for the *big* trip to California.

Dad realized that he was probably going to have to walk away from his job security at DuPont. He had been steadily moving up the ladder of job positions; some coworkers even believed that had my father stayed with DuPont, he would have become the CEO. So, in essence, everyone in my family made sacrifices for me. My dad not only was forced to start over for himself, but for his entire family of five. The process of finding employment in California, giving up a home that he had purchased through his G.I. Bill loan, and uprooting every conceivable seed that had been planted was quite an undertaking!

They decided to put their home on the market, even though they would probably take a loss on the sale. They didn't have a lot of equity in it, and there was no longer the beautiful maple tree in the center of the lawn. In fact, they found out very quickly that it was too costly to remove the tree altogether, as its roots snarled all over the entire property. The FOR SALE sign was posted next to the huge tree stump, so my mom stuck a potted plant on the stump. (I'm sure *no one* noticed the tree after that, Mom.) There was tremendous stress in the Jewell household, but there was also much hope and anticipation.

We were booked on Pan Am Airlines and arrived in California a couple of days before our appointment with Dr. Jacques. It was a long trip that included a layover in Chicago, with us finally landing in Los Angeles around midnight. Diana and Charlie were at the airport to greet us. I actually slept for the entire car ride from the airport to Lancaster. Diana mentioned what a wonderful, good baby I was. Mom laughed, saying, "Most of the time." She explained that I was probably just coming down from a sugar rush, that all I had to eat on the plane were cherry Life Savers. How symbolic that cherry Life Savers kept my little tummy filled on this lifesaving trip across the country . . . especially considering that what would follow wasn't always going to be a bowl full of cherries.

Mom and Diana stayed up for a while visiting. Diana was thrilled to have her Aunt Olga staying with her. There were not that many neighbors, unless you counted all the jackrabbits that roamed freely. The desert was beautiful though, and as Mom passed the large bay window, she couldn't help but notice the dark sky filled with what looked like a hundred stars. "Wow! Are there always this many stars in the sky?"

Diana explained that it was one of the most mesmerizing and calming aspects of the desert, seeing all the cosmic stars twinkling on a clear night. "You might want to focus on one and make a wish," she said. Mom searched for the brightest star she could see that night and wished for her daughter to get the best possible care she could have. In a way, I already had.

The next morning, Mom carried me into the kitchen where Diana had prepared breakfast for us. Diana couldn't help but notice that I couldn't hold my head up very well. It was obvious to her that even though I was a little past 18 months old, in some ways I was developmentally at the age of six months. Mom explained that yes, I was delayed, but that with the right doctors and therapies, I would catch up. Like most people, Diana had never heard of cerebral palsy before and hadn't quite known what to expect. Frankly, there is no way to totally prepare for seeing an 18-month-old baby developmentally equivalent to a six-month-old. Diana couldn't hide her pain at seeing my head still bobbing like an infant's.

Mom had grown accustomed to receiving shocked responses from family members, friends, and even total strangers. But sometimes, my sunny smile actually put others at ease instantly. In the face of everything, I was a happy baby. This was something that inspired Mom daily. The strong front that

Mom showed the world was genuine, but she was only human, and sometimes she did cry herself to sleep, praying that God would keep showing her the way. It was now February 12, with my long anticipated doctor appointment two days away. Charlie had arranged to take the day off so he could drive us there himself.

It was a clear windy morning in the desert that day. The sand swirled, and tumbleweed sometimes crossed our path, but there were no major delays. The beautiful scenic drive against the backdrop of the purple sky took a little more than an hour. Finding a parking space proved somewhat challenging, although it was free — unlike in medical parking structures today, which demand a week's salary for an hour's stay.

When we entered Dr. Jacques' waiting room, there were at least three other children who hadn't been seen yet. We signed in and waited. Finally, just before noon, my name was called. Dr. Kenneth Jacques was a soft-spoken man in his mid-forties. He took his time to ask a lot of questions. He finally said the words that Mom had been waiting to hear, "Geraldine definitely has cerebral palsy. In fact, if you don't mind, I would like to officially diagnose her at a symposium later on this afternoon at UCLA."

The symposium was attended by 300 medical students. At 2:30 p.m. I sat on top of a table, strapped in a little chair, and showed all the classic symptoms of cerebral palsy. I was diagnosed before an attentive audience — that was my first stage appearance. I was unaware of the seriousness of my first performance and pretty much laughed and giggled the entire time, to the delight of my audience. I didn't get a standing ovation, but there was applause as Dr. Jacques acknowledged Mom's willingness to have me diagnosed for them that afternoon. I'm sure I mistook the applause for my own performance, and if I could have taken a bow, I'm sure I would have.

I was diagnosed with having a combination of athetoid, ataxia, and spastic cerebral palsy. Even though Mom had suspected this was the case all along, it was nevertheless painful to hear it so clearly. These words carried a lot of weight; I now had a label. There was a sense of relief that I was finally diagnosed, but there was also a sharp pang. There were so many questions with no immediate answers. Would I develop speech soon? Would I be able to sit up on my own? Would I learn how to walk? All these questions and many others raced through Mom's mind. Dr. Jacques had the same answer for all of them: "We will have to wait and see."

The fact that I was diagnosed so young was a blessing. It gave me a gigantic head start in getting the intervention and therapies that I would inevitably need throughout my lifetime. The earlier the issues are addressed, the more likely they can be worked with. Some of us will never have speech or be able to walk because of the extent of the injury to the brain. But even in these cases, early intervention will still make a difference. My parents always said that if they had to do it again, they would. Diagnosis was just the beginning of a long process that was challenging every step of the way. No family can ever remain the same after having a "special needs" child. The entire family dynamic changes forever.

Diagnosis is just the beginning. Once the reality sets in, there is the heartbreak that every parent must feel after discovering that their baby will never be normal. There is the unspoken guilt that transpires, where the parents believe it is somehow their fault the child has a disability. If there are siblings involved, there is even more guilt to contend with. Does the child with the disability pick up on the guilt as well? I think so, but I also believe that with so much focus revolving around the physical achievement, however big or small, becomes a priority over emotional developments that inadvertently are put on the back burner.

After my stage debut at UCLA, Mom took me to Los Angeles twice a week to have physical and occupational therapy. We would board the train to L.A. in Lancaster at 6 a.m. every Tuesday and Thursday. Then we'd catch a cab to UCLA. Mom always stayed with the therapists, observing and learning how she could assist me. Each day I made a little more progress in developing my motor skills. I worked hard, fighting against the spastic and involuntary movements that oftentimes kept me awake at night. Falling asleep was never something that came easily to me. My right arm would always be flinging from one position to another, as if it had a mind of its own. No matter how tired I was, my arm was "awake." This was challenging because I worked so hard and tired quickly.

The therapy kept both Mom and me busy, and the excitement that our family would be back together again very soon kept us going.

CHAPTER TWO

A New Life Out West

The boys were out of school, and the day had finally arrived for them to leave on their *big* trip across the country. Dad, my Uncle Ed, the boys, and Kim all piled into Dad's 1955 black two-door Chevrolet Handyman station wagon. Luggage was piled sky-high on top, with the rest of their belongings being transported by a moving truck. Our home with the maple tree stump finally sold; everyone was ready to join Mom and me in California. Dad and Ed took turns driving, enjoying the scenic trek across the country. Most nights they slept in the car or camped out, although a couple of nights they stayed at a YMCA. My brothers collected various two-cent postcards, capturing all the landmarks they traveled past.

They saw the Great Lakes, the Ozarks, and pretty much all of the old famous Route 60. My brothers got a kick out of seeing real Native American reservations and tepees. The average price of gasoline in 1958 was 14 to 19 cents per gallon. The trip captured a slice of Americana when life was still considered as simple and wholesome as apple pie. David insists that they even traveled through a small town that looked exactly like Mayberry! He remembers the pop machines, being able to get an ice-cold cream soda for a nickel, and Black Jack gum for four cents. My brothers missed Mom and me, but this cross-country trek was so much fun, they weren't in the greatest hurry to get to Lancaster.

After eight days of zigzagging across the country, the guys finally reached the California border. In about five hours, they would be arriving in Lancaster. It was a beautiful day but very windy. When the Santa Ana winds are not whipping up some firestorm disaster, there is a rare beauty to the smell and feel of these winds. I always loved them as a kid. Even when their strength would knock me off balance, I laughed and tried to get back up again. Kim didn't quite know what to make of them. She stuck her head out the car's back window and barked at the invisible force. When they pulled into a service station about 20 miles south of Lancaster, my brothers walked Kim so she could pee, but she barked at the wind the entire time. Dad was hoping Kim would eventually calm down, but he also knew that this was a whole new experience for her, and that it may take her a while to get used to this climate. He had to get used to it as well; I'm sure that deep in his psyche, he felt like barking once in a while too!

The last 20 miles into Lancaster reminded Fred of the Old West, and he kept expecting to see some cowboys and Indians. David kind of scoffed at his little brother's excitement. "There were probably real cowboys and Indians over a hundred years ago! But the only cowboys and Indians we're gonna see out here are actors!" At the time, Fess Parker's *Davy Crockett* was the craze for millions of kids across America, and Fred had a raccoon tail hat. As they drove into Palmdale-Lancaster, the 103-degree heat was scorching. They pulled into Charlie and Diana's small driveway, lined with boulders and cactus plants, and the front door flung open. They were greeted by everyone. There were a lot of hugs, kisses, and tears. My mom held me high in her arms so I wouldn't get trampled. Diana grabbed me so Mom could hug my brothers.

The next morning, Diana and Mom were up early. Dad knew that he needed to be educated more about my therapy, so he drove Mom and me to UCLA to see for himself what I was doing. Dad was truly amazed at how hard I worked. He also noticed the other children with cerebral palsy who were receiving therapy as well. It actually bought tears to his eyes, seeing these beautiful, innocent babies struggling so hard, while their bodies seemed to have no navigation. How could God allow such pain?

Even my father's strong John Wayne persona couldn't belie his sadness. As he looked closer, though, he became aware of something that his own pain hadn't previously allowed him to see. Through the entire struggle, these children were not unhappy, especially me. I was cheerful, cooing and gig-gling with joy that my daddy was there watching me. From a very early age, I was a people pleaser, wanting to perform my best and make others proud of my accomplishments. Like most children, my daddy's approval meant the world to me, and it was always something I strived for.

For the next month, Dad diligently sought work, filling out one appli-cation after another. The boys and Kim enjoyed playing in the desert, building forts out of small boulders, scraps of wood, and tumbleweed. The tiny house in Lancaster was a bit cramped, and we soon moved to Long

Beach. Dad managed to secure a temporary job as a cook at one of the hotels in downtown L.A. He was a good cook, and even though it was hardly what he envisioned himself doing, he knew he had a responsibility to provide for his family. He was hired because he had been a cook during his tour of duty in the navy. However, he was not a short-order cook for long; he knew this job wasn't his true calling.

Soon we got some very exciting news. On August 1, there was an opening in a very progressive school for children with cerebral palsy. I was immediately accepted into the program, which was taught by Ms. Hazel Olds and was in Long Beach. I was finally going to get aggressive therapy five days a week, along with intensive academic schooling provided by Ms. Olds. Dad managed to find a small two-bedroom apartment on Ohio Street. Everyone was getting ready to make the next big move, except Kim. One night, as Diana came into the house, Kim ran out without her leash. Diana called her, but Kim was in sheer delight in what I'm sure she perceived as blissful freedom.

Unfortunately, Kim went from a state of sheer delight into a state of absolute blindness from the fast-approaching headlights of a small truck. Diana was horrified when the vehicle, unable to stop, struck Kim, and hoped against all hope that Kim would survive her severe injuries. My dad carried Kim home, and she died in his arms as tears streamed down my father's cheeks. He knew how devastated everyone was going to be and felt powerless in not being able to save her. Everyone was heartbroken at losing our beloved Kim. Even I was aware of the loss. I had learned to steady my right arm by grasping onto Kim's ear. Kim just moved with me, never pulling away. Even though I was still pretty much nonverbal, David swears that he heard me say, "Where's Kim?"

The move to Long Beach went very smoothly. Everyone welcomed the much needed space and privacy. Besides, Diana had found out that she was pregnant with their first child, my sweet cousin Juliana. Long Beach came just in the nick of time. The little apartment with a round, royal blue stained-glass window in the hallway was a new beginning.

I started attending school with Ms. Olds. The school didn't have any bus transportation, and Mom hadn't applied for a driver's license in California yet. She usually wasn't one to be afraid of anything, but driving in California terrified Mom. So, as it was, I took a cab to and from school. It wasn't exactly a limo, but it might as well have been. I wouldn't have known the difference. Ms. Olds proved to be the greatest influence in my life. She did not believe in babying toddlers just because we had cerebral palsy; she firmly believed that we had to be pushed and had to work hard. If we were spoiled, we would only become lazy and wouldn't have the tools to overcome as much as we could otherwise. She was a drill sergeant, and her school was boot camp.

Hazel Olds was way ahead of her time. She made up her mind to build the strongest possible foundation she could for the first four or five years of our schooling, because after that it was out of her hands. Some parents pulled their children out of her program because they felt Ms. Olds was too hard on her pupils. Mom held the same standard as Ms. Olds, so I was never pulled out, even when I threw an occasional temper tantrum. Five days a week, from nine in the morning until three in the afternoon, I received physical, occupational, and speech therapy and was provided a huge head start academically as well. I loved learning new things and looked forward to going to school each morning. Hazel commented that because I accomplished everything so quickly, she actually had a hard time keeping up with *me*. For the most part, I had a pretty good attitude, except I hated having to use the standing table. It was a wooden work table that I was locked into, forcing me into the standing position. My legs wanted to fly out in every direction, which made standing up difficult. Even when I was harnessed into the sitting chair, my feet were buckled down for the same reason.

Dr. Jacques wanted me to wear braces all the way up my legs, but Mom wouldn't allow that. She wouldn't even compromise with the shorter braces that only went as high as below the knees. My mom was right on the mark with most things regarding my development, but I have always felt she made a mistake here. Had I been allowed to wear the lower leg braces, I would have walked straighter overall. I think my mom's reasoning was twofold. She did not want me to become "brace dependent," and subconsciously she didn't want me to look even more disabled than I was.

Shortly after my second birthday, I was chosen as a poster child for AID, which was an umbrella organization that raised funds for such charities as the Crippled Children's Society, United Cerebral Palsy, and the March of Dimes Foundation (to name a few). From September through December, my picture was in every post office across the nation. In 1958, I was the Shirley Temple of handicapped children. There were several local newspaper articles that featured me and all the wonderful things that were being done for children like me, who went to Ms. Hazel Olds's preschool. Of course, these spots had no monetary value but were another early sign of my future in the public eye. I seemed destined from the very start to become an entertainer.

I hardly led the life of a child star, but there were some psychological similarities between child stars and children with special needs. Child stars tend to view themselves as special, set apart from other children. Special needs children deal with very much the same thing, only they don't get paid for being different. Instead of going to the studio every day and having Louis B. Mayer as a boss, I went to my special school every day and had Ms. Hazel B. Olds as my boss. While child stars were learning their lines, I was learning to walk.

In 1960 I could finally walk by myself. I had spent the last two years getting extensive therapy and schooling from Ms. Olds. By mastering the parallel bars and orthopedic walker, I graduated from the crummy standing table. I only had to wear a protective brown leather and foam helmet, similar to a boxing helmet, for protection.

Home life at this time was good, except that Mom knew intuitively that Dad had to find a job that was more secure, higher paying, and more suitable for his ability and talent. When Dad was a teenager in Buffalo, he used to hang out at the police station and made friends with many of the local officers. At that time, they allowed teenagers to ride along in their patrol cars, giving them a window to experience the life of a police officer. Dad had dreamed about having such a career, but when he returned from serving in the Second World War, he was married, in love with my mom, and had two small boys to think about. For Dad, being a police officer was always a pipe dream.

One morning, Mom showed him an ad in the paper for a job at Westminster Memorial Park and Cemetery.

"What do I know about the cemetery business?"

"Jack, with that Jewell charm and your dashing good looks, you are a born salesman!" Going door to door selling plots and caskets? My dad was aghast at such a profession! That is . . . until he saw how much the starting pay was: $2.25 per hour! Besides, their fourth child was due in four months. My dad knew nothing about the cemetery business, but his charm always got him a long way. After his interview at the cemetery, he was hired.

By this time, the tiny two-bedroom apartment was getting too small. We had acquired two cats, Gunsmoke and Maverick; my brothers were getting bigger; and then my little sister, Gloria Elaine Jewell, was born. We moved to Garden Grove, which was closer to where my dad worked in Westminster. It was a brand new housing development, and we got to see our new two-story, five-bedroom home being built from the ground up. From my perspective, it was like moving into a mansion. The move was a milestone for my parents, who were full of pride and excitement at showing off their new home. Every curtain and bedspread was made by my mom. In fact, until I was in the third grade, Mom made most of the dresses I wore to school.

One of the most exciting things we experienced in moving to Garden Grove was that there were frequent air shows nearby, put on by the U.S. Navy's Blue Angels. We used to sit out on the lawn and watch with awe as the pilots did their magic in the sky. Granted, it was loud, but it never bothered me since I was hearing impaired. However, we did have to tearfully find new homes for Gunsmoke and Maverick because every time the planes flew overhead, both cats would be cowering under someone's bed. I guess there are pros and cons to everything. We gained some fabulous air shows but lost our two kitties. It's not like we could have gone to the air force and said, "Cut that out, you're scaring our cats!"

CHAPTER THREE

Changes, Challenges, and Choices

Nineteen sixty-one was an exciting year. John F. Kennedy was voted into office, which was every Catholic's dream, except my father's, as he was a staunch Republican. We had just moved into our brand new home in Garden Grove, and Dad was thriving in the cemetery business. (Turns out, death is big business!) My brothers were both in high school, and after I graduated from Hazel Olds's program, I was attending school in Santa Ana. At the time, Carl Harvey Elementary was the only school in Orange County that catered to children with special needs. The school was three hours away, so I was the first child to be picked up in the morning, at 6 a.m., and the last child to be dropped off. At age seven, I literally spent as much time on the bus as I did in school — six hours on the bus, six hours in class. Luckily, for two of the three years of my extensive bus travel, I had a sympathetic driver, Mrs. Kay Arden. Kay felt bad that I had to spend so many hours on the bus. After all the other children were dropped off, she always stopped and bought me a cookie and carton of milk. It was our little shared secret.

I missed Ms. Olds but was making new friends at Carl Harvey. My closest friend was Christine Kellogg. Christine had polio and was in a body brace. She wore full leg braces, a torso brace, and a neck brace. Talk about heavy metal! Many special needs children are very bright. Christine was intellectually gifted, and this is what sparked our friendship. Christine and I were at the top of our class academically, so the one thing we both hated was taking naps after lunch. We weren't tired, and we felt naps were a waste of time. Our wish was granted, and while our classmates were resting, Christine and I got to sit out in the hall doing schoolwork together.

There were many children in my school that had learning disabilities as well. So, in each classroom there were always many levels of development going on simultaneously. There were 12 or 13 children per classroom. Those who did not have learning disabilities tended to gravitate toward one another and vice versa. Of course, as in any group of children, there was a pecking order. Previously, I had only been exposed to children with cerebral palsy, and now I was going to school with children who had polio, spina bifida, muscular dystrophy, and autism. I always felt that this was one of the gifts of being in special education: you developed empathy and appreciation for the diversity of all children.

At home on the weekends, I enjoyed playing with my new baby sister, Gloria. I loved her — that was a given — but I was also jealous of her. I had been the baby of the family for so long and now someone had taken my place. I knew that while I was at school, Gloria had my mom's undivided attention. My envy caused me to act out from time to time. One time in particular landed me in *very* hot water. While Gloria was napping, I climbed into the crib with her, with a jar of A&D ointment in tow. I covered the whole top of Gloria's head with it. She looked like one little greaseball with curls. Hiding the evidence, I got out of the crib, washed my hands, and went back into the bedroom to look at my greasy little sister. I called Mom, pretending to be *shocked* at what Gloria had done to *herself*! The only thing that shocked Mom was that I could have been so devious. I was punished by having to kneel in the corner (well, at least she didn't lock me in Ms. Olds's old standing table). Mom knew that I was jealous, but she told me that I had to learn to deal with my feelings, just like all children do.

My third and last year (1964) at Carl Harvey was very painful for many reasons. Dad couldn't afford the mortgage on our big home in Garden Grove. David was not going to graduate from high school and he was moving out at age 17, and I was going to have to say goodbye to my best friend, Christine Kellogg. It was a lot of change in one year, and nobody likes change. We moved to Fullerton, putting me in another school district. My new special education school was Woodcrest. Initially I didn't like going to Woodcrest nearly as much as I enjoyed Carl Harvey, but I soon made new friends and settled into the new environment. However, academically Woodcrest never even came close to the program at Carl Harvey.

The first time my parents took Gloria (who was then six) and me to see our new home in Fullerton, we were both disappointed. We had just come from a two-story five bedroom *mansion* and were moving into a small three-bedroom one-story fixer-upper. We didn't understand why we had to move there; the Jewell finances were never discussed in front of us kids. The only thing that remotely put any kind of a smile on my face was the big orange tree in our new backyard. "Wow, we have our own oranges!"

Not only did we move into a smaller home, but David was moving away to Seattle, Washington. David and Dad never did see eye to eye and fought often. I think in many ways my brother was too sensitive for my dad's macho expectations. David loved to draw, act in plays, and sing. Dad wanted him to play football and box. In the end, after David left home, he simply joined the army. As horrible as this choice was during the Vietnam War era, I believe that unconsciously he was hoping this would finally make my dad proud of him. David and I were so close that it crushed me to watch my oldest brother leave.

I was also breaking David's heart, holding onto his leg, begging him not to go. "Geri, stop it . . . I have to go. I can't live under the same roof with him!" I had known this for years, but I couldn't help feeling that he was abandoning *me*. "You still have Fred and Gloria. Stop being a baby!" I tried to be strong, but David made my world special in many ways, like letting me ride on his handlebars to the fairgrounds in Long Beach, playing all kinds of games with me, and watching television together on Friday nights, eating popcorn. He took the training wheels off my bike when Dad wouldn't allow it and taught me how to ride without them. He even created a magical world of imaginary people who lived under the house. There was the Great Pumpkin, Big George, Zelda the Good Witch, Ichabod, and the Blue Fairy, who lived in David's sapphire ring. I told David that if he left, all the mystical people would be gone, too. "Geri, you know that was a game," he replied. On some level I knew that, but these games filled a gnawing sense of loneliness that I felt. I didn't have any friends in our neighborhood, as I was ridiculed and mimicked by most kids. If the magical people left with David, who would be my companions when Gloria or Fred were off with their friends?

Truthfully, my best friend in the world was Gloria. Gloria loved me, and from the time she was able, she looked out for me. She was three years younger, and had friends of her own, but quite often she allowed me to tag along with her friends. Gloria accepted me unconditionally, even though I did things that were kind of mean. Once, at Disneyland, Gloria was afraid of the Dumbo ride, but I was controlling the car and made it go really high while Gloria screamed for me to bring Dumbo down. Ah, what power I had! Even though I was not always sensitive to Gloria being a wimp, she was almost always sensitive to me. She knew that I experienced the world differently and always tried to be sensitive to those differences. For example, when we played school with our dolls, we always played "special ed." All our dolls had to have one disability or another. We crafted wheelchairs out of shoe boxes and leg braces out of Popsicle sticks and elastic hair bands. A couple of dolls were made blind by pushing their eyeballs deep into the sockets and coloring over them with crayons.

I had tremendous talent in making elaborate tents in the backyard with old blankets, clothespins, and chairs. When Gloria wasn't there to play in the tents with me, I often played by myself. One game I used to play was "Vietnam." I was totally unaware of the true reality of 'Nam; I was only trying to imagine where my brother David was. I had a wild imagination and was able to shut out emotional pain by retreating into a world of make-believe friends.

Mom thoroughly enjoyed her children and was forever thinking of creative ways to make our memories special. For example, one Christmas Eve while Gloria and I were asleep — not dreaming of sugar plums but rather Hostess Cupcakes, Twinkies, and Ding Dongs — Mom and Fred were up late with a Super 8 camera "filming" Santa Claus to prove to Gloria and me that he was real. Yes, Geri, there is a Santa Claus! In Mom's film version, Saint Nick was smoke! That was how he got down the chimney. When the film was developed, Gloria and I watched in awe as the magical smoke swirled around the Christmas tree, while gifts piled higher and higher. The film certainly didn't use high-tech special effects, just Mom off camera, smoking many cigarettes in front of a fan, blowing the smoke in whimsical circles toward the tree. Fred operated the camera, turning it on and off, as one more gift was placed under the tree. This convinced me there was a Santa Claus . . . for longer than I care to admit.

What changed for me psychologically as I got a little older was that I became more acutely aware of how different I was from other children, and I began to compare myself unrealistically to Gloria. I was always watching Gloria with scrutiny, because in my mind, Gloria was normal and I was not. Gloria did nothing herself to perpetuate my low self-esteem; she couldn't have been a more loving sister. But she wasn't teased because of a disability.

After we moved to Fullerton, one of the things that changed for the worse was that the neighborhood kids harassed me almost daily. They mimicked my movements and called me "retard" and "spaz." Their cruelty ate at me. Then, of course, there were adults who reinforced my feelings of shame. I believe that the ignorance and stupidity of an adult can be more harmful and influential than anything another child could do. Because I was still being bussed to another school district, there was again no social setting for building friendships in my own neighborhood. I tried becoming friends with Katherine, a girl who lived down the street from me. We played together once in a while, and I thought I had a best friend like Gloria had in her friend, Janet Tokarz. However, Katherine told me that her mom didn't approve of her playing with me, and if she were caught, she'd get in trouble. One day her mother came storming out of the house, grabbed Katherine, and told her right in front of me that she couldn't play with me. Katherine was torn and could only react with sadness.

After pushing Katherine inside, her mother came back outside and shouted at me, "I told you not to play with my children! Do not play with Katherine anymore! I don't want you touching our property! Go find kids like yourself to play with!" I was absolutely crushed and wished so badly that I could be normal like Gloria. However, I rarely vocalized my sadness because I knew deep down that nobody could do anything about it. It was my shame, and I would find ways to cope. Luckily, my family tried to make my life as normal as they could. Mom ensured that I had a happy childhood and never treated me any differently than she did Gloria. Dad could be a strict disciplinarian, but he adored his little girls, taking us to the beach or the public pool, bike riding, even kite flying. While in Fullerton, we acquired another German shepherd, Kelly, who enjoyed walking to the park with us and on hot summer nights we'd sometimes take her along to Fosters Freeze for ice cream. Both Gloria and I loved it when we got to do these things with our daddy.

Meanwhile, Dad wasn't getting the promotions that his boss had promised him, so Mom was forced to go to work, at the post office as a letter carrier, to supplement Dad's income. Sometimes when Mom had to work on a Saturday, Fred would babysit, and it was a treat when he would take us to 31 Flavors, the ice cream parlor where he worked. Gloria would agree that we had the best brothers in the whole world. But more than anything else, we loved it when Dad took us to work — the cemetery.

I loved playing the organ in the chapel, or walking around the graveyard, reading all the names on the tombstones, wondering what kind of lives these people led and how they had died. I was especially intrigued by the children who had died so young. At school, a lot of my classmates had died, and I mistakenly believed that if you had a disability, you were going to die young. It didn't bother me though, because the pat answer that I always got when one of my friends had died was that they were very special to God, and He wanted to bring them back to Heaven. Secretly I was always hoping that I was special enough for God to want to take me back too, as I didn't fully grasp the concept that CP was not degenerative, and that my lifespan would not be affected by it. Mom used to get so upset whenever she had to break the news to me that one of my classmates had died, but I often ended up comforting her, repeating what I had been told, that it was okay because they were with God now.

One particular Saturday, Dad had told me that I could not play the organ in the chapel, that I had to stay in his office and color. When asked why, he told me that there was an inspection going on, and he didn't want any kids wandering around. It was true, but he failed to mention that there was also a service taking place in the chapel. Thinking I could dodge the inspectors, I sneaked into the chapel, assuming no one would even notice me. Instead of entering from the front, I went in through a stairway in the back, which led directly to the pump organ in the foyer. Once inside, I could play to my heart's content, and nobody would ever know.

However, because of my hearing loss, I was oblivious to the funeral service taking place below so I turned on the organ and started playing one of my favorite songs, "Home on the Range." The mourners were shocked by the music that filled the room from above, and someone finally yelled loud enough to get me to look down. As soon as I realized what I'd done, I knew that I had to get out of there *fast*. I ran down the stairs as quickly as I could and didn't stop until I made it to Dad's office. I sat down at his desk with my coloring book and crayons and pretended I'd been there the whole time. Unfortunately, "Home on the Range" was one of five songs I knew how to play, so he knew the ghostly organist had been me. I was banned from the chapel for a month.

Gloria loved going to work with Dad, too. The day before Veterans Day and Memorial Day, she helped him put flags on the graves of persons who served in the military. One Christmas, my sister and I noticed that some graves had a lot of flowers, wreaths, even small Christmas trees, while other graves had nothing. We began moving stuff around, spreading the decorations more evenly among those graves that seemed forgotten. It was a thoughtful gesture, but Dad said we had to put them back the way they were, that it wasn't for us to be the "Robin Hoods" of the cemetery.

However I felt about Fullerton, it would be my home for the next 13 years. I was able to make some new friends at Woodcrest, but I just didn't know how to make friends in my own neighborhood with kids my own age. There was one boy down the street, Johnny de Vaux, who was my age, and was always sweet. In fact, he rescued me more than once from bullies who were harassing me. For different reasons, we shared a commonality of being misfits. His parents were divorced, and back then, divorce was frowned upon, and kids had to deal with ridicule and prejudice. Had Johnny been a girl, we probably would have played together, but, nevertheless, he always looked out for me.

In truth, I was a tomboy and felt more comfortable playing with the boys. At school, I could always be found on the playground with the boys. I never felt comfortable being a girl. From as far back as I can remember, I wished I had been a boy. Whenever I would go into my world of make-believe, I always chose to be male. I hated wearing dresses, or, God forbid, ribbons or bows. I had to wear dresses to school, and I could never get out of them fast enough after school, changing into my play clothes. Having cerebral palsy was hard, but having to be a girl was even harder in some ways.

In my mind, I was Beaver Cleaver trapped in a girl's body with cerebral palsy. Gloria was completely the opposite, a very feminine little girl who loved ribbons and bows. The stark difference between us was obvious, and on some level it reinforced my feeling of inadequacy. Again, this was nothing that Gloria did to me. It was just that I was always comparing myself to her. She was *perfect* in my mind. Also, whether or not it was because Gloria was a girlie-girl and I wasn't, I secretly believed that somehow I wasn't really totally a girl. I thought perhaps that God changed His mind and made me a girl at the last minute, but left all those little boy feelings in me. What I was unable to comprehend at such a young age was that my sexual orientation was also different from Gloria's; I didn't come to understand that until I was in college. One time when Gloria was on a softball team, I was so jealous, but more because she got to wear a uniform than the fact that she got to play softball. All I wanted was the cool baseball cap and the shoes with cleats.

Gloria often felt bad about me not being able to do the same things as her, but sometimes the situation was reversed. There were a lot of things that I got to do that Gloria couldn't. For instance, Easter Seals financed a summer camp for children with disabilities. I got to go to Camp Paivika in the mountains for two whole weeks. The only reason I got this wonderful privilege that particular summer was because Easter Seals paid for it. Dad and Mom were just making ends meet and couldn't afford to send Gloria to camp, so they tried to compensate in another way, letting her have a "vacation" with our neighbors, the Powers, for the weekend. The Powers were both in their late seventies. Gloria has always said that between Mr. Power passing gas and belching, and having to sit through Kathryn Kuhlman and the *Lawrence Welk Show,* this was no vacation — it was borderline child abuse. My poor sister had a horrible weekend while I was riding horses and making arts and crafts.

If Gloria got a cute bracelet or hair band, I couldn't care less. I didn't want them. I wanted a cap gun or a cast metal race car. Whenever we went to Disneyland, Gloria always opted for a cute little bonnet, whereas I went for the raccoon-tail hat. Gloria and I were as different as night and day in many ways, and as we got older, these differences grew more and more apparent. But Gloria and I always remained close. We loved each other deeply, and that helped because we had to share the same bedroom. Both of us wanted our own bedroom, but until Fred moved out, it wasn't possible.

In the meantime we tolerated each other as roommates. For one, I was a chronic bed-wetter until I was about 12, and I have no doubt that Gloria was sick of the smell of urine. I remember that when we got bunk beds, I was mad that Gloria got the top bunk, but the decision had nothing to do with me having cerebral palsy, it had to do with me wetting the bed. Seriously, how would you feel if your sister peed on you from the upper bunk? Eventually, I came to love the bottom bunk, as I could tuck a blanket underneath the top bunk, all the way around, and pretend I was in a tent in the mountains.

I remember one night when Mom came into our room, it was particularly chaotic. Toys, clothes, even candy wrappers: it looked like a tornado had whipped through our bedroom. Mom was furious and said we would have to spend the whole weekend cleaning our pigsty. After Mom slammed our door, I whispered to Gloria, "We have to clean up this mess right now! If we do it *now*, let's face it, we will have a much better weekend!" But we couldn't make any noise or turn on the light. It was almost 10 p.m., and we were supposed to be in bed. We didn't need to get into any more trouble than we were already in. So, I devised a plan.

We had a little night light by the floor. We quietly looked at each item next to the little night light and then put it in its proper place. It was slow and tedious, but we knew it would improve our current disapproval rating with Mom and Dad. In fact, to speed up the process a little, I invented a little song that we sang *very quietly* over and over again: "We have to get done before Daddy gets home!" And we did. Our room was so immaculate the next morning Mom almost forgot why she was so angry. She was all ready to dole out our punishment, but it was as if she had entered the wrong bedroom! She was amazed that we could have done what we did the night before, especially that we did it so quietly. We told her how sorry we were that we'd let our room get so bad. That afternoon, Mom bought us both bubbles to blow outside, and Dad never found out about the state of our bedroom.

CHAPTER FOUR

Innocence Interrupted

Even though I had cerebral palsy, it didn't really slow me down as a kid. In fact, it probably made me more determined than ever to physically achieve things. I had been conditioned from the age of 18 months to push my body to the limits. I was not afraid of falling, and I did so often. Nothing really serious ever came from my falls, except one time when I was eight. I was still living in Garden Grove at the time. Dad had bought Gloria and me a swing set. One weekend, Mom and Dad took us to Japanese Gardens, an amusement park like SeaWorld. I was awestruck by the bears that could swing so high on a swing that they actually went all the way over the top of the bar, without falling! When I got home I was determined to do it; if a bear could do it, then so could I. Using all my strength and weight, I kept swinging higher and higher until I went over the top just like the bear at Japanese Gardens, and I almost achieved it — until my one hand slipped and I came crashing down to the ground, flat on my face!

I had left a rake lying under the swing set, with the prongs facing up. Dad always told me that if I was going to play with his garden tools, I had to be responsible and put them away before moving onto something else. And did I? Of course not. As my face hit the ground, one of the prongs from the rake had caught my mouth. I knocked out three of my front baby teeth and almost sliced my entire tongue in half! There was blood everywhere, and I was in a state of sheer panic! Without a second to lose, the very first thing I did was put the rake away in the garage, even hosing off the blood. I was more afraid of getting in trouble for leaving the rake out than of losing my tongue.

After the rake was in its proper place, *then* I screamed! I was rushed to the hospital on Mom's lap with David holding one towel after another to my mouth, trying to stop the gushing blood flow. It took 16 stitches to sew my tongue together. I was in the hospital for a whole week (they didn't have

HMOs back then). The doctors were afraid to let me go home right away, because my balance was not the greatest (you're kidding . . .) and they didn't want me to fall and tear all the stitches out of my tongue.

They had to put me under to sew my tongue back together. It was the first time that I was given anesthesia, and my mom became really concerned because I stood up on my hospital bed, hallucinating. She was holding onto me with all her strength, begging the nurses to strap me to the bed. They finally did when they witnessed it for themselves. I was standing up on the mattress, my eyes wide open, screaming, "I gotta hide the rake!" over and over again. When I finally did wake up, Mom asked me if I recalled dreaming about a rake. At that moment, I was extremely grateful that my tongue hurt too much to talk. In fact, I didn't tell anyone the truth about that rake until my adult teeth came in. I figured by that time everyone would be so excited that I had teeth again, how it really happened would no longer be such a big deal.

I was never hospitalized for anything else, other than having my tonsils removed. I was an avid bike rider and mastered the jump rope, which was a part of my physical therapy to help improve my coordination. I loved climbing the monkey bars and used to pretend that I was competing in the Olympics. Physical achievements had always garnered applause, so I was forever trying to improve my personal best.

Aside from learning how to walk, mastering the skateboard was about the most exciting thing that I accomplished physically. All I wanted for my twelfth birthday was a skateboard. My parents had reservations but figured that I would probably just ride it sitting down and grow tired of it quickly. They knew if they didn't get me a skateboard, they'd never hear the end of it, knowing I'd say, "You don't think I can do it!" They didn't want to hurt my self confidence. These decisions were always hard for my parents, but this time the risk paid off.

I not only stood up on it, my skateboard preoccupied much of my playtime. The minute I'd get off the bus, I would run home, change my clothes, and whiz around the neighborhood until I got tired. I even set up obstacle courses on the sidewalk with empty soup and coffee cans. When Mom told my doctor that I was a true athlete on the skateboard, he laughed, thinking that Mom was only wishing that were the case. That is, until she brought me and my skateboard to his office and he witnessed it for himself. Nobody could ever quite wrap their head around how I could do it. On the skateboard, my balance was perfect; without it, CP dictated how well my balance was going to be. The skateboard, and my bike, gave me a sense of freedom that I never had in just walking or running. When I was riding it, I didn't have CP. No kids laughed at me. Somehow my brain shifted gears and allowed me the pleasure of these fast-paced physical activities, which CP normally would dominate. I didn't care *how* I did it; I just did it (long before the Nike slogan).

In some ways, the bike and the skateboard created an escape from the ridicule I encountered from many of the kids in the neighborhood. I can remember begging one bus driver to please drop me off in front of my house, so that I would not have to walk several blocks home. I didn't know it at the time, but he was taking advantage of the fact that I was ambulatory, because by law, a special needs child had to be dropped off at home. He accused me of being lazy, but in truth he was lazy and saving time by not taking me to my doorstep. My reason for not wanting to walk was because without my bike or skateboard to make a fast getaway I had to endure the circle of children who'd mimic me and call me names all the way home.

I continued attending Woodcrest Special until I was 15, so I was still bussed to school. I loved all my friends at Woodcrest, and even today I keep in touch with some of them. However, because we were bussed to school from all over Orange County, it was rare that we got to see each other outside of class like children who live closer together. Even though I had great friends while in school, at home the loneliness would creep in, especially as I was approaching my teen years. As Gloria got older, she would often be off with her friends, and I retreated into my make-believe world, creating stories in my mind, as I rode on my bike for hours on end.

Of course there were my new friends who moved in across the street. June Allen was 16 when I was 12, and although she was old enough for my parents to hire her to babysit Gloria and me, June and I became friends and remain so to this day. June was a lonely teenager, and I was a lonely preteen. I loved visiting her family because in the afternoon they always had freshly baked cookies, popcorn, Scrabble, and I could watch the daytime soap *Dark Shadows*, which I was not allowed to watch at home. When they moved away, I was deeply saddened at losing her.

I still tried to play with Katherine but at the risk of facing the wrath of Katherine's mother: I chose to ride my skateboard and roller skates on the other side of the street. One afternoon while Fred was babysitting, he told me I could ride my bike as long as I didn't go past Katherine's house because if I did I would be out of his view and he wanted to see me at all times. I did as I was told: I proceeded to do a U-turn in Katherine's driveway, to come back down my street. Just as I did the half circle in the driveway, Katherine's mom, Mrs. Bismuth, turned on the street from around the corner. She slowly followed me in her dark green Rambler. I kept pedaling until I was caught between her and a parked car. She leaned out of the window of the car and began screaming at me.

"How many times have I told you to stay off my property? What, you don't understand?" I could only stare at her, mortified that I was being yelled at in front of the whole neighborhood. "Are you *retarded*, Geri?" Up until then, I was only called retarded by other kids, never by an adult. The question reduced me to tears. I lifted my bike onto the sidewalk, and in a moment of CP shame, I walked my bike home. Instead of using the kickstand, I threw my bike to the garage floor and ran into my bedroom, hiding under the bed. Fred heard the bike crash and saw me running into the house. He thought that maybe I had fallen off the bike or something. When he entered my room, all he could see were my shoes sticking out from under the twin bed. He grabbed my ankles and pulled me out. I was hysterical now, screaming for him to leave me alone.

"What is the matter, Geri? What happened?" I blubbered out the whole ugly incident, and said I hated CP and I hated Katherine's mom! Fred did his best to comfort me. He had to rescue me from other kids that tormented me many times over the years, but now an *adult* was tormenting me! He was infuriated. He marched all the way down to Mrs. Bismuth's house and pounded on her front door until she opened it. At age 17 and left in charge of his sisters, Fred wasn't about to let this moron get away with what she just did to me. When "Mrs. Bitchfit" opened the front door, he raised his voice to her, asking her if she was insane. She explained to Fred that she couldn't allow me on her property, because if I fell, it would be a liability. Fred was appalled and continued to yell at her.

"Oh, is that why you chased my sister down the street in your car, because you were afraid she might fall?" She slammed the door in Fred's face, saying that she didn't have to listen to him. Fred brazenly opened the door and called her a bitch and a goddamned idiot!

Mrs. Bismuth was shocked. "I will *not* have that language used in front of my kids!" she yelled back. "Wait until your mother gets home. I will tell her what kind of language came out of your mouth, young man!" Fred didn't care. He knew she was in the wrong, and he could have said a lot worse. Sure enough, as soon as Mom pulled into the driveway, Mrs.

Bismuth came storming into our yard to tell her what horrible language Fred had used in front of her children. However, Mom had already heard what had gone down, as Fred called her ahead of time, letting her know.

Mom was very cool and calm. "I know the whole story, and quite frankly Fred was only looking after his little sister. Maybe he could have found another word to use, but based on the fact that you *followed* Geri on her bike while you were behind the wheel of a *car*, I can't think of a better word for my son to have used. Now, if you will please get off my property . . . and try not to trip, as it could be a liability." Mrs. Bismuth was shocked that Mom didn't see it from her perspective. Before she made it down the driveway, Mom gave her one more thing to think about. "How does it feel to be ordered off someone's property?"

Of course, Fred was reprimanded for using such language, but Mom wasn't about to give any satisfaction to our crazy neighbor. Later that evening when my dad arrived home, Mrs. Bismuth marched right up our driveway again, this time to complain to my dad. Man, was she barking up the wrong tree. My dad told her that he didn't care to engage in any conversation with her, and that whatever occurred, he would stand by his wife, so if she'd already spoken to her, there was nothing further to discuss.

"Do you want to know what your son called me?" she asked haughtily.

Dad laughed and said, "It's probably not half as bad as what I'm going to call you if you keep pressing this!" She turned and huffed home.

The following year was 1969, and I was 13. The Bismuths had finally moved away. Life was good. I learned how to play the organ so well in the chapel that for my birthday Dad and Mom bought me a toy organ to play at home. That year is etched in my psyche for many reasons besides the Bismuths moving. On the morning of June 23, 1969, I poured myself a third bowl of Lucky Charms cereal. Dad had just finished reading the paper and was off to work. When I read the paper, I normally skipped all the important boring stuff and went directly to the comics, but this morning I got the shock of my life. The headline screamed, "Judy Garland Found Dead." I couldn't believe that Dorothy was dead! I read the entire article, perhaps the first newspaper story that I *ever* read from beginning to end. I actually found myself crying like I did when President Kennedy was shot on November 22, 1963, or more recently, when Bobby Kennedy had been assassinated on June 6, 1968.

In the world that extended far beyond my own, these three events earmarked my consciousness. I led a very sheltered life, as most children do who are trapped in a special education environment, which provides a hard shell of protection from the real world. However, some events could still break through that barrier. I didn't fully understand why Garland's death impacted me so greatly, but I was stunned that she didn't live happily ever after like her character Dorothy Gale. Like most American children of the '50s and '60s, I always looked forward to watching *The Wizard of Oz* once a year on CBS. It was a magical tale that gave hope to children, whether they were fighting the Wicked Witch of the West, or the wicked Mrs. Bismuth. Even though there were no tornadoes in Fullerton, there were those Santa Ana winds!

Judy's death was so shocking to me that I was determined to find out what happened to my "hero," so to speak. I began reading up on Judy Garland, and so began my fascination with showbiz. I was surprised that, like me, Judy lived in Lancaster in her early years, auditioning and trying to get roles and singing gigs until she was finally signed to MGM. I started reading anything I could get my hands on that was about celebrities and Hollywood. At 13, I had made up my mind to go into show business. I wasn't sure yet in what capacity, but I had a single-mindedness about it that I rarely wavered from. I read about Fanny Brice, Charlie Chaplin, Fatty Arbuckle, Lucille Ball, and Bob Hope, to name a few. Television had always been an escape for me, and now that I began my quest to understand the people behind the "magic," I unconsciously also began to groom my own psyche to accomplish my goal of becoming an entertainer.

The summer of '69 would continue to rock my world, providing a turbulent springboard into the next era. Like most Americans, I was glued to the television on July 20, watching the moon landing. Wow, what a groovy thing to witness! I loved the idea of walking with no gravity, as I would never fall again! In fact, for Christmas that year, one of my favorite gifts was from Fred — a Skipper doll wearing a NASA space suit!

But the summer wasn't over yet. The world was becoming more and more bizarre. It was an awful lot to process for anyone, much less a child living in a chrysalis state of special education. Even before the historic Woodstock, there was the unforgettable morning of August 7, when the news covered the story of the Manson murders in the sleepy area of L.A. known as Benedict Canyon. Sharon Tate was an *actress*. How could these terrible things be happening to people in the very profession that I intended to enter? I would watch the evening news, trying to make sense of the violence, rioting, and prejudices in the world, but I was too sheltered to fully comprehend the seriousness of what we were going through as a nation.

David was finishing his tour in Vietnam, and Fred followed in his footsteps by also joining the army. (David finally came home in December 1969, and Fred left to begin his tour shortly after that.) Through the evening news with Walter Cronkite, I could imagine but never truly understand what a horrible place my brothers had to be in. I remember the solemnity of Gloria and me going to the store with Mom and buying items for the care packages that we'd prepare with Dad, and writing our letters that were sent weekly to David, and then later to Fred. David saved one letter I wrote in 1969 that he particularly held dear. "Dear David, How are you doing? Please ask your boss if you can come home. We miss you. I have some bad news. Our pool broke down! That's the bad news. Well, I have to go to bed now. Like, Geri." When I read this letter years later, I realize how young I was at 13. The letter reads as though a seven- or eight-year-old wrote it. I was only then beginning to see that the world was not as safe as I had believed, but I also wasn't willing to give up my cream-puff perception of the world. Where was Batman when you needed him?

In the midst of all the upheaval of the summer of '69, there was one field trip that I would remember for the rest of my life. The Crippled Children's Society had sent notices home at the end of the school year: for those who wished to go, they were going to bus 20 special needs children to Hollywood to visit Universal Studios. The trip would cost nothing for the parents; only volunteers were needed to help push wheelchairs. I just *had* to go! My brother Fred came along, offering to help. It was his very last outing before joining the army. I was beside myself with excitement. Universal wasn't as commercialized then as it is now. It was more like visiting a movie studio than a theme park. For me, it was a dream come true.

What I remember most about that day was seeing Lucille Ball's dressing room. I actually got up into her big makeup chair, pretending that I was getting ready for a television show. Fred quickly grabbed me out of the chair when he saw an employee heading our way. After all, it was roped off. But that hadn't stopped me. I wanted to feel what it was like to sit in the big chair like Lucy! Had someone told me in 1969 that one day I would be sitting in a makeup chair similar to Lucy's at Universal, I would have laughed. Although, while riding the tram, I commented to Fred that someday I would have my own parking space there too, and sure enough, one day I did.

I pretty much knew what I wanted to do with my life. I wanted to be a comedienne, an actress, and a writer. The only other thing I considered was becoming a nun. I didn't yet realize that there were no disabled nuns.

(Disability is considered a "health" issue by the Vatican, and one has to be "healthy" to serve as a nun.) I figured I stood a better chance at becoming an actress. And that way I could still *play* the role of a nun.

My last year at Woodcrest was as sheltered as usual, and academically I fell behind. It was a shame that I got trapped in the system because I was very intelligent but never pushed in any way. I was also hearing impaired and that was often mistaken for not comprehending or paying attention. I was fitted with hearing aids at 13, but they gave me so much feedback that I hardly ever wore them.

Emotionally, I was younger than my chronological age. My head start with Hazel Olds was torpedoed during my time at Woodcrest Special, there were two exceptions to the rule. First, I was integrated briefly for two hours a day in a regular sixth grade classroom, and second, I was allowed to attend summer school in 1968 at a regular junior high school. However, to my disappointment, I was right back at Woodcrest Special in the fall. I never understood why, and this academic move hurt my self-esteem. In retrospect, I believe it had more to do with government funding than anything I did or didn't do. The more children with special needs that were enrolled at Woodcrest, the more funding they received. I had very little say in my own education, or about what I could or couldn't do.

Also, after my stint at summer school, my teacher had written in my progress report that I was not doing well, and it was better that I be with children like myself. Even though I worked very hard and received two Bs and an A (in English), the teacher felt that it was too difficult for me to keep up with the rest of the class. Furthermore, he said that I ate lunch alone and did not engage socially with the other students. I did speak when I was spoken to, but I did not seek out relationships, preferring to isolate myself by sitting alone and reading. Since when is *reading* considered a problem in the realm of education?

My recollection of that summer is totally different from what that teacher wrote about me. I was proud of myself for completing all of my assignments and was thrilled that I didn't have to take the bus to school. In fact, Dad bought me a brand new lock and chain so that I could ride my bike to school. I couldn't have been happier with my newfound challenges and independence. I even rode home fast enough to catch a brand new soap opera on ABC, *All My Children*. True, I was slow at seeking friendships. I was still quite timid about approaching non-disabled children. But I rarely had lunch *alone*. I often had lunch with Judy Garland or Anne Bancroft, or, on occasion, with Johnny Carson. I wasn't the first child to be as content in a world of make-believe as with real people. I felt that my fantasy world was harmless as long as I finished my schoolwork, and I always did.

Going from the luxury of riding my bike to school back to riding the bus was a cruel joke in my mind. However, there was nothing I could really do about it except surrender and make the best of it. I may have had to give up my bike, but I didn't have to give up fantasizing that the bike was really a motorcycle, and that MGM had taken it away from me. (My bosses at Metro felt that the motorcycle was much too dangerous. So it was back to the stretch limo.)

My last year at Woodcrest ended up being a good one, though. We had a new teacher, Mrs. Snyder. She was very similar to Hazel Olds in that she was a no-nonsense kind of teacher, trying her best to prepare us for entering high school. She also had a child with a disability, so in addition to her degree in Special Education, she had intuitive understanding as a parent of a special needs child. She was a rare gift in her field, and she had a big influence on me. The most valuable question that she asked us was what we wanted to do when we grew up. A few of my classmates were clueless and really didn't think beyond the following week. However, most of us had dreams and aspirations like any other child would.

When we told her what we wanted to be, she created job assignments. Perry, who was a hemophiliac, wanted to become a doctor, hoping to find a cure for his disease so others wouldn't have to live like he did. I wanted to be an actress and a writer. One of my best friends, Steve Hughes, shared my enthusiasm for the arts. Steve and I were given the assignment of writing three plays and putting one on before the end of the school year. For an hour every day, we each worked on our job assignments. Steve and I were given the supply closet, set up as a makeshift office. Our names were taped on the door with black and gold stencils to make it look like an actual office. Mrs. Snyder made room in the little closet for a table, an electric typewriter, a stack of paper, and several bottles of Liquid Paper. Steve and I had to be "at work" at 1 p.m. each day. If we were late, we were fired! I had already made up my mind that we were working for Universal Studios, but of course I had to keep my fantasy to myself. I would never risk explaining my inner dialogue, as I knew people would think I was nuts. What I was doing unconsciously all along was creating a mindset for my future. Regardless of my current circumstances of being a little girl with cerebral palsy, I would someday work in Hollywood!

In fact, it was in this last year at Woodcrest that I began a semi-regular correspondence with Carol Burnett. Like so many other people, I loved Carol. I observed how people loved her, and that they didn't laugh at her, but rather *with her*. I identified with Carol's awkwardness and loved that she made something of herself. Over the next five years, I wrote her around 15 times, sending her poetry and telling her that I wanted to be an actress like her someday.

On one occasion, I wrote to her explaining that I had had an involuntary movement and accidentally dropped her signed photo in the toilet. I tried to blow-dry it, but it was basically ruined. "Could you please send me another one?" She did! Taking the time to write me back meant more than Carol could have possibly ever known. The correspondence reinforced my dream that anything in life is possible.

CHAPTER FIVE

The Highs and Lows
of High School

The first day of high school is exciting for everyone, but having spent my entire school life shuttled to special education, entering the ninth grade had an even greater significance for me. The fall of 1971 was definitely the most exciting time in my life up to that point. I didn't have full inclusion, but half of my classes were mainstreamed. The rest were classes taught by a staff of special educators and aides. At the time, Troy High was the only high school in Orange County, California, that catered to students with special needs. So even though I was leaving Woodcrest Special behind, I was once again going to school with kids that I had grown up with. All the special needs students had the same homeroom at Troy, known as the OH (orthopedically handicapped), Room 509.

Whether we were freshmen, sophomores, juniors, or seniors, we gathered in Room 509 each morning. Our lockers were in there as well. The separation wasn't designed to intentionally segregate us; rather it provided a physical convenience to students with mobility issues. However, I always hated not having a locker on the campus quad like the other students. I was so tired of being different, yet I would always be different, and whether I liked it or not, Troy was going to reflect that truth back to me. Because my brother Fred had graduated from Troy, I thought that I would walk in his footsteps of popularity. But first, I had to learn how to dress!

On the first day of school I wore what looked like a Catholic school uniform, completely adorned with navy blue knee socks and black-and-white saddle shoes. I carried a *Partridge Family* lunch box. When I got to school, I realized that I looked more like a little girl than a teenager. I had to figure out a way to *blend in* a little more effectively. I couldn't do the makeup, platform shoes, or minidresses (nor did I desire to). The only thing that made any sense to me was to go for an androgynous look like the pop icon himself, Mr. Cassidy! (Yes, I'm afraid David Cassidy was my fashion and hair consultant.)

My two favorite classes were, without question, my drama class taught by Mr. Moore and my English class taught by Mrs. Hansen. The classes that I deplored were Adaptive Physical Education and a class called Practical Arts, taught by Mrs. Gartin. Adaptive P.E. was simply insulting for someone who had mastered a skateboard! However, I was not allowed to enroll in a regular girls' P.E. class. (In my senior year I finally got my way, joining a girls' badminton class.) For the life of me, I couldn't find one thing practical about the Practical Arts class, and Mrs. Gartin was worse than Mrs. Bismuth! We couldn't stand each other and to have to be in one of her "special" classes irked me to no end.

However, one of the main objectives of the Practical Arts class was to work on various projects to raise money to go on some fabulous field trips. If there were any perks to being a part of the OH Department, this was definitely one of them. One of the trips we took was to Washington, D.C. It took the students and staff two years to finance the trip, and all 48 students, 12 aides, and six teachers went to Washington in April 1973. Unbeknownst to anyone at the time, my class stepped right into the middle of one of the biggest scandals in American political history. Yes, Watergate. We were all booked at the Howard Johnson Hotel, and I could see the famous Watergate Hotel from my sixth floor hotel room. It was an amazing time in history, and the trip in itself was quite an accomplishment when one stops to consider that high school students with disabilities made a 3,000 mile trip across the country all prior to any ADA law!

The first obstacle to overcome was finding an airline that would accommodate all of us. There was tremendous concern about accommodating that many people with disabilities on *one* flight. Mr. Moss, my favorite teacher, cut the deal with American Airlines. The supervisor explained that it would be a safety hazard. Meaning if the plane should go down, how would they help 48 passengers with disabilities? Moss's answer was that if the plane went down, chances were they would have a hell of a lot more than 48 passengers with disabilities! That cocky answer closed the deal with American.

It was an exciting trip for everyone. We were most excited about meeting President Nixon. The bus pulled up to the White House followed by a small Ryder truck that transported all the wheelchairs. Everyone got off the bus, and the wheelchairs were unloaded from the truck. We were all ready for our exciting tour of the White House and to meet President Nixon. And then . . . the meeting was canceled. For whatever reason, *after* we all assembled on the White House lawn, we were informed that we would not be able to meet with the commander in chief. Not only that, but it was not possible for us to have a tour of the White House either. It could have very well been a "disability issue," meaning that the difficulty of having so many wheelchairs touring the White House at one time suddenly became apparent.

I believe that even if we were unable to tour the White House at the very least, the president could have come out on the lawn and shaken hands with everyone. After all, in a short time my class would all be eligible to vote! But in retrospect, Nixon probably wasn't concerned with any future votes, as his only concern was just finishing this term in office. Furthermore, he probably wasn't able to meet with my class that afternoon because he was busy burning audio tapes.

In any case, we all got back on the bus and went to the Washington Monument instead, for a picnic lunch. In spite of the dark clouds that hung over President Nixon at the time, this particular day in D.C. was absolutely gorgeous; even the cherry blossoms were in full bloom. President Nixon wasn't the only one who was under surveillance at the time, though; I was too. Mrs. Gartin was watching me like a hawk. The group photo that was taken of my class on the White House lawn is proof of that: Mrs. Gartin is strategically standing right next to me, and I'm not smiling. Here I was, my first visit to the White House, and I wasn't smiling! I admit that I was moody and didn't fully grasp the joy of such an incredible event. I was a teenager, and sometimes I acted like one!

I seemed to always be "in trouble" for one thing or another. My classmates played a whopper of a joke on me. A student aide managed to buy two six packs of beer. I was asked if I could hide the beer in my room and to bring it to the "big party" later that night. I was wise enough to ask, "Why me?" but not savvy enough to guess the real answer.

They explained that I would be the last person anyone would suspect to have beer in her room, and because I was ambulatory, I could carry the beer up the stairs, instead of taking the elevator and getting caught. They gave me the room number of the party. I was flattered that they trusted me enough to do this and thrilled that I was invited to their party. I climbed five flights of stairs with a pack of beer in each hand. This was quite a challenge having cerebral palsy. It felt like some kind of physical therapy, coupled with the anxiety of getting caught! I finally made it to the twelfth floor and found the room number. I knocked on the door a couple times, anxiously waiting to get inside with the beer. When the door opened, Mr. Moss was standing in his pajamas. "Oops, wrong room," I muttered and turned away quickly. Moss grabbed my arm before I could get away. He took the beer and escorted me back to my room. Well, at least it wasn't Mrs. Gartin's room. She would have called the attorney general!

Earlier that day, before the beer fiasco, Jay White, one of my classmates who had muscular dystrophy, asked me if I could please spray some "dry shampoo" on his hair and comb it. I didn't understand why he would want to use dry shampoo. He explained that it was because it was so easy. I thought it was disgusting, so I decided to put Jay's head in the sink and use "real shampoo" while Jay insisted it wasn't a good idea. What could be so difficult about washing someone's hair over the sink? What I didn't understand was that once I put Jay's head in the sink, because of the muscular dystrophy, I couldn't lift his head out of the sink! We argued for a while as Jay's face weighed heavily against the soapy wet porcelain sink. I wasn't strong enough to lift his head, so I had to go get help. I called security, hoping that they could lift his head out of the sink and not tell any of the teachers what I'd done. But when security came up to the room, so did Mrs. Gartin. Oh, what a scolding I got this time!

In spite of everything, I still had a wonderful time in D.C., and this trip to the capital was only a prelude to many other trips to Washington, D.C., in the future. Not only would I eventually get that tour of the White House, but I would speak there too.

All teenagers struggle with the growing pains of life, but for a teenager with cerebral palsy, these years can be devastating. Part of my problem was that my expectations were so high. On some level, I thought that attending a regular high school meant that I would be totally accepted with open arms, and that didn't happen. In truth, I didn't have enough social skills to successfully take advantage of the opportunities of inclusion. It was like experiencing the excitement of ski season in Aspen, Colorado, for the very first time, but all you packed was a bathing suit, goggles, and a beach towel.

So, as it was, I swam through high school. I loved my drama class and was cast in the production of *The Teahouse of the August Moon*. I was absolutely thrilled with *Teahouse* as it allowed me to be in a production alongside my "groovy" classmate, Paul McKay. (I had almost as huge a crush on Paul as I had on David Cassidy.) In *Teahouse*, I played the role of an elderly Japanese woman. I only had two lines, but my part in the play was memorable to say the least. My first scene opened with me sitting on top of a real Jeep on stage. During the blackout on opening night, I was so nervous sitting there waiting for the lights to come on, that I had involuntary movement and accidentally kicked the turn signal on the Jeep. So, the first thing the audience became aware of in the pitch darkness of the theater was the flashing green light and clickity click click of the left-hand turn signal. The audience laughed; my teacher, Mr. Moore, didn't.

The next thing that happened was even funnier, but again my teacher wasn't laughing. Explaining my character to his superior, my castmate Tim Prager said, "Don't worry boss, she won't fall off, she's tied on." He then proceeded to shake me, showing that I wouldn't fall off the Jeep. On opening night, he shook me a little too hard, and I fell off the Jeep. I started laughing as Tim quickly adlibbed his next line, "Don't worry boss, she won't fall off again!" The audience laughed hysterically. When you do live shows, anything can happen. As an actor, you are trained to keep moving no matter what. When I fell off the Jeep, one of my thongs (the kind you wear on your feet) fell off my left foot. In the following scene, which was hundreds of miles away from where my character was, it was still lying onstage. Without thinking, I ran out to pick it up right in the middle of a scene I wasn't supposed to be in. Not only did they use a real Jeep in the play, but they also used a real goat. When I fell off the Jeep, the goat peed onstage. There wasn't any time to mop it up until intermission. When I stupidly ran into the next scene to retrieve my shoe, I slipped in the goat pee and went sliding into the right wing! The audience roared.

My next scene got even more unintended laughter. It was a party scene in Okinawa. I had no lines and was only supposed to be dancing slightly (I was an elderly character). I was dancing, totally unaware that my kimono bun had come undone. I was only wearing my bra and panties and was flaunting myself in front of the entire audience! Tim and Paul attempted to cover me up, moving in front of me, trying to block any direct view of me flashing myself.

After the show, Mr. Moore took me aside, scolding me for my infractions, and reminded me never to walk into a scene I was not supposed to be in. "If you drop something onstage, leave it there!" He also explained to always wear something under my kimono just in case something should come undone. He reminded me that *The Teahouse of the August Moon* was not a comedy and said I had somehow turned it into an episode of *I Love Lucy*. I tried not to smile. I accepted my well-deserved criticisms, but I did enjoy the impromptu laugher I had created. Subconsciously, I was already developing my talent as a comedic actress. I always remember my moments in Mr. Moore's drama classes with affection, and many of my classmates would remember me as well. Paul McKay is now my hairdresser, and years later, Tim Prager invited me to London, where he is now living and working as a film writer. He also has a son with cerebral palsy.

Throughout my childhood, I endured countless embarrassing moments. So many that I just had to laugh; it was either that or crawl in a hole of utter humiliation and cry. I believe that every great comedian carries enormous pain, and they learn to make jokes as a way of dealing with adversity. On a very subtle level, comedians try to vanquish the pain of others so that they may never have to feel the pain that they have felt in their own lives. I learned early on that laughter could defuse a potentially painful situation. For as long as I can remember, I've always had a knack for making people laugh. I didn't mind creating the laughter at my own expense, but it was a crushing blow when other children taunted me, mimicking my cerebral palsy.

The most embarrassing "side effect" of CP is when I lose control of my bladder. When this happens, it can be mortifying! Most of the time I wet my pants laughing too hard. I had a wonderful sense of humor (and still do), but it was a blessing and a curse at the same time. I could hardly be angry at those who made me laugh, *but* there were times when it was actually done intentionally, and they would not let up until I was soaking wet! In high school, this happened at least twice a week, if not more often. Even when I was in Washington, D.C., it happened. I was sitting in the restaurant of the Howard Johnson Hotel with several of my friends in a booth. I laughed too hard and peed. The place was crowded, and I didn't know how I could possibly leave without suffering much embarrassment. So I sat in that booth until well after 11 p.m. when I felt that the place was empty enough for me to make a "pee line" to the elevator. When the doors opened, none other than Mr. Moss was standing there grinning. He had been alerted about my situation and came looking for me so he could escort me to my room. He just couldn't help but laugh, and in the brief moment of shared laughter, I forgot how humiliated I was and peed again!

Another time, while I was swimming in the Troy High School pool, I endured another embarrassing moment. I was with many of the students from the OH Department. Aides, teachers, and students were messing around. The teachers and aides would carry a student with a disability on their shoulders, and the object of the game was not to fall off. I got knocked off a couple of times, but I was determined to show my strength and kept getting back on Mr. Moss's shoulders. The third time I got back up, the class started cheering for me. Everyone kept yelling my name and pointing at me. I was so proud of myself, waving my arms in the air . . . until I glanced down and noticed that the top of my bathing suit had fallen off, and I was riding topless! Everyone was shouting for me to go underwater, but being hearing impaired all I could hear was "Geri!" I then kicked Mr. Moss as hard as I could, attempting to break hold of his grip. He thought I was having involuntary movement and held on tighter. He finally looked up, laughed, and promptly let me go. I didn't ever want to come out of the pool! In my mind, I thought of an old *Twilight Zone* episode where two children jump into a lake and enter another world that isn't as painful as the world they actually live in.

One moment will always stick with me as one of my funnier laughing experiences. During my senior year in high school, I needed some extra credit toward my GPA, so I volunteered at a preschool facility run by Lorraine Shaw. The classroom was located at St. Joseph's Catholic Church in Placentia. This was a wonderful experience. I made a great friend (Jane Holler) who was another student volunteer from Troy High School. Lorraine Shaw was not only loved by the preschoolers, but also by us volunteers. She was a beautiful woman inside and out. Supportive and creative, she was a shining light to all.

It was right before the school holiday break in 1974. Christmas lights glimmered and twinkled on many homes and businesses. No, we didn't have the white Christmases that colder climates enjoyed, but we did have the twinkling lights and some rotating Santas waving from rooftops. Lorraine was feeling sad because she couldn't afford a tree that year for the children to decorate. Jane, myself, and the other volunteers decided to have a car wash one Saturday to raise money to buy a Christmas tree for Lorraine's preschool. We got permission from the church to hold it in the parking lot and were allowed to use the hose. Even though it wasn't the holy water that we could get *inside* the church, we nevertheless felt it was just as blessed, as it was going to help raise the money we needed to surprise Lorraine with a Christmas tree.

We arrived in the parking lot early Saturday morning with lots of old towels, buckets, soap, Windex, and vacuums. The church was even generous enough to let us use their extension cords. We displayed a big poster board advertising to all the dirty cars on the road that we would clean them, making them as shiny as the next ornament hanging from the tree that we were trying to raise money to buy. Whatever our gimmick was, it worked. Cars began to pull into the parking lot early. It was so exciting thinking about the gift we were all going to give Lorraine. We charged $1.50 per car to clean it inside and out.

The day was off to a good start, and we all got very wet and soapy. The dirtier the cars, the more fun it became. Everything ran relatively smoothly until about 2:30 that afternoon, when a nun pulled into the lot in her very old red clunker. I didn't know enough about cars to know the year or make of it, but I knew it had to be almost as old as I was! I was also thrilled that I got to wash a nun's car. I pretended that I was a nun and was doing penitent work, and that she was my Mother Superior. All I can say now is that thank God she really wasn't, because what happened next would have probably had me excommunicated from the church.

The first thing I noticed was proof of her vow of poverty. This was the oldest car I had ever seen, and extremely dirty as well. I couldn't wait to show her a beautiful, clean car when she returned. I was a little stunned at all the clutter on the floor and began tossing it, including an empty can of 7Up and candy wrappers. (Nuns eating junk food seemed like a sin, but hey, nobody's perfect!) Next, I began vacuuming. As I vacuumed, I happened to glance up at the ceiling. It looked totally filthy, like it had several layers of mucky embedded dirt. I decided to vacuum the ceiling as well. I was curious as to what color it really was underneath all the yellow, brown, and gray layers of whatever it was. As I put the hose to the roof, it sucked off a section of the padding and revealed the bare metal frame beneath it! My heart raced as I wondered what kind of trouble I was going to be in when Mother Superior returned.

There was now a huge gaping hole in her ceiling, and there was no way I could cover it up. Instead of just stopping and letting it go, I decided that if the material sucked off so easily, maybe the best thing to do was to vacuum all of it off. At least then, she might not notice the big hole that was there. I also justified it as getting rid of some serious unholy mucky muck. So off came the rotted padding, revealing nothing but the metal frame. I didn't believe it could get any worse, but it did! Next, I pulled the car up further to the hose. Unfortunately, her car was manual; I took Driver's Ed, but for the life of me, I couldn't remember what exactly a clutch was or what to do with it. All I knew was that when I turned the key, the car bounced and jerked all over the place. It felt as though the car was possessed (*The Exorcist* was the hit movie that year) or had cerebral palsy just like I did!

Now, I was terrified that I had somehow broken her car, as well as stripped her roof off. And then, with the car convulsing all over the place, the situation struck me as insidiously funny. I couldn't stop laughing. It's like that feeling of being totally overwhelmed. You want to cry and laugh at the same time. And . . . I laughed so hard that I peed. The front driver's seat became soaked with urine. Fearing the hour when she would ask me for the keys to her car, I knew I couldn't lie and just hoped to God she was in the Christmas spirit. As she walked toward me, I prayed for mercy.

Her black-and-white habit looked imposing and frightening, and her rosary beads swayed back and forth in the wind as though they had a life of their own. Suddenly, I wished I could be like Sally Field and fly away to some far-off land. The next thing I knew, she was standing right in front of me, requesting her keys and handing me two dollars. Quickly I mentioned there was no charge, that I had accidentally vacuumed her roof off . . . and that I peed in the driver's seat. She glanced at the bare roof, the wet seat, and simply said, "Thank you." I thought for sure she misunderstood and repeated myself. "Never mind, child, your heart was in the right place, and you were honest about it." She then made the sign of the cross and told me that she would pray for me. She got into her old clunker, sat right in my pee, said, "Merry Christmas!" and drove off.

In the end, we raised almost $30, enough for Lorraine's Christmas tree and even had money left over, so we bought some ornaments too. She was overwhelmed that we did this for her, and all of us remember her crying softly.

My years at Troy were enriching in many ways, but it was a continuous game of academic and emotional hopscotch. I had so many gaps in my development. Years of being sheltered in the special education system resulted in difficulty handling all the challenges that come with being a teenager. I realized that I would have to overcome special education and I saw myself as a survivor of that system. All survivors have gaps in their development, whether physical, psychological, emotional, or spiritual. In order to survive, one cannot always be focused on each stage of development at all times. Often I found myself trying, on some level, to fill the holes of my development and, at the same time, appear as "normal" as possible.

In Mrs. Hansen's ninth grade English class, it became quite glaringly obvious that I was not at the ninth grade level. I was able to follow direction well, but processed information differently. Mrs. Hansen was perceptive enough to nip it in the bud, working with me closely and teaching me how to not just read a book, but comprehend *what* I had read, and write about it with clarity. My favorite books were those that were assigned by Mrs. Hansen: *The Grapes of Wrath*, *Up the Down Staircase*, and *Of Mice and Men*. With her guidance and patience, my greatest strength became my ability to write. I will always be grateful for her willingness to work with me.

My experience with Mrs. Hansen was completely new to me: instead of lowering the bar so that I could pass, she expected me to rise to the challenge. Every single one of the teachers who treated me this way impacted my life greatly, creating a little more self-confidence in me each time. However, socially, emotionally, and psychologically, I continued to flounder through high school. Because I had always put my "non-disabled" counterparts on a pedestal, I kept lowering my own self-esteem. This was something that I did to myself, and it became more intense when so many of my peers validated my feelings of inadequacy.

I think I actually went out on two dates in high school, both times with boys whom I had known throughout my childhood, Steve Hughes and Randy Bradley. Like me, they had cerebral palsy, so it was a "familiar" comfort level. Randy and Steve were more like buddies than potential boyfriends. I share a bond with most of the kids I grew up with that's unlike any other bond in my life. We have an unconditional love and acceptance of one another that exceeds any of the superficial boundaries we've created for ourselves.

Troy High School also marked the first time Gloria and I went to the same school. I honestly was a bit envious of her, in my mind, Gloria was perfect and there was no way I could live up to my sister's image. I literally became known as Gloria Jewell's sister. Guys would say, "Wow, you're Gloria's sister! Gloria is beautiful!" These remarks made me proud of her, but tormented me at the same time. In all fairness to my sister, it is always a two-way street. For her, it was not always easy having a sibling with a disability. She once told me, years later, that she had considered trying out for cheerleading while in high school, but didn't because she was afraid it would crush me. She would always try to be sensitive to me and tried to buffer my pain of inadequacy as best she could.

One Christmas in particular, I was feeling really blue that I didn't have a boyfriend like Gloria did. Gloria reached for a small gift under the tree and handed it to me. It was to me from her boyfriend, Richard. I was so surprised, and even more so when I opened it. It was an almost duplicate ring of the one that he had just given Gloria. As inadequate and lonely as I felt at that time, that gift filled my heart with so much joy! For Gloria and Richard to have that much sensitivity for me spoke volumes; my sister was just as beautiful on the inside as she was on the outside. Sometimes, I think Gloria's "disability" is that people are so stunned by her looks, they don't realize what a beautiful heart and mind she has as well.

Chapter Six

Escaping CP Land through TV Land

Sexuality has been a stumbling block for me for as long as I can remember. There was never any open conversation about sexuality at home, and hardly any education in school about sex. I was left mostly with my limited understanding of what "sex" was. Even in the ninth grade, I still believed that you could get pregnant from being kissed. My family was never very demonstrative, and I didn't have many opportunities to date, so my ability to form healthy and accurate conceptions of sexuality was virtually nonexistent.

When I was about 12, I was lying on my parents' bed while Dad was in the bathroom getting ready for work. I opened a drawer next to the bed and found several packets of condoms. I had no idea what they were, so I opened one up out of curiosity. To me, it looked like a very boring balloon. I blew it up, rubbed it in my hair for static cling, and put it up on the wall. I then added two more. I couldn't wait for Dad to come in the room, because I thought this was so funny and that he would laugh. Dad was taken so off guard seeing a display of blown-up condoms on the wall, he didn't know quite what to say. He scolded me for going through his drawers and took the balloons off the wall. I knew that I was not supposed to be going through his drawers, but why was blowing up a few colorless balloons such a big deal?

He told me they weren't balloons, but when I pressed the issue, he wouldn't tell me the truth about what they were. Finally . . . he told me they were big toe warmers that men wear under their socks in the winter. I felt bad that I had wasted three of his big toe warmers. Dad then sat down on the bed and opened up two more, putting one on each big toe. Putting on his socks and shoes, he went to work with a condom on each big toe. When I reminded him years later what he did that day, he couldn't stop laughing. I didn't know what they really were until I was 18.

I do remember seeing one educational film in class about the facts of life. It was shown at the very end of the school day, with very little group discussion afterward. My hearing loss prevented me from making out everything clearly and, like most who are hearing impaired, I filled in the gaps the best I could to make sense of the film. The film was mostly animated, which made it even harder for me to understand.

To say that I didn't fully comprehend the concept of sexuality was an understatement. Did I have questions? Of course I did, but asking questions about anything was very difficult for me. I would be filled with tremendous anxiety, and I have walked away from many conversations kicking myself for not asking the questions I wanted to. In part, I believe that my terror of asking questions came from my deep-seated fear of being perceived as having a mental disability as well. I was called "retarded" so often as a child that a part of me came to believe that I was. My actual intelligence didn't matter; emotionally, I felt as though I had missed the Smart Boat when it had docked.

There were many reasons I had problems with sexuality. There is a myth that people with disabilities are asexual. But much more than that, my issues arose from the fact that I was molested by a friend of the family at 17. It only happened once, but like most survivors of molestation, the pain can sometimes take a lifetime to heal. Because Adam was such a close and trusted friend of my parents, I didn't even know how to comprehend this intimate violation. I felt guilty and, like most children who are molested, I never considered that his actions had nothing to do with anything I'd done.

One night after everyone had gone to bed, Adam made his move. If my dad had not been at work that night, Adam may not have ever done what he did. I tried to keep a "cool" veneer, unable to comprehend what exactly I should do. My mind kept questioning why this was happening; I hadn't even been kissed by a boy yet. This one assault gave way to even further feelings of inadequacy and shame. After getting over the initial shock of being violated, I finally found the courage to leave the house that night. Taking my mom's car, I parked on a nearby street, waiting until I saw my dad coming home from work. I slipped in the door and went to bed knowing I was safe now. I did not tell my parents of the incident until many years later.

In 1999, Adam contacted me via e-mail and apologized, explaining that he had been drunk and hadn't meant to take advantage of me. He had felt guilty about his actions ever since and wished to repair the damage that had occurred. Truthfully, I could not find it in my heart to forgive him at that time because I still hadn't reconciled my own pain. Today, I do forgive him completely and hope sincerely that he has forgiven himself.

For the most part, my high school years were just a series of one adventure after another and I obviously was never "damaged" to the point of being afraid to go after my dreams. In fact, one such adventure involved Mickey Campbell. Mrs. Campbell worked in the OH Department as a teacher's aide, helping any teacher or student that needed her. She was a sheer delight, one of those rare angels put on this earth who make every day a little sunnier than the last. She was "groovy" in every sense of the word. She laughed easily and was compassionate at the same time. Like many students, I would often seek her out when I needed advice, and I became very close to Mickey. She was a lovely woman with snow white hair, and her blue, blue eyes always had an infectious glint. She was everyone's June Cleaver.

One night, several of us students decided to toilet-paper an OH teacher's home. I was a part of this, and so was my friend Pam, one of the student aides. Papering houses was a big fad among teenagers in the '70s, so I was thrilled to be a part of this cool adventure. We all climbed into a van and headed to Sav-On Drugs where we purchased about 40 rolls of toilet paper. On the way to Ms. Burling's home, we decided to swing by Mrs. Campbell's house and kidnap her. It was probably the most out of character thing that she had done in her entire life! Can you imagine June Cleaver papering Donna Reed's house? It was exhilarating throwing rolls of toilet paper into the trees late at night. And, of course, no one ever thought of the mess to be cleaned up in the morning. Just as we were throwing the last roll, we noticed Ms. Burling's car coming around the corner. Everyone dashed to the getaway van. In a panic, I couldn't gauge my movements and ran straight into a pine tree!

The next morning I had a swollen nose and two black eyes. One of my first classes was with Ms. Burling. When she asked how I got the shiners, I couldn't even make eye contact with her. I couldn't lie, though, and told her I ran into a tree on Friday night. Ms. Burling dropped the subject and resumed teaching class. I thought I was off the hook. When the bell rang, Ms. Burling told me I wasn't excused. What I didn't know was that Ms. Burling actually *saw* me run into the tree and was giving me a chance to tell the *whole* truth. I finally admitted that I had papered her home, but couldn't bring myself to mention anyone else who was involved, especially Mrs. Campbell. I simply told her how sorry I was and that I'd never do it again.

I lied. The second time, my friend Pam and I did it alone. I didn't want to do it, but Pam had a very strong influence on me. She *always* seemed to get me in trouble in high school. She convinced me that we should paper Ms. Burling's home again. I went along, and my guilt went with me. After each roll was thrown into the trees, I kept thinking that we should stop. Thankfully, we didn't get too far into it when Ms. Burling and her parents drove up their driveway. Pam and I ran, but then I heard a bloodcurdling scream! I stopped in my tracks. I turned around, going back to the scene of the crime while Pam yelled for me not to.

When I got there, there was a lot of screaming and crying. I started cleaning up the best I could, apologizing to Ms. Burling. Her father came running out of the garage with a pitchfork, wildly removing toilet paper from the trees. I met his anger head-on as he aimed the pitchfork at me. Ms. Burling frantically grabbed it, trying to calm her father down, saying it was just a teenage prank. She told me to leave, "Now!" and I did.

The following morning I met with Ms. Burling, but I got something far worse than being expelled. What she told me that morning was a lesson I would never forget. She said that she never expected us to do the same thing twice, otherwise she would have explained further after the first time. "First, this is my parents' home, not mine. So, even though the papering was directed at me, my parents felt it was directed at them. I know that everybody is papering houses these days, but it doesn't make it right. I am sorry that my parents reacted as they did, but it was not without a very valid reason. You see, both of my parents lost relatives and friends in Jewish concentration camps in Germany. When you papered their home, psychologically it felt as though they were 'marked.' It is this same horrible feeling that they felt in the Second World War. I know that was not your intent, and rationally they do understand that, but because they were subjected to such horrors in their lives, their psyches will never be the same."

I felt horrible that I had caused such duress and asked if I could apologize to them personally. She insisted that it was better left alone, but that she would let them know how sorry both Pam and I were. I never papered another house and never forgot the lesson.

My years at Troy High were enriching in so many ways. I developed relationships with several teachers: Ms. Burling, Mrs. Hansen, Mrs. Ekedal, Mr. Barnett, and Mr. Moss. Each relationship provided me with tremendous growth and confidence. In fact, I am still close friends with Blaine Moss. Throughout my ups and downs in life, Blaine Moss has always been a constant. Mrs. Ekedal allowed me to be in her girls' badminton class in my senior year. I wasn't any good at the game, but just doing my best was all that was expected of me.

When I think of my high school years, I'd have to say that the forefront image is of the television lineup. It was as if my mind took a detour to TV Land to avoid my inadequacy and an emotional fear of sexuality. *The Waltons, The Brady Bunch, The Partridge Family, Medical Center,* and *The Carol Burnett Show* were all emotional safe havens, creating a sort of fusion in my mind.

In my junior year I ordered four tickets to *The Carol Burnett Show*. The tickets were free, but to me they were worth gold. I was going to meet my idol! The only thing that could have made me more excited was if David Cassidy had been my date. I took three friends with me — two student aides (Lori Medford and Lance Walker) and a friend from the second grade on, Audrey Lang. Although Audrey and I had gone to school together since Carl Harvey School, we never lived near each other. Being bussed to school, you don't have the same after-school socialization that other children experience. So in a sense, going to *The Carol Burnett Show* was really the first thing we did together outside of school. She loved Carol Burnett, so this was an exciting event for both of us. It was a huge undertaking — four teenagers driving from Orange County to Los Angeles and going to Television City, CBS Studios.

As fate would have it, the particular episode being taped is now a classic, the one that included the parody sketch of *Gone With the Wind* in which Carol wore a curtain rod on her shoulders. Because Audrey was a wheelchair user, the usher let us in before everyone else. We had to enter the studio from a different area where there was an elevator. It was the same entrance used by employees, so I actually saw Carol Burnett's huge studio behind the soundstage. It was like walking through Lucille Ball's dressing room at Universal when I was 12. I was walking on air. You can imagine our disappointment when the usher led us to the back of the studio, nowhere near the stage. I was beside myself. Like millions of other Americans I had grown up watching *I Love Lucy*, and I knew I had to pull off a "Lucy" to get a better seat. In my best deaf speech that I could conjure up, I told the usher that I was deaf and needed a front-row seat, so that I could read lips. The ploy worked. The usher moved us up to the front row. I was ecstatic.

My dream of actually meeting Carol Burnett was going to happen. I even brought along a research paper I had written on Carol for my English class. If I could get Carol to autograph it, then perhaps I'd even get a better grade. Oh, this was too good to be true! Then the shining moment: the music started and Carol walked on stage. "Bump up the lights!"

Carol started her familiar banter with the audience, answering questions in a way that only Carol can. I had my hand up, anxiously waiting to be called upon, but it didn't happen. The lights went down, and the show began. I was disappointed. My friends kept telling me to snap out of it and enjoy the show. I tried, but just couldn't let go of missing my *one* chance to talk to Carol. Explaining it to Audrey, I said, "She looked right at me, why didn't she call on me?"

Halfway through the taping, something magical happened. Many times with a show taped in front of a live audience, a sketch may have to be done more than once. In this case, Tim Conway strayed from the script (which Tim did frequently) and had Harvey Korman laughing hysterically. They ended up having to take a break and do the sketch again from the top. In that time, Carol started walking toward me. I was chatting with Audrey, still griping about not being able to talk to Carol. Audrey replied, "Well, you better think of something to say real quickly, because she's coming over here right now!"

Before I could say, "Oh, she is not . . ." Carol extended her hand, introducing herself to me and my friends. "You must be Geri!" I was shocked that Carol knew who I was! But my having cerebral palsy was a hint: I had been writing to Carol fairly regularly and had told her about my disability. She was able to put two and two together and arrived at the correct conclusion. She even thanked me for my poetry that I sent her periodically, saying that she always put my poems up in her office for everyone to see. Carol even signed my research paper, which garnered an A+ grade. If that wasn't enough excitement for one evening, we also shared an elevator ride down with Harvey Korman.

Going to *The Carol Burnett Show* was even more exciting than my high school graduation, but my graduation was also something I would never forget (nor will many other people who were there). It is a milestone for many, and my parents were thrilled that I was graduating. They were a bit apprehensive about my future, but at least I had my high school diploma and a driver's license. The latter was even more remarkable, as Mom had to write our state congressman to make sure that I was not discriminated against in driver's education. I have often marveled at this gift of independence my mom gave me.

When it came time for the senior class to graduate, I got the most delightful surprise of my life. Steve Wayland, a friend from my drama class, asked if he could walk with me in the graduation ceremony. It wasn't an invitation to the senior prom, but it might as well have been. I was walking on air. Steve had asked *me* to walk with him. I did suspect that Mom may have been behind it, as Steve's father worked with her at the post office, but I didn't care one way or the other.

I got dressed in my red cap and gown and felt on top of the world. The graduation took place in the gymnasium at California State University Fullerton across the street from Troy High. This was a generous privilege that Cal State had offered Troy ever since the high school opened in 1966. However, my class of '75 was the last class ever to be granted that opportunity. What we did not only embarrassed the school board and angered Cal State, but garnered an article in the *Orange County Register* the following morning.

As the families excitedly filled the bleachers, the graduating students were outside in the hot early evening, waiting to be signaled in. As with all high school graduations, not everyone was taking it seriously. Some students do, but others just go through the motions to please the parents. Some students were drunk, others were high. I wasn't either but, as always, looked like I was.

As the procession was gathering, there were students handing out everything from rolls of toilet paper, confetti, and plastic pop guns to paper sacks with *live* pigeons. Many students refused to be a part of it (including Steve and me), but there was no stopping those who did. The pranksters just thought it would be hilarious, and what were *they* going to do about it? Not give them diplomas? Besides, there was really no way to identify the students who were involved from those who weren't.

The moment had arrived, and the double doors finally opened. The graduating students shuffled in to their assigned seats exactly as rehearsed the day before. The music, "Pomp and Circumstance," began to play. It was very exciting for me to graduate even though I was clueless about what the next chapter in my life held. All the students were seated in the gymnasium waiting for the signal to create havoc, oblivious to the consequences. Our principal, H. L. Looney (seriously . . . that was his name), was at the podium speaking highly of this class of '75. In the middle of his speech, a motorcycle roared in behind him. The student riding it was totally nude! Streaking was a fad in the '70s and this person took it one step further, doing it on a motorcycle and making a fast getaway.

Everyone reacted with shock and laughter at the nude biker dude. Students shot pop guns and threw toilet paper and confetti onto the platform. The pigeons were let loose into the closed gymnasium. The poor birds had nowhere to go. They were diving in and out of the crowd, some mortally wounded flying into the walls in a state of panic. People were screaming. It was like a scene from Alfred Hitchcock's *The Birds*. Principal Looney was actually hit in the head with a roll of toilet paper. Considering the shit that was being pulled, toilet paper seemed appropriate. He solemnly said that he was no longer proud of the entire class of '75, embarrassed more than anything. The next morning, I read an article in the *Orange County Register* about how unruly my class had been, and that Troy High would never have the luxury of using the Cal State Fullerton Gymnasium again. But I was just thrilled to have graduated. I proudly hung my tassel on the rearview mirror of my mom's old rusty Biscayne, gazing at it with awe.

CHAPTER SEVEN

Waiting in the Wings
of College

The summer of '75 should have been a pleasant one. After all, I had a high school diploma and a driver's license. Upon graduation, I had to meet with my counselor from the California State Department of Rehabilitation, a state agency set up to assist persons with disabilities to secure employment, attend trade school, or pursue higher education. State Rehab's role was to evaluate our abilities, credentials, and interests and determine which course of action to take. I was an average student with a willingness to do something with my life. I breezily let my counselor know that I wanted to be a nun, an actress, or a psychologist. He informed me that State Rehab could not work with the Vatican. So, the nun idea was shot down rather quickly.

An actress with a disability wasn't even conceivable in 1975, so they weren't going to support a pipe dream without promise either. But the California State Department of Rehabilitation did have a good track record of assisting qualified students with disabilities in a career in psychology. What my counselor didn't share with me was his own opinion of this child/woman who sat in front of him with all her nonsense and immaturity. My animated answers fed into his assessment that I was not ready for higher education, so I was placed in Goodwill Industries, a sheltered workshop where a proper assessment could be made about what kind of employment suited me. Goodwill ran a program that tested and evaluated people with special needs in various job skills.

I had to ride the bus again for that entire summer at Goodwill (Mom needed the car for work). I could deal with riding the bus, but putting me in a special employment setting irked me to no end! I was constantly written up for having a bad attitude. I thought my supervisor, who was condescending and dismissive, was the one with the bad attitude, especially when she told me to stop flaunting my sexuality and teasing my male coworkers.

"What sexuality?" Had she taken the time to listen to me, she would have realized it was the other way around.

I was given a banana with "Blow Me" written on it with a Sharpie. I honestly didn't get the implication: how did they know that I hated bananas? I also was given a condom in a little gift-wrapped box with a note attached, "Save it for a rainy day, or meet me later." I was so confused. Why would someone give me a toe warmer in July? I just ignored these stupid gifts, but my lack of reaction ended up annoying the aggressor more. At the end of the two-month period, my supervisor had written on my state record that I could not be trusted with male coworkers, was a model child (meaning I followed direction but was unable to make adult decisions on my own), had a below-average IQ, had an attention span of 15 minutes, and had problems with authority. The only good thing my record said was that I had a flair for the dramatic and could write well.

I kept complaining to my counselor that I was misunderstood and misplaced. He only halfheartedly listened to what I was saying; he took me out of Goodwill and placed me in a keypunch class. I had to punch a lot of information onto these cards that were fed through a machine. The "key" to the success of keypunching was speed. Even my teacher was surprised that I was chosen to learn this job skill. Cerebral palsy caused my hands to jerk all over the keyboard. There was no way that I could do this line of work and told my counselor on the second day of class just that. Once again I was "a problem to be solved" for State Rehab. It was toward the end of August, and my counselor was at odds on how to find employment for me. They finally agreed that maybe a junior college might be the answer. I had a choice — Cypress or Fullerton Junior College. I chose Cypress because it was farthest away from home. The greater distance made me feel more grown up.

As it turned out, Cypress had a wonderful department for students with special needs and actually had a van providing transportation to the students who needed it. Cypress College was the best thing that had happened to me since Troy High School, and my parents couldn't be happier that I was going to college. Mom knew that my poor motor skills could prevent me from getting employment, and that my best bet was my mind, even if it was questionable how "realistically" I chose to use it. The State Department of Rehabilitation paid for all of my books and transportation. There was no tuition for junior college back then. If I successfully completed junior college, State Rehab would then further my education, financing a four-year university degree. It was up to me to register for classes. After perusing the different majors that I had to choose from, I selected accounting. It wasn't that I really wanted to be a CPA, but from State Rehab's perspective, accounting was a realistic goal, and they had had a good success rate of people with CP finding employment with such a degree.

I took basic 101 classes just as all freshmen did, but also several theater classes. When I signed up for them, I didn't realize that these classes were not going to be *approved* by the state of California. I thought that it would be fine; I didn't stop to think that the classes you enrolled in had to coincide with your declared major. Once I became involved in the Theater Department, I was hooked. I knew I wanted to be an actress/writer. I was extremely stubborn: even though State Rehab told me that I could not be a theater arts major, I felt that if I could sneak in through the back door they'd come to realize their error, and everything would be fine. I didn't even consider that the government had very strict guidelines that I had to abide by.

I worked on various productions and Mom let me drive to school on some evenings when I was prop manager for *One Flew Over the Cuckoo's Nest*. I even ran the spotlight for *Oklahoma!* (although I didn't want that job). I still sought out teacher/student relationships and tripped along emotionally as I tried to find my place socially in a world that I just didn't fully grasp.

At this point in my life, I was also in complete denial sexually. My peers were now adults, and I was not. Though I was 19, I vacillated emotionally from ages 10 to 16, and because the necessary steps in emotional development did not occur, I always hit a ceiling. I excelled in other areas though, like in creative and analytical thought processing, which made the gaps in my emotional development even more difficult for instructors to understand. Some instructors questioned whether my written work was plagiarized because it was not in sync with where I was emotionally. This adult/child dance has plagued me my entire adult life.

At least while I was in college, I didn't have to deal with any of the cruel intentions of those who later took advantage of me when I moved to Los Angeles to embark on a career in the entertainment industry. My precious time in college was a godsend in many ways, allowing me to buy a few more years of development before becoming a stand-up comic. I was 19 years old, but looked like a high school freshman. I was starved for attention, not knowing how to fulfill my needs without alienating people by being too needy.

I was doing well in all of my classes, with the exception of algebra. I just didn't know how to wrap my brain around math (still don't). Also, writing the long math formulas was always arduous and time-consuming because of my cerebral palsy. After failing algebra two semesters in a row, my instructor assigned a student tutor to help me with the writing and comprehension. This helped a lot, but never to the point where I understood the mathematical process. It was as if the logical part of my brain was short circuited. I even cheated on my final exam out of fear of failing, but I rightfully failed algebra again for the third time! Good thing I was on track to become a CPA!

Wanting a career in the entertainment industry defied all logical thinking, even though my gifts accentuated creativity and abstract thinking. It never even occurred to me that I wouldn't achieve my dream; I just dove in and had faith. I once described how the "courage" to go after my dreams really paralleled the story of the bumblebee. A bumblebee shouldn't be able to fly as its body weight is too heavy for its tiny wings to carry, but the bumblebee does not know this, so it goes ahead and flies anyway. I knew I was destined to become an entertainer and blinded myself to any obstacles in my way. It was never a question of *if* I would succeed, but rather *when* and *how*. When I stepped on the stage, this bumblebee just buzzed around in a state of natural euphoria, allowing God to work through me.

For now, though, I still had a lot of growing to do before arriving in Hollywood. I enjoyed going to college, and loved my theater arts, and creative writing classes the most. I managed to keep a B average in all of them. I also had to take a public speaking class. I did so well that my instructor used my "persuasive" speech for many years as an example of an A+ quality speech. Despite my success in the class, I withdrew from it because I hated being videotaped! My instructor, Mr. Swenson, asked me why I was so upset. I tearfully told him that when I watched the playback, I looked like I had cerebral palsy! "Well, you do!" It was one thing to have CP; it was quite another to look at it. It is a wonder that I still went into the field that I did, but my success was no surprise to Mr. Swenson. He knew that I had the ability to speak well and persuasively. But I never became comfortable with watching myself.

The State Department of Rehab finally caught on to the fact that I wasn't actually taking any courses to support my "major." Why was I purchasing books like *History of World Theater*, *Acting 101*, *Movement for Stage*, *Monologues for Women*, and *Lighting 101*? I honestly thought that as long as I went to school, I was keeping my end of the deal, and I felt that eventually State Rehab would realize that theater arts was my true calling and come to accept *my* choice of a major. That's not how it worked, and I was called on the carpet to explain myself (and that carpet wasn't red).

I begged my State Rehab counselor to fight the head office in Sacramento. I promised that I could deliver an impressive GPA and get letters from all my instructors who would describe glowingly my ability to excel in a career in theater arts. Even though the attempt failed, I did manage to get several instructors to write those letters for me. It made no difference to the government. I had to change my major or Rehab would stop giving me support. It was just as well, because the Theater Department chairman, Kaleta Brown, was at her wit's end in dealing with my immaturity. She was very hard on me when she needed to be, but she was also supportive when necessary.

At one point, the Theater Department hired a new teacher, Dennis Dowling. He was really "hip," wore his hair long, and bragged to students about all his connections in Hollywood. I wrote a pilot for a television series for Mr. Dowling's screenwriting class. He told me that he had shown it to some friends of his at CBS and that there was the possibility it would be sold. I was ecstatic and told everybody that Mr. Dowling had set up a meeting for me at CBS Studios.

What I didn't know was that he was making the whole thing up. Kaleta found out about Mr. Dowling's false promises to several students, not just me, and he was promptly replaced by another instructor. I was devastated that it was all a lie and asked Kaleta why someone would do that. She explained that she didn't understand it completely, except that Mr. Dowling had a deep need to feel important. "But if it was all made up, wouldn't we eventually have found out?" Kaleta sadly told me that he probably would have made up a string of new lies about CBS delaying things, and eventually he'd probably say, "CBS changed their minds, but look how far you got!" She was truly sorry that he had played with her students' emotions, and also added, "There are a lot of Mr. Dowlings in Hollywood, and maybe this served as a lesson to not believe everything everyone says to you."

I felt bad and knew that Mr. Dowling's letter to State Rehab was worthless. I accepted that, but was humiliated that I had told my whole family that I had a meeting at CBS. Instead of admitting to everyone that I had been duped, I continued the charade, attending a "meeting at CBS" the following week. I got all dressed up in a business suit and packed a briefcase with several copies of my pilot. I got in the 1969 Biscayne Chevy and drove to Huntington Beach where I attended a matinee. I sat alone in the movie theater watching the movie *One on One*, written by and starring Robby Benson.

Afterward, I went to the beach and sat on the pier watching the sunset, making sure enough time had elapsed for me to have driven to CBS Studios in Los Angeles, had a meeting, and then fought traffic coming home. When I got home, I told Mom the truth about what had happened. I realized that by lying I was no better than Mr. Dowling.

After school let out in the summer of '77, I was frustrated that State Rehab was making me change my major away from theater and back to the one I declared on my application and upset that Kaleta had told me that I had to grow up. She scolded me, telling me that at this point I didn't have the skills to be hired anywhere and that emotionally I was a *baby*. She chose that word intentionally, knowing it would motivate me to prove otherwise. I left Cypress College, determined to find a job just to prove Kaleta Brown wrong. It wasn't a mature reason to seek employment, but at least I would discover how difficult it was for a person with a disability to find work, especially in 1977. Mom wasn't pleased that I was trying to get a job with zero skills or experience. "But I have to prove that Kaleta is wrong!" Mom was at her wit's end. It was so painful for her to watch me go through one employment rejection after another.

"Jesus Christ, Geri!" she said. "Just change your major and allow State Rehab to finance an education for you!"

"No, I can get a job just like Gloria and my brothers!" At that, I would storm out of the house to go fill out one more job application.

This went on for two months, and I became more depressed each time I wasn't hired. The last thing I tried to do (besides getting a job at Del Taco) was join the army. My brothers had done that, so I saw no reason why I couldn't join as well. In a way, I didn't see myself as disabled, and when I was forced to, I fought against it, refusing to accept the boundaries that had been placed around me. It was this very quality that made me fiercely stubborn, but also set me up for constant disappointment.

The army recruiter clearly thought it was hilarious that I was asking to join. After telling me they wouldn't take me, he said mockingly as I left, "Geri, wait . . . why don't you go next door and try the marines?" I knew he was joking and wasn't even offended. I mumbled something about writing a letter to President Carter and went home, depressed again.

Mom was sitting in the living room, familiar with my routine of coming home dejected with tears in my eyes. She tried her best to cheer me up, but knew that I was being totally unrealistic. She begged me to call my rehabilitation counselor so I could return to school in the fall. But I ignored her. I stormed into my bedroom and collapsed onto my bed, sobbing in complete frustration at not being understood. But my mom *did* understand, and she realized that tough love was the only thing that would snap me out of my ridiculous behavior.

Marching into my room, she pulled me off the bed by my hair and dragged me into the hallway. "What is the matter with you? You tried to join the army? Are you nuts?! You are not like your brothers, and you are not like Gloria! Goddamn it, Geri, you have cerebral palsy! Don't you get it? Nobody is going to hire you!" She slapped me across the face and began to cry. I just shut down and went back into my room. I stared at my reflection in the mirror, resenting what I saw and angry that everything came back to the CP. I wanted to run away from home, but I knew I had nowhere to go. Besides, anywhere I went, I'd have to take cerebral palsy with me.

In that moment of fury, every ounce of pain and guilt that Mom bore rose to the surface. It wasn't that she was truly angry with me. I was doing the best I could within the realm of my understanding. Mom had always dreaded the day when I would have to face the music and grow up. The time had come. The pain that both my mom and I felt on that day was the tremendous grief that always accompanies the journey of a special needs child and his or her parents. It will play out differently for every family depending on what the disability is, the family dynamics, and the personalities involved, but a day will come when no one can deny those overwhelming emotions. For Mom and me, that moment sparked a new understanding between us, and our relationship grew, filled with deeper love and respect.

A couple of weeks later, I finally decided to go back to school in the fall, changing my major so that State Rehab would finance my education. I switched to Fullerton Junior College for psychology. One of the reasons I switched schools was because I'd never taken a theater arts class at Fullerton, and I figured it would be easier for me to stay on my non-theater path. I knew that State Rehab would drop me in a heartbeat if they found out I was still a closet thespian. Like an alcoholic stays away from liquor stores, I tried to stay away from the stage, where I'd risk falling off the wagon. Thankfully though, I relapsed.

Even though I didn't attend Fullerton for as long as I attended Cypress, Fullerton was just as rewarding, and I was able to form some very solid relationships that changed my life. I had known John Holton from riding the van to Cypress College from time to time. He transported students with special needs to both Fullerton and Cypress. John and I always enjoyed each other, but we didn't embark on a real friendship until I started going to Fullerton. It was at this time that John introduced me to Alex Valdez. Alex was dependent on John for transportation because he was legally blind. He and John were close friends, and I soon became friends with both of them. Besides attending Fullerton, Alex was also doing stand-up comedy in Hollywood. When Alex discovered that we shared that same passion for the arts, he and John made it possible for me to take my own journey down Stand-up Lane.

Alex first had aspirations to be a musician, but knowing there were already famous blind musicians like Stevie Wonder, Ray Charles, and Jose Feliciano, he figured he had a much greater chance at finding fame in stand-up comedy. What Alex then had to face was that by introducing me to the craft, I became his competition.

But first I had school to think about. I loved Fullerton Junior College and the new friends that I was making. Fullerton J.C. is a beautiful, old campus. It is large enough to feel like a college, yet small enough that walking was not a physical hardship. I absolutely loved it, even though while I was there I had nothing to do with theater or the performing arts. Truthfully, if there were ever a window of time that could have changed my life course, this was it. However, *fate* had other ideas.

I was still living at home, and while I missed the theater, I was enjoying all my new experiences. My favorite class was a psychology course taught by Dr. Jerry Hershey. His class was a favorite among many students. Dr. Hershey was one of those teachers that most of us only have once in a lifetime. When you opened the classroom door on the first day of school, you were greeted by him handing out Hershey's chocolate kisses to everyone. The lights would be dimmed, music was playing, and plants were situated everywhere. If any student were lucky enough to have had the "Hershey Experience," you would never forget it.

Jerry was an imposing man of six foot two. His eyes were deep-set and he was extremely intelligent, compassionate, and caring. In 1977, Jerry wore his curly black hair shoulder-length with long sideburns.

The first morning of his class I almost made it to the door, but I lost my balance and fell down the stairs. I was taken to the school nurse, who bandaged up my left hand and fingers. I missed the class entirely, and didn't return until the next class, a couple of days later. What I didn't know was that a student had witnessed my tumble and told Dr. Hershey that there was a "drunken" student who had fallen down the stairs outside his classroom.

Dr. Hershey sighed at the thought of a student being drunk at seven in the morning. He had no way of knowing at the time that I wasn't drunk, but that I had cerebral palsy. When I actually did show up for his next class, he still had it in his head that I must be that drunk student who fell down the stairs, and he was stunned that I was drunk again! It wasn't until after class when I introduced myself, that he realized I had CP. I apologized for missing the first class and explained what had happened. He also learned that the reason I was staring intently at him during class wasn't because I was drunk and struggling to comprehend what he was saying, but rather I was hearing impaired and trying to read his lips. The two of us laughed at the misunderstanding, and it was the beginning of a friendship that lasts to this day.

Jerry soon figured out that I really wanted to be an actress more than anything else. He revealed to me that before he changed his major to psychology, he was a theater arts major at UCLA. He told me that he had gone to school with Carol Burnett, and there was a part of him that always wondered had he not quit, would he too have found success as an actor. But he believed there are no mistakes in life, that he was actually meant to be just where he was, and that he loved his work as a teacher immensely. He also knew intuitively that my calling was in show business, and that I needed to find a way to follow it. The fact that Dr. Hershey went to school with Carol Burnett at UCLA and he was *my* teacher was all I needed to believe that maybe fate *was* pushing me to become an actress.

During my Fullerton years, I moved out of the house for the first time. Dad was not happy about me moving out, but Mom knew I wanted to go and told him they needed to let me spread my wings. When John Holton pulled up the driveway to load my bedroom furniture onto the truck, my dad was in the kitchen playing solitaire. With each piece of furniture John loaded onto the truck, Dad became more and more irritated. When John carried one of my two prized bookcases out of the room to load it onto the truck, Dad couldn't contain himself any longer. He bolted out of the kitchen and yelled at John to take the bookcase back to the bedroom. I knew if Mom had been home, he wouldn't have said anything, but she wasn't.

I was so angry. "Dad, they're mine! You bought them for me for my eighteenth birthday!" Dad pursed his lips and again ordered John to unload the bookcase. Dad explained that it was true, they were mine, but only if I lived at home. If I chose to move out, I'd lose the bookcases. At the time, I just thought that my dad was being selfish and small. Defiantly, with tears,

I told him he could keep *his* bookcases. I would move without them! At that point, Dad realized his game plan had failed. He knew how much I loved those bookcases and thought for sure that if I couldn't take them with me, I wouldn't move out.

That's where Dad underestimated me. With or without the damned bookcases, I was going to leave. I was stubborn, as always. Knowing my dad, he probably regretted making an issue over the bookcases and probably had tears in his eyes as he thought of his little girl with cerebral palsy moving out into the big cruel world that he and my mom had protected me from so far. (Jeez, I was just moving eight miles away!)

Thelma Jackson was my very first roommate, and we enjoyed each other's company. She was a lot older than me, and she was a lesbian. Although there was a certain attraction, we did not really take it to any level beyond flirting. Thelma and I had found a cute little two-bedroom apartment close to Fullerton College and not far from my parents. I was on my own, yet close enough to them in case I needed anything. John Holton lived on the same block, across the street.

Soon after I moved out, however, I realized that some of my dad's concerns were legitimate, like how was I going to pay half the rent and utilities? But he didn't have to worry; I had a plan. (Not a well thought-out plan, but nevertheless a plan.) I went down to the local Social Security office and applied for ssi (supplementary security income), Medi-Cal (health insurance), and food stamps. I actually had applied for this when I was 18, but was turned down. They told me that I wasn't disabled enough to qualify for such benefits, and that I should get a job instead. Not knowing anything about how the system worked, I was not able to receive retro income for those two years of not receiving benefits. At 20, I was told that because I didn't follow through with the first claim, I had no proof that I had actually been turned down. "Just because you 'talked' to someone in our office, doesn't hold any water as far as having any tangible proof," they said. This time, I was not turned down and began receiving supplementary security income for the first time. I was surprised, however, that the total of the monthly income was so low. The agency informed me that I would receive $147 a month. Our rent alone was $360 a month. The supplement covered my half of the rent, but left me with only $27 for additional expenses. That was when I was told by the agent that if I had a more severe disability, I could qualify for more money to be able to pay an attendant. "How much more money?" I asked.

"That depends on how much work the attendant does for you."

"But how do *you* know how much my attendant does for me?" (I said this like I actually had one.)

"We conduct an assessment. Someone from our office visits your home and observes how much the attendant has to do for you; how many points you receive during this determines how much more money the government will pay you." The following week a field officer showed up at my apartment to evaluate my needs.

In my mind, all I had to do was convince Thelma to pose as my attendant. Thelma agreed as long as whatever I got, she would get some of it for her role as my attendant. Thelma and I were looking at this as sort of a play (non-union). We rehearsed our roles for several days. Thelma was a seasoned actress herself, but she left the Hollywood scene so she could return to Orange County and get a degree in psychology. For this brief afternoon, she was back to honing her acting skills once again. Did I feel guilty? Oh, God yes, but I justified it as compensation for the two years I was cheated out of receiving benefits. Besides, who could live on $147 a month?

At two o'clock sharp, the doorbell rang. A kind, middle-aged government worker introduced herself to a very disabled me and my attendant, Thelma. My gait was far more pronounced. I put grease in my hair and wore my hearing aids dangling, as if I was unable to put them behind my ears. My speech was slurred and I drooled occasionally. I had severe involuntary movement and spoke in a childlike manner. In order to keep up the performance that lasted a little less than an hour, we tried not to make eye contact with one another, for fear of laughing. After the assessment was completed, the agent added up all the points, which gave me $75 a month more than I was already receiving. It wasn't nearly as much as I thought it would be, but then again, it was hardly an Oscar-winning performance.

Meanwhile, at school, I had to take a required human sexuality course. When I took the first exam, I turned it in with not one question answered, only my name and class at the top of the page. The instructor talked with me later, asking me if I had read the material. I said that I had, but that I had no interest to read anything further, and that I was just going to withdraw from the class anyway. She asked me what was so frightening that I couldn't even take an exam. I explained that I couldn't talk about it, but she made me talk, trying to get past my walls. This was the moment when I had to tell someone a secret that even my own parents didn't know. Tears came to my eyes when I tried to explain that I was different than other women. "What do you mean?" she asked.

"Well, I am attracted to other women."

"Geri, it's okay if you're gay."

"That's what my roommate tells me, too! But she *is* gay! I'm not!" I actually told her that I had a half penis, something that was completely untrue, but I had convinced myself of it in an attempt to grasp the concept of sexuality based on what I was taught — if women are attracted to men, and only men are attracted to women, then I must be a man.

I didn't know how to express being gay. I just thought that I must be a male hiding in a female body. Due to emotional immaturity, lack of socialization, isolation caused by hearing loss, and poor self-esteem, I was unable to comprehend what same-sex attraction really was. My instructor realized how confused I was, and she tried to simplify this complex issue with a step-by-step approach. She knew it was time for me to come to terms with my sexuality, so she set up an appointment for me with a gynecologist. "Let's find out for sure whether you're male or female, and then we'll take it from there."

I kept my promise and followed through in seeing the "sex" doctor, but I was nervous about the *shock* the doctor would have upon discovering I was half male. I had to lie on the table and spread my legs wide open, placing my feet in what appeared to be stirrups. Tears rolled down my cheeks as I lay there feeling like a freak. When the doctor finished her examination, she told me to get dressed and to step inside her office with a big oak desk. I went in expecting to be told what I already knew, that I would never be able to have sex like normal people.

The doctor had a big, easy smile on her face. She said that I was 100 percent female, and that I was perfectly able to have intercourse. I wasn't prepared to hear *that*. Now what excuse could I conjure up to not have sex with a man? Did this mean I really *was* gay? The doctor showed me a book with color pictures of various vaginas (no monologues, just vaginas). They came in all shapes and sizes. There were no half penises, only vaginas that were as diverse and unique as every other part of our bodies. She gave me a big book called *Our Bodies, Ourselves*. It was a gift. "Read it," she said, "and learn to accept yourself as a sexual being." Unfortunately, it would take a lot more than just reading a book to achieve inner peace and comfort with my sexuality, but it was a start.

In retrospect, I always felt that if I had not become famous, I would have more than likely led a quiet gay lifestyle in Berkeley and would have been content, but as it was, within a very short period of time, I found myself known to millions on a G-rated show. Struggling with my sexuality was very frightening, especially when there was so much pressure from the gay community in the '80s to be out of the closet. What many people in the gay community don't always understand is that being out should be a personal choice. For some people, it isn't the healthiest option. It's really hard to come out of the closet if you don't even know for certain what closet you're in. So I stayed in the closet for a very long time, trying to grow . . . and wondering what outfit I'd wear when I came out.

CHAPTER EIGHT

Sneaking into the Store
and Stealing the Spotlight

After flunking anatomy and physiology, I finally decided to turn to Alex for guidance in doing stand-up comedy instead. He educated me on how to write a five-minute comedy act. I wrote my routine on a Friday afternoon and went onstage for the first time the following Monday night at the Comedy Store on Sunset Boulevard in Hollywood. John drove both Alex and me to Los Angeles. Everyone was excited! I was terrified as well, hoping that I wouldn't forget my material. I was so into remembering what I wrote that I didn't even think about the venue in which I was going to perform.

All I knew was that I was doing my routine at a place called the Comedy Store. In my mind, it could have been an Albertsons, or Ralphs, or Rite Aid; a store is a store. I figured I would be standing in some aisle telling jokes. When we arrived at the Store that night, it finally registered that this was a nightclub, not a Kmart. We went in the back entrance and were greeted by Alex's friend Danny Mora, who ran the Original Room at the time. The Original Room is one of three stages at the Comedy Store. The Main Room is the largest, seating 800; the Original Room seats 200; and the smallest is the Belly Room, seating 100. Interestingly, today all the comics perform in all the rooms, but back then, only female comedians performed in the Belly Room; and even though everyone wanted to perform in the Main Room, club owner Mitzi Shore only allowed me to perform in that room once.

Danny had already spoken to Alex and knew I was coming. It was decided that I would show up at the back door, and when Mitzi was *not* in the room, I would be brought to the stage. Danny didn't want my act cut short based on any prejudices the owner may have had. So, from that first night in late October 1978 until about May 1979, I was whisked onstage only when Mitzi left the room.

Every comic will always remember when he or she first performed. Whether you killed or bombed, you will never forget it. Alex and John taped my act that night on a little portable cassette recorder. I still have that tape today, and when I play it back, I never cease to wonder where I got the guts to do what I did. At that time, my voice still carried a medium-high child-like pitch. If I didn't know my real age, I would have thought I was listening to a 13-year-old. In fact, I didn't look much older.

I stood in the back hallway, nervously waiting to be called onstage. Fear and anxiety gripped me; I wanted to perform, flee, and pee at the same time. After the applause trailed off from the previous performance, the emcee introduced me. He got my name right, and where I was from correct, but because my name was Geri, he assumed that I was Jerry and introduced me as a male. "Our next performer is Jerry Jewell. He comes all the way from Fullerton, California. Please give a warm applause for him!"

When I walked onto the stage, you could hear a pin drop. The next sound was muffled whispers as everyone was trying to wrap their brains around me. I could barely wrap my brain around myself, so I can only imagine how the audience was taking it all in. There was instantly an "elephant in the room" energy. My God, she thinks she is a male! And she's really on some heavy shit, or drunk, or even disturbed. All these thoughts and whispers were floating around the room, waiting anxiously for me to break the silence and say something funny.

I was so nervous that I forgot to correct the emcee's gaffe in introducing me as a man. I was only praying that my intense stage fright wouldn't cause me to forget my lines. My very first line that night was "I don't know about you, but I've heard an awful lot about the gays who have been coming out of the closet lately [hmm . . . maybe she's a transgender] but what you probably haven't heard about are all the cerebral palsy people who have been coming out of the closet. [Nervous laughter.] But let's just keep this between you and me. I don't want a lot of people to know about me. Especially Anita Bryant! She may even get on another bandwagon and start a campaign saying, 'We've got to stop these cerebral palsied people from teaching in our public schools! They will influence our children, and before you know it, all our children will be walking like this' [mimicking my own CP walk]." The audience roared!

That first sound of laughter was music to my ears. It was the green light to go into my next bit with a little more confidence. "A lot of people are surprised when I tell them that I can drive. In fact, I think I drive *better* than

I walk!" More laughter. I was tackling the elephants, one joke at a time. "Some people even think I'm drunk. The thing is, when I really am drunk, I walk perfectly straight!" Now I was on a wonderful four-and-a-half minute roll, just a couple more jokes, and I could leave the stage. As much as I was enjoying the experience, I wanted it to end as quickly as possible. Some comics need to have lights flashing, signaling them to wrap it up. Not me, if I was told to do five minutes, I did five minutes, sometimes four-and-a-half. Why? Because as much as I loved being onstage, I hated it at the same time.

But my first night was amazing. My next line was to pull my jean suspenders down to reveal my now famous T-shirt, "I DON'T HAVE CEREBRAL PALSY, I'M DRUNK."

"Did you know that this cost me thirty cents a letter? I wish I had polio, it would be a hell of a lot cheaper." The audience went wild. Then I closed my act that night by saying, "I believe that you can do anything you want to do in life if you want to bad enough. That's why I'm going to be a brain surgeon!" I got a standing ovation. It was one of those surreal moments in life that can only be experienced once. No matter how many successes we have thereafter, nothing is sweeter than that first night of doing stand-up comedy. Well, only if you kill.

The following Monday night I couldn't have been more excited about returning to the Store for a repeat performance. However, the "magic" didn't happen, and I bombed. I became horrified when the laughter didn't follow the jokes, and people were staring at me as if I were nuts. I hadn't yet learned how to handle any kind of silence, how to shift gears or ad-lib. Every line that worked the week before died a quiet death on this night. I walked off the stage feeling humiliated and ran out of the nightclub, continuing down Sunset Boulevard, with Alex and John yelling for me to slow down.

When they did catch up to me, I was bawling and told them that I never wanted to do stand-up comedy ever again! Alex held me in his arms, saying, "Geri, you have got to toughen your skin! So you bombed tonight, so what? Some nights will be wonderful and some nights you will feel like shit, but if you expect to be great every single time, forget it. Even Bob Hope bombs." I was astonished to hear that.

"Really? Bob Hope bombs?"

Alex laughed, and said, "Many times; although I'm sure every time he performs, he *hopes* he doesn't."

I had experienced a standing ovation, then hissing and booing only a week later. This was my journey now. Every Monday night I would perform at the Store. I also went with Alex and John on other nights to watch Alex perform. Alex nicknamed me Dinky Face, and both John and Alex looked after me like big brothers. We were inseparable until I moved to Los Angeles about seven months later.

I never had to wait in line on Monday nights, hoping I'd be a part of the potluck show. I was always guaranteed a spot, just never guaranteed what time. We usually arrived around 8:30 or so, and sometimes I wouldn't get to go on until 11 or 12, but I couldn't care less. It was the beginning of a grand adventure, and there was no going back. Like every other amateur comic, I wanted fame. At that time, so many of us wanted to be the next Robin Williams. He was riding high on *Mork & Mindy* and we were all in awe of what he had accomplished. Being able to witness his brilliant comedic genius on stage was a true gift for us. Robin oftentimes showed up at the Store unannounced and wowed the crowds.

Everything seemed to happen at lightning speed for me between October 1978 and October 1980. In this two-year period, my life changed dramatically. Each time I performed, I got some additional attention one way or another. While most performers pay a publicist for publicity, I never needed to. I was so different that publicity followed me.

I also created opportunities for myself by aggressively seeking them. One of the greatest examples of that was when I called the organizers of the United Cerebral Palsy Weekend with the Stars Telethon in the spring of 1979. I had been doing stand-up for a little more than six months and didn't really have any more than ten minutes worth of material, but that didn't deter me from trying to get on the local CP telethon in Los Angeles. I called UCP and they gave me the phone number to the production office. After initially explaining to the producer that I wanted to appear on the telethon over the weekend, I was told that the talent portion of show had been booked months in advance, and that there were no open spots for any more talent.

"But . . . I have cerebral palsy!"

"I thought you just said that you were a stand-up comic!"

"I am . . . and I have cerebral palsy too."

"What kind of jokes do you tell?"

"Cerebral palsy jokes, what else?" He then asked me for my phone number and explained that someone would get back to me. So I had some milk and peanut butter toast, and sat by the phone waiting for the call. Truthfully, it never even occurred to me that they might not return my call.

Within the hour I got a call back. I think I spoke with Marty Pasetta. He asked how long I had been doing comedy. I didn't want to say that I was a novice, performing on amateur nights for roughly five months. I wanted to sound as though I had been around the block. I lied and said that I had been doing comedy for over a year and had even been on *Carson*. He said he never saw it, and I responded, "You're kidding. I can't believe you missed it!"

I had his attention now. Again I was reminded that I could *not* actually perform, but if I was willing, I could volunteer to answer the phones for the local L.A. segment. Possibly their local host, Greg Mullavey, could interview me on camera. I was asked how palsied I was, and if I had problems writing or hearing. I said I had moderate CP with no problem hearing or writing, which seemed to appease him. I was to show up at KTTV Studios in Los Angeles at 10:30 p.m. My name would be at the gate on the volunteers list. I hung up the phone, at first ecstatic and then panicked — how was I going to hear on the phone, take pledges, and write addresses down when I was hearing impaired and wrote slowly? I mean, I could barely hear *him* on the phone, and had asked him to repeat the address of KTTV several times. I almost called back to cancel, but I decided to go through with it. All that mattered at this point was performing on television!

I immediately called John Holton, as I had to make sure he could drive me to Los Angeles on Saturday night, and to my relief, John could do it. He couldn't believe this was happening. I confessed that I was only supposed to answer phones and take pledges, but I could possibly be interviewed by the host. He said, "Well, this is certainly going to test your acting ability. You don't hear well enough to do that, and how are you going to write at lightning speed?"

"John, don't worry about it, I'll figure it out."

"What, you're planning to be healed by Saturday night? If you do get healed, you won't have an act, so either way, you're in deep shit!" I knew he had a point, but the show must go on.

Saturday night arrived quickly enough, and John came by to pick me up around 8:30 p.m. We decided it was better to get there early, rather than late. The traffic to Los Angeles from Orange County was always unpredictable. We figured if we got there too early, we could just go to Denny's to kill some time. I kissed my mom goodbye, and both she and Gloria waited anxiously for my first television appearance. They both promised to stay up until they saw me on television answering phones. Mom hoped I would get at least one minute of television exposure.

John and I arrived, and I was all dressed up, waiting for my shining moment. Then security informed me that I was not on the celebrity guest list. John just watched, totally amused. I acted shocked that I wasn't and asked the guard politely to look on the volunteers list, that perhaps my agent (of course) screwed up. He looked and said, yes, indeed, I was on the volunteers list. "Well, obviously it was a mistake. Can't you just put my name on the celebrity guest list?" John couldn't believe the balls I had to ask that. Truthfully, I didn't believe it either! The security guard said that he didn't have the authority to do that, but that if I went into the celebrity green room, he was sure someone could help me.

We parked the car and followed the directions to the celebrity greenroom. We started to open the door but someone stopped us, pointing to a flashing red light above it. We couldn't go in until the red light was turned off, because they were live to air. I panicked, thinking we weren't going to get in. Then it stopped flashing, and John and I entered a very hushed studio. There was a form on the table, which I was asked to fill out. It asked for my social, my agent/manager, what union I belonged to. I wrote that John was my manager, and that I belonged to the Screen Actors Guild, the American Federation of Television and Radio Artists, and Equity. John rolled his eyes, especially when I wrote of my appearances on *Carson*. But before John could convince me to erase all of the bullshit, a production assistant came up to me, introducing himself. He didn't quite know what to make of me, because I had no interest in answering phones and only wanted to do comedy.

I bluntly asked him what time I was going to perform. He knew he had to mentally shift gears here. He explained that they had a problem: someone had not shown up to answer phones and take pledges, and he was wondering if I could fill in until the other person arrived. I was fully aware that I was filling in for *myself*, but I wasn't about to admit it. So, I told him that I would take this other person's place *only* if I could do three minutes of stand-up afterward. He excused himself and returned a few minutes later with an answer.

He returned carrying a cardboard placard displaying my name, GERI JEWELL, in bold, black capital letters. He explained that it would be impossible for me to do stand-up comedy, but that they would seat me in the celebrity panel row of phones, and the host would briefly interview me on the air. I agreed, knowing that he knew what I was up to. I still wasn't about to give up my plan of doing comedy, not just yet. The next thing I knew, I was sitting in the front row of the celebrity panel and the cameras were rolling.

I was learning very quickly that with every plan A, you needed a backup plan B, and in my case, also a plan C and D. I cannot recall who the other celebrities were on the panel, but I remember thinking, "Now what?" Of course my phone began ringing. I answered maybe a total of four calls. I was so frustrated because I was having so much difficulty hearing and writing. I turned to my celebrity neighbor more than once to ask if she would please take my call. Then I was spared by a cutaway to the national broadcast with John Ritter.

I called Greg Mullavey over to me and begged him to let me do three minutes of stand-up comedy when we were back on the air. "Come on, Greg, this is United Cerebral Palsy, and I have cerebral palsy! Let me show my strengths, not my weaknesses. Please, just three, or even two minutes of comedy! I promise I'll be funny." I could see Greg's mental wheels spinning. He said he would try, but couldn't promise anything. He returned five minutes later, saying that when we're back on the air, he was going to take it upon himself to introduce me. He told me that I could do three minutes of stand-up comedy. "I am putting my job on the line here, so don't take advantage of me. *Three minutes*, not a minute longer." I promised that I wouldn't go over, and I have never forgotten that break or the trust that he instilled in me not to go wild with his gift.

Greg surprised everyone in the studio that evening by straying from his scripted dialogue and introducing me. He handed me the microphone and backed away. Knowing what I know about "production" today, Greg must have been sweating bullets. Tom Ritter (now my dear friend) was in the control booth that night, and he told me that he will never forget that night as long as he lives. He said he never saw so many mouths fall open at one time. The confusion, frustration, and anger were palpable. "What in the world is he doing?" followed by "And who in the hell is Geri Jewell?" All the while, I was telling cerebral palsy jokes. Tom said that everyone was ready to kill Greg and wring my neck. That is . . . until all the phones started to light up. People were calling in with their donations, saying how much they loved that kid, Geri Jewell.

I have never had the opportunity to thank Greg personally for taking such a risk with me, although I have told this story countless times to audiences over the years. It was a pivotal moment in my life, because Greg followed his gut instead of his orders. I just thank God I was funny that night, or else we both would have been in big trouble. Just for the record, I kept it under three minutes by 10 seconds. He was happy, I was happy, UCP was happy, and Mom and Gloria were sitting at home laughing and crying.

CHAPTER NINE

My First
"Funny Business" Manager

After I appeared on the local segment of the UCP Telethon, it felt as if I had been swept up in an undercurrent. No matter how much I resisted and wanted to pull back a little, there was no time to reflect. I kept the momentum of performing one show after another, knowing intuitively there was no going back to ever being Gerry Jewell, the little CP kid. From the time I arrived at the Comedy Store in October 1978, I was Geri Jewell, the inspirational, CP comedian.

Shortly after I performed on the UCP Telethon, I performed in New York City and on Long Island. I was featured in the Calendar section of the *Los Angeles Times* and appeared on a local morning talk show, *Two on the Town* with Steve Edwards. Steve Guttenberg was also on the show that morning. The show stands out in my mind for two reasons: first, it marked a time in history when there was an oil shortage, and we were waiting in long lines at the gas stations. And, after both *Two on the Town* and the telethon aired, I received a letter from the State Department of Rehabilitation, congratulating me on my "successful career." My case was officially closed. The State Department of Rehabilitation, despite never supporting my desire to go into show business, took credit for me finding employment. However, because they had closed my case, if I failed as a comedian and needed their assistance again, I would have to go through the process of "reopening" my case instead of already being in the system.

At this early stage of my career, I hardly had succeeded, but at least my notoriety was picking up tremendous pace. I performed at both Fullerton College and Cypress College, and my now famous T-shirt, "I DON'T HAVE CEREBRAL PALSEY, I'M DRUNK," was getting permanent sweat stains and fading quickly from so many washings. I still have that shirt today, and sometimes I cringe because cerebral palsy is not spelled correctly! I've had the condition my entire life and didn't even know how to spell it. I also could have saved 30 cents had I left the "e" out of "palsey."

I had begun receiving fan mail, often addressed to newspapers that were kind enough to forward them to my post office box in Fullerton. My roommate situation with Thelma hadn't worked out, so I was back with Mom and Dad. After failing the first time I tried independent living, I was a little gun-shy about trying again so soon. However, the time to move out again came quickly enough, and this time I left Orange County for Los Angeles.

The first thing I did there was meet with a manager, George. He had read the article about me in the *Orange County Register* and had come all the way from L.A. to see my next performance at Fullerton College. After the show, he introduced himself, giving me his business card, and asked me to call him about representing me. I called him the next day, making an appointment with him for the following week. I still have that business card and remember thinking how magical it was that his company was called Rainbow Productions. In my mind, I equated it with Judy Garland, my idol. As crazy as the thought was, I was right on some level. Many people took advantage of Judy in her lifetime, and George was about to take advantage of me.

I drove up to L.A. the following week and was very impressed that he had a Mercedes Benz in his parking space. He wanted me to sign on immediately. Looking back, it was foolish of me to sign *anything* without having an attorney look at it. I didn't even show the contract to my parents because I didn't want to feel like a child again. What I refused to acknowledge was that I *was* a child. Even worse, I was a child with cerebral palsy in "LaLaLand." George recognized my vulnerability right away and knew which buttons to push. Subconsciously, I saw George as a father figure, and just like the relationship with my own father, I did as I was told (most of the time).

I believe that with or without George, I would have made a name for myself. After all, I had already acquired a certain amount of success on my own. Had that not been true, George would have never heard of me. However, because so much more success came about *after* I had signed with him, for a long time I believed that George made me a star.

Truthfully, I didn't really understand much of the contract that I had signed with him, and just trusted that he *loved* me, and would look after me. This childlike way of perceiving George was extremely conflicting; I honestly didn't understand the difference between a business associate, a father figure, a friend, and even an unrealistic crush. I hadn't had the life experiences or relationships to have the maturity of a young adult.

My family, especially my mom, was anxious that they couldn't help or guide me through a world in which they had no experience. That old saying, there's no business like show business, is pretty much true. I did not grow up in a show business family. I didn't turn to them because I wanted to stand on my own two feet, and I didn't want to be controlled. The funny thing was, George was controlling me, and I was oblivious to it.

I gave George power of attorney and also agreed to pay him 75 percent of my earnings: 25 percent of my earnings were taken as management fees, and I then turned over another 50 percent because of a partnership clause in the contract. I remember questioning that 75 percent of my earnings seemed high. He explained that it only looked high because I wasn't taking into consideration the 50 percent of *his* income that I would be earning from all of George's projects, productions, etc. For the record, I never saw one cent of earnings from his business ventures. My 50 percent partnership money, as well as the remaining 25 percent that I was left with, was supposed to be put into an account called Jewel Productions. If I needed money for anything, I had to ask George for it, and he would then write a check out to me from that production account. However, I soon found out that I would be forced to jump through a lot of hoops to get every check.

George insisted that I stay on the government dole of ssi long after I was legally entitled to it. I lived on ssi, and whatever I was paid from actual performances went directly into Jewel Productions, in which I was a partner with George. One of the reasons he gave me for staying on ssi was that if I started to earn "bigger" amounts of money I would become spoiled, it would somehow ruin me as an artist, and I would no longer be genuinely funny. Because I gave George power of attorney, I basically gave him the legal right to cash all checks that were made out to me. Other than a rare check that was written out to me from that account, I was not made aware of any of the activity that occurred and did not actually see any of the legal documents of this account until two years later.

After I signed with George in 1980, my life changed rapidly. I was now not only doing stand-up comedy, but also doing motivational speaking. I was earning anywhere from $100 to $500 for speaking gigs. I never saw these checks; they went directly into the Jewel Productions account. I knew it was illegal to stay on ssi and to be gainfully employed at the same time. George explained that when the government caught up to me, I would be so wealthy that whatever I owed them would be a drop in the bucket. I was scared of breaking the law, but totally oblivious to the consequences of my action, and trusted that George knew better than I did. Confusing? Now you've just experienced a glimpse of how confused I was!

Aside from the financial confusion, I was also dealing with conflicting sexual feelings. It became more and more obvious to me that I was attracted to women, not men, yet I was terrified of these feelings and felt shame and conflict. I wanted to be straight so badly and thought that perhaps I just hadn't found the right guy. I even thought that George might be Mr. Right. After all, he loved me, right?

I was a tomboy, and George kept stressing how important it was for me to be more feminine. If I was going to be a star, I had to start dressing like a lady, not an androgynous little boy. He told me once after inspecting my bra that it wasn't feminine enough. I figured that if he cared so much about what kind of a bra I wore, perhaps he'd marry me in time. I actually remember him fondling my breast once. I never interpreted it as sexual harassment; I just thought it was his way of showing me how to be a woman.

My "false image" and "true image" were at war with one another internally. I became somewhat compartmentalized in order to cope with so much trauma in my young adult life. It was a quandary that in one instant I discovered the power and joy of performing, and in that same instant, I was being beaten down by the very disability that brought me to a place of acceptance. On the one hand, cerebral palsy quickened the pace toward fame, but on the other hand the gaps in my development were kicking me in the face.

At one point, George had one of his two girlfriends take me to the garment district in downtown L.A., and she picked out two dresses, pumps, and a purse. After that, we went to get my hair done, makeup, and nails. I even had my eyebrows plucked! It was a scene right out *My Fair Lady*. If I didn't have cerebral palsy, I am sure I would have had to walk balancing a book on my head as well. It took years to compensate for my lack of grace, to walk a little softer, and learn how to wear appropriate attire.

Aside from appearances, I performed as many nights as I was able to. By the second half of 1980, I was only working one or two nights a week at the Comedy Store. Luckily, Jo Ann Maher approached me, inviting me to perform at her club, the Comedy Cave located on La Cienega Boulevard. It actually looked like a cave, being underneath a disco, with female mud wrestling upstairs. Jo Ann provided a club for comics when they couldn't get time at the Store or the Improv on Melrose. Mitzi Shore had told Jo Ann that she was uncomfortable around me and didn't think I was right for her club. Because Jo Ann believed in me, she let me perform at the Cave frequently.

George came to some of these shows, but not many of them. I still saw Alex and John occasionally, but after I moved to L.A. we didn't hang out like we used to. Jo Ann was my newest friend, but she left the scene in late 1980, not resurfacing until 2004.

If there was ever a time when the hard shell of special education was cracked profoundly, it was when Charley Metcalf, a pied piper of sorts, skipped into my realm of existence. Interestingly, Charley (C.W.) didn't like George at all, and told me so. Ironically, George did like Charley, especially when he wrote a review of my act in the Who column of *Oui* magazine. He also liked that Charley got me to move to L.A., since it actually saved him the hassle of doing so himself. George didn't mind Metcalf's influence over me as long as it didn't interfere with his own control of me. Even though I didn't give much thought to Metcalf's opinion of George, I believed almost everything else he told me. Years later, Metcalf admitted that he was full of shit most of the time, but his magical, whimsical touch of genius gave him the appearance of being a guru of sorts, and I was his follower.

I remember the night I met C.W. at the Comedy Store. It was a full house that night. Alex, John, George, and a whole camera crew were there, filming a national segment of ABC News. It was a story about the booming comedy club scene, and how young hopefuls were flocking the stage on amateur night hoping to be discovered and land a series the way Robin Williams had. As fate would have it, I just happened to be in the lineup that night. I hadn't known that I was going to be filmed for national television.

This particular night, I tried two new jokes. I hadn't learned the rule of never doing *new* material. One should never try out new material on national television — instead, stick with what you know works. Second, don't steal another comedian's joke, and then tell it on national television. Yes, I stole a joke, and it was the last time I did! I felt so bad, and even worse at having to call Bob Nelson in New York and tell him that I did *his* impression of a Q-tip on ABC national news. All the Q-tip impression required me to do was to put a white fluffy cotton ball hat on my head, close my eyes turn around, and say, "Now I am a Q-tip!"

I honestly thought it was harmless "borrowing." With Bob being in New York, I thought it was safe to do one of his *many* impressions in Los Angeles. Out of all of his numerous impressions, that he'd hardly miss one Q-tip. As it was, millions of people saw *me* do an impression of a Q-tip and it instantly became *my* joke. I called Bob the very next day and apologized for stealing his Q-tip. I told him he could have any of my CP jokes he wanted and promised never to steal any material ever again. He was very sweet about it, but pointed out that even if I was in Omaha, Nebraska, I should never steal another comic's material; it'll get back to them one way or another. However, the Q-tip joke was now mine, due to the kindness of Bob Nelson. Eventually, I even added an impression of a *dirty* Q-tip (wearing a brown fluffy cotton ball hat).

Even if I hadn't stolen Bob's Q-tip, I still wouldn't have forgotten that night, because it was when I met Metcalf. After the show he introduced himself and was interested in interviewing me for the Who column in *Oui* magazine. *Oui* is a men's adult magazine published in the United States featuring explicit nude photographs, centerfolds, interviews, other articles, and cartoons. I didn't know French, so when he said *Oui*, I was seeing it in my mind as *We*. I had no idea it was a magazine like *Playboy*, or I probably would have said no. Truthfully, the column was fine, it's just that you had to thumb through a lot of naked women before you made it to my article.

That night, C.W. told me that I had met my match. I wasn't sure what he meant, but he said that you cannot bullshit a bullshit artist. I thought perhaps he knew I had stolen the Q-tip joke, but over the years I've found that *he* didn't even quite know what he meant when he said it. I do know this though: C.W. went onto national fame as a motivational speaker and an expert in laughter therapy. He is one of the best storytellers I have ever come across in my lifetime.

I've often wondered how my life would have been had I not met C.W. or George. I know there are no accidents in life, and that if we learn something from a relationship, then it has served its purpose. Both C.W. and George were men that I trusted without question. The difference between the two of them was that although they both lied to me, C.W. always had my best interest at heart. George, on the other hand, only had his own interests in mind, and was driven by greed and deception.

CHAPTER TEN

Another Suitcase, Another Hall

I didn't always know where I was moving, and nobody else did either. I was a nomad. One of the reasons I could move so easily to Los Angeles was because I didn't have furniture to haul; the bulkiest thing I had was my ten-speed bike. Dad told me not to take it and warned me that it would probably get stolen, but I stubbornly refused. It was time for me to grow up, to leave Orange County and Disneyland behind, and come to Hollywoodland.

My parents were terrified about me moving to L.A., but they knew there was no holding me back. This time around I didn't even *want* the bookcases. All I had with me in the Biscayne Chevy were some clothes in a suitcase, toiletries, a backgammon set, a tape recorder, my books, and my bike. It was all I really needed. C.W. told me I was going to be famous, and when that happened, I could buy all the bookcases and books that I could ever want. It was an adventure, and I didn't want to be weighed down by too much *stuff*. I was a free spirit, and had I been born five years earlier, I probably would have been a flower child, hitched a ride to Berkeley, and done acid.

As it was, I was a child of the '70s. I drove myself to L.A. and I didn't need to do acid because the trip I was on was mind-boggling enough all by itself. The first place I stayed at was in Venice Beach with C.W. and his wonderful wife, Sharon. Sharon also danced the C.W. dance for many years, supporting him and his whimsical ways without question. They set up a little cot for me in the corner of the living room. It was a very small, quaint apartment overlooking the Venice canal. C.W. hung a little mobile above the cot with crystals that caught rays of sunlight through the window.

Rainbows danced above my head every afternoon. C.W. said these were the auras of angels.

C. W. Metcalf had a lot of charm and charisma. He had an uncanny ability to draw people into his energy field by making them feel better about themselves. If you pumped gas, he would make sure that you knew you were God's gift to the world at the pumps. For every person he built up, he lived vicariously through them, finding a sense of fulfillment by helping others.

I usually performed at night, sometimes not getting home until two or three in the morning. C.W. and his writing partner, Harvey Brenner, wrote a script especially for me for an existing series on PBS called *The Righteous Apples*. Although *The Facts of Life* was my first big break, it was not my first sitcom. In the episode, I was the girlfriend of D.C., played by series regular Joey Camen. The episode was titled "Love Has Two Left Feet" and featured C.W. and Harvey's dry humor at its best. In it, D.C. took me home to meet his parents, and they got really upset — not because I had CP but because I wasn't Jewish! It was groundbreaking subject matter, but because it was on PBS, it didn't garner the same attention as it did on *The Facts of Life* soon after.

I lived with Sharon and C.W. for almost three weeks. In that time, I did *The Righteous Apples* and was featured on a segment of *In Search Of . . .* with Leonard Nimoy, about therapeutic humor. During that happy month, however, my bike was stolen. I was so upset and wished I had listened to Dad. C.W. suggested that my dad probably came up to Los Angeles and stole the bike himself just to give his warning some credibility. He was joking, of course: my parents didn't know where I was living. They knew I was staying with Sharon and C.W. but had never met them.

While I was blubbering to C.W. about my stolen bike, he decided to shift gears. "Jeez, what a big baby you are! Geri, you're on your way to stardom and all you can think about is your damn ten-speed bike. I'll tell you exactly why it was stolen. Because somebody else needed it more than *you*. It's that simple, Jewell. Let it go. Besides, whoever has your bike probably did you a favor. Had you actually had the chance to ride it here in Venice, you would have been hit by a bus or something, and that, my friend, would have put a damper on your comedy act." I sullenly agreed with him, but it didn't make me any happier.

"Okay, let's talk about Carol Burnett," he said, wisely changing topics. "You want to work with her, right?"

"Yeah, so?"

"Then you can't sit here whimpering over a lost bike. Call Carol and say something like, 'I'm here; when do we go to work?'"

"Metcalf, are you nuts?" I didn't even know her phone number.

"Then go to her house!"

"I can't just show up on her doorstep; besides, I don't have her address."

Metcalf laughed and said, "Well, kid, I *do* have her address." He wasn't joking.

"Do you have David Cassidy's address?" (Hey, it was worth a shot.)

"No, I don't, but Carol might. Ask her." He handed me Carol's address in Beverly Hills.

The next day, I drove my olive green Biscayne Chevy to Carol Burnett's house on Alpine Drive. Every home in the neighborhood looked like a mansion; every lawn was perfect, and the palm and pine trees towered high into the sky. There were no cars parked on the street, except for a couple of gardeners' trucks and mine. Back in 1979, the term "stalker" hadn't been popularized yet and there were no anti-stalking laws in place. But looking back on it, I think I stalked Carol Burnett.

I sat in my car on that day for roughly three hours, although it felt like an eternity. I wasn't waiting for Carol to magically appear, but rather I was terrified to actually go up to the gate. I must have walked up that driveway and then run back down to my car at least 10 times. At one point, a police cruiser drove by. I thought for sure someone had called the cops on me, but he didn't stop. I smiled and waved to him, thinking it would make it look more like I lived there. He'd probably had seen many fans do the same thing I did and just laughed to himself.

It was getting dark, and I was getting hungry. I tried one last time to ring that buzzer. My heart was beating fast. First, I was scared of not knowing what to say, or, more important, how Carol would respond. I finally pushed the buzzer, but in response all I heard was a bunch of crackling words, and I didn't have the guts to ask the box with a camera on it to repeat itself. Defeated, I turned and left. While walking back to my car, I made up some dialogue in my mind so that I could drive away with a little dignity intact. That evening, I told Metcalf that the butler said Carol was out of town. Of course, I wasn't even sure she had a butler, but it sounded good. I reassured him that I would try again, but I had no intention of ever returning to Alpine Drive. To this day, I am not really sure if it actually was her house. C.W. did have the propensity to lie. For all I know, he could have gotten the address from one of those vendors on Sunset Boulevard who sold $5 maps to the stars' homes.

I didn't live with Sharon and C.W. for long because the quarters were too cramped, and three wasn't considered company. It became Charlie's mission to find me another place to stay. I never even stopped to ask why C.W. wanted to help me. It just felt wonderful that this new friend of mine believed in me as much as he did. The next place I lived was at the Hyatt Regency Hotel on Sunset Boulevard, right next to the Comedy Store. The location was perfect, the maid service was convenient, and the view was spectacular! However, after only four days at the Hyatt, C.W. knew it was time to move on. It was much too expensive so he found me another place to live: a wine cellar in Venice Beach.

C.W. told me that a friend of his lived there and that he was going to Canada for a couple of months. I was welcome to stay there for free until he returned. He gave me the key, telling me not to bother anyone in the main house, just go through the side gate and open the door to the wine cellar. It wasn't really a wine cellar, as it was above ground. It was one room with no kitchen. It had a wall with nothing but racks of wine, a king-sized waterbed, a small picnic table and bench, and a tiny bathroom with a shower. Best of all, it was free!

It was a cool place to live — until someone walked in one day, looking bewildered, and asked me what the hell I was doing in *his* house! I tried to explain to him that I was given permission to stay there until my friend came back from Canada. The man standing in front of me looked at me as if I was insane, and my having CP didn't help. "What friend, and who gave you this key? I don't know who you are, but if you're not out of here by this evening, I am calling the police." Needless to say, I moved out quickly! I was also pissed at C.W. for lying to me. He would only say that he was stunned that his friend had lied to *him*. He said that he would find me another place to live, which he did. To be honest, I can't believe I managed to live there for a few days before the owner discovered me!

I spent a couple more nights with C.W. and Sharon before he straightened things out. This time he found me a place in Westwood. I moved in with a single mother and her two toddlers. I cannot recall the children's names, but their mother's name was Lee Ann. It was another ideal place to live, as it was only $100 per month and was about two miles from the Comedy Store West, the newer location in West Hollywood. Lee Ann was going through a divorce and was struggling to make ends meet. She had the two kids share one bedroom while I rented the other child's room. It was all furnished with children's furniture. Letters of the alphabet were painted on the wall, and characters from *Sesame Street* adorned the bedspread.

At this time I was working another club as well, the Improvisation on Melrose in Hollywood. Between the Cave, the two Stores, and now the Improv, I was sometimes able to work six nights a week. Politically, comedians were not supposed to play both the Improv and the Store because the owners, Budd Friedman and Mitzi Shore, were in competition with one another. You were expected to make a choice, showing loyalty to one or the other. It worked for those who got a lot of spots at one or the other, but those of us like me, who didn't get many spots at either, cheated and did both clubs, always hoping the other club wouldn't find out.

Then, Budd Friedman started booking me regularly at the Improv. In fact, he was giving me more stage time than the Comedy Store and Comedy Store West combined. I felt a little guilty since I had started at the Store, but I also had to survive.

I had been working at the Improv for about a month when I was approached one night by a handsome man named Jack King. Jack had the look of a knight in shining armor that most women fantasize about. He was undeniably handsome: over six feet tall with a football-player physique. He sat down next to me at the bar and started talking to me. I was actually stunned that someone as handsome as him was having a conversation with *me*. Men usually didn't give me the time of day. He basically said that he loved my act, and that I was going to be a star. He asked me if I had a manager and I said yes.

Somewhere during the course of the conversation, he shifted gears, asking me how old I was and if I was a virgin. I told him the truth: I was 22, and yes, I was a virgin. He acted shocked. "I can't believe someone as beautiful as you is a virgin!" He gave me his card and asked me to call him so we could discuss management. I explained again that I already had a manager and a contract with George. Jack said contracts were broken every day. He walked me to my car.

He held my hand on the way out and again commented on how beautiful I was. I was embarrassed when we got to my old beat-up Biscayne. He then kissed me on the lips. When I reacted with resistance, he apologized, saying that he forgot how young I was. He went on to explain that if I hadn't been a virgin, he would make love to me in a heartbeat, but since I was, he had to be respectful. He then opened my car door and reminded me once again to call him.

I drove back to my little room in Westwood and climbed into a twin bed with a Big Bird and Cookie Monster quilt wrapped around me. I was fraught with anxiety. I asked myself: what do I do with this situation? On the one hand, it would prove to George that I was a beautiful woman and someone else "wanted me," but on the other, I just wanted to remain safe under the covers and make people laugh. I couldn't put my finger on it, but something didn't feel right, and I was scared.

I called George the next morning, letting him know that a dashing man in his thirties wanted to make love to me. George laughed, saying that it was a line. A part of me knew that it probably was, but my ego resented that he didn't believe anyone could truly be attracted to me. At least that is how I *felt*. Because I had such low self-esteem, I wanted so badly to just prove to myself that I was desirable, even though I didn't really welcome any of the advances that were being made.

That very afternoon I placed a call to Jack to set up a lunch date. I was not going to allow myself to act like a scared little girl. I was relieved when Jack didn't pick up the phone. I left my number on his machine, telling him that I had called about getting together for lunch. He called me later that evening. I felt like I was in control until he shifted gears, wanting to pick me up for dinner that evening instead of meeting for lunch the next day. Instinctively, I panicked. I told him that I was waiting for Mitzi Shore to call me. Jack laughed and asked me who the hell I thought I was, that Mitzi would call *me*.

He also reminded me that we had met at the Improv, and if Mitzi was calling me then I must be two-timing both Budd and Mitzi. So I told him that I was joking, that the real reason I couldn't go to dinner with him was that I'd had three wisdom teeth pulled that morning, and that I wouldn't be able to eat anything until the following morning. (I didn't think one wisdom tooth would be serious enough to get out of dinner.) Looking back, it's funny that I had chosen my wisdom teeth, because I certainly wasn't demonstrating any wisdom in this situation.

Jack's response to my pulled teeth excuse was "Then we'll go out for ice cream, okay, little girl?"

"I'm not a little girl!"

"Then stop making up stupid excuses, and act like an adult!"

I wanted to hang up on him, but I told him where I lived instead. When he arrived, I was surprised to see that he was wearing sweats. I thought that this was a business meeting, and he was dressed to go jogging. I think the restaurant we went to was Bob's Big Boy, located on Westwood Boulevard within walking distance from the Comedy Store West. It wasn't exactly a romantic night out.

He mentioned how good I looked for having three wisdom teeth pulled. He smiled, saying that he didn't notice any swelling or bruising at all. It was a very awkward conversation, and it got even more awkward by the minute. When the waitress brought us the menus, he told her that I was only going to have ice cream. So that is what I ordered, even though I knew that he knew I hadn't even been to a dentist. When our food arrived, his demeanor changed again. I thought we were going to discuss my career, when all of a sudden he teared up, informing me that he needed to tell me something very painful. I was not able to see how he was so blatantly playing me.

Next, Jack dropped a bombshell. He told me that he only had three months to live. Being hearing impaired, I thought perhaps I misunderstood him. "You have how long to live?" He became irritated that he had to repeat himself, but did so anyway. I heard the same words, *three months to live.* He dabbed his eyes with his napkin. Truthfully, I almost laughed. The man looked radiantly healthy. The possibility that he was dying seemed about as plausible as the story of me having my wisdom teeth removed that day.

Searching my mind for something to say that was going to be "mature," I told him that he could do a lot in three months! His self-pity immediately disappeared, replaced by anger that I could be so insensitive. I felt stupid and guilty, not realizing that was *exactly* how he wanted me to feel. He continued to tell me that not all diseases have their own telethon like mine did. Some people don't have the love and support that people with cerebral palsy have. I told him that I was sorry, and then asked him what disease he had. He looked at me again, and quietly told me that I'd just asked him a very insensitive question. Little by little, he was eating away at my self-confidence.

When he was paying our check at the cash register, I backed away from him, and tried to think of how I could get out of there. He caught me and yelled, "Where are you going?" I winced when everyone in the restaurant looked in my direction. Even the cashier raised an eyebrow. In a condescending manner, he told her that I got confused sometimes, and pointed to his head. I was pissed and asked him why he said that. He told me it was because he thought I was going to run off, acting like a child again. When we got in the car, I mumbled for him to just take me home. Very little else was said, and I was relieved when we finally turned the corner onto my street.

However, instead of driving down the block to my house, he pulled over and parked. I assumed he was just mistaken, and told him this wasn't where I lived. He laughed, pointing out to me what a child I was. He explained that mature men and women like to sit in the car and get to know each other better. "Haven't you ever been on a date?" I felt so ashamed and embarrassed for not knowing how to act or what to say. He continued to ridicule me, saying that I used my adorable little cerebral palsy to hold audiences in the palm of my hand, "Yet, intimately, you're retarded."

"I am not!" I protested.

He then pulled his sweats down and put my hand on his penis. "Let me show you what adults do." He held my hand tightly and moved it back and forth. "Just keep doing that. . . ." He then unbuttoned my blouse and undid my bra. I started crying. He screamed at me to stop, but I couldn't. He then reached across me and pushed the door open. "Go on, get out! You're a little girl! Go find your mommy and daddy!"

Holding my bra and blouse closed against my bare breasts, I quickly walked toward my residence. He did not rape me, and I was grateful for that, but I was mortified and ashamed, exactly how he wanted me to feel. I thought it was over, but then he got out of the car and started running to catch up to me. I thought that he was going to grab me, but he went ahead of me, and then walked backwards all the way up the street, calling me names. He whistled and called me a "doggy," among other things. I prayed that a police cruiser would drive by, just like one did on Carol Burnett's street, but no such luck this time.

When we got to the door, I was shaking more than usual and couldn't put the key in the door. He grabbed the key and imitated me missing the keyhole repeatedly. Then he got very serious again, like he had been earlier. He said how disappointed he was in me, how he was hoping to discover a mature compassionate young woman, only to find out that I was just a baby. He told me that he had lost his wife recently in a car accident and really needed someone to talk to.

He then put the key in the door, but before I could get inside he told me not to tell anyone what had happened, that if I did, I could kiss my career goodbye. He reminded me that he knew I was playing both the Improv and the Store. "You say anything to anyone, and you won't have *any* club to work in." He also threatened me by saying that he knew where I lived, my phone number, and my license plate number. "I know a lot of people. Remember,

Geri, this town is really small, and if you choose to stay in this business, we'll meet up again." As I was just about to go inside the door, he called my name loudly from the sidewalk. I looked over to see him mooning me.

In retrospect, I realize he was only revealing what an asshole he was.

However, in the moment I was unable to look at it so objectively. I had no idea that he was probably just as threatened by me — because I could tell people what he'd done — is why he had to intimidate me. If I could have only realized my own power, I would not have given it away so easily.

After I climbed into bed, I was unable to sleep. I felt like crying, but I didn't want to wake anyone up, so I grabbed my car keys and drove aimlessly, screaming and crying, hating myself, and hating my body, punching myself in my thighs, trying to numb the pain. I did not get back home until daybreak. My tank was as empty as I felt inside.

CHAPTER ELEVEN

Nice Dreams

I avoided performing at the Improv at all costs, knowing that was where Jack sometimes hung out. I still performed at the Store and the Cave, but I had to build up my self-confidence all over again. It was during this time that I found a new place to live. I no longer felt comfortable living at Lee Ann's, and besides, I think one of the kids wanted his bedroom back.

I am not completely sure where I met Robert Schimmel, but I think it was at the Comedy Cave in 1979. Schimmel was a brilliant writer and stand-up comic, and he was looking for a roommate to help share the expenses of his two-bedroom apartment in Hollywood. It was located on Genesee Avenue, just off Melrose. Fairfax High School was across the street, and there was a video arcade nearby that I would later frequent.

For $100 per month, I rented a furnished bedroom from Robert. He had recently separated from his wife, who retained custody of their daughter. We were both vulnerable and in a lot of emotional pain, struggling to find our place on Hollywood's Walk of Fame. We were good company for one another, and I can remember spending many nights until the wee hours of the morning at Canter's, the famous deli on Fairfax Avenue. There was nothing better than a hot bowl of chicken noodle soup in that deli at two in the morning on a cold winter night.

It wasn't long before Robert found yet another roommate who needed a place to live. Raul just slept on the sofa in the living room. He was another comedian — imagine three comics living under the same roof. It was the gender reversal of *Three's Company*. Instead of Jack, Chrissy, and Janet, it was Geri, Robert, and Raul. I decided after a couple months that Raul should have the second bedroom. Robert didn't agree with the plan. He felt that I shouldn't have to sleep on the sofa in the living room. I agreed: I didn't want to sleep in the living room, either. I wanted to rent the closet off the living room, underneath the staircase. Initially, he thought that I was joking, but I wasn't. I loved the idea of my bedroom being the little closet under the staircase. (I was the original Harry Potter!)

Robert balked at the notion of such lunacy, but when he wasn't home one afternoon I moved all my things into the closet and put all of Raul's things in the second bedroom. I laid a mattress with a sleeping bag down on the floor, with my pillow placed at the high end of the ceiling so that when I sat up in the morning I wouldn't bash my head on the staircase. I hung my clothes like I would in any other closet and had plenty of shelving for the rest of my things. A single lightbulb hung from the ceiling with a pull chain. To make the room look bigger, I put up a poster of Paris on one wall and Hawaii on the other. I couldn't have been happier with this arrangement. I felt secure, and my room was easy to clean.

Robert, on the other hand, felt bad about it, and he got a lot of flack from the other comics when they heard that he was renting me a freaking closet! Everyone had a hard time believing that it was my idea. Robert lowered my rent; after all, my bedroom was actually smaller than a half bath, so he figured it was the least he could do. What people didn't understand is that from the time I was a small child, I loved cubbyholes and closets. I think it was the result of spending the first three months of my life in an incubator. Even today, I still feel more comfortable in a closet than in a large room.

I remember when my parents came up to visit me and met Robert for the first time. He was mortified when Mom and Dad saw my "bedroom."

"Mr. Jewell," he said, "this was not my idea. Geri wanted the closet, and I gave her a discount, and she has access to the rest of the apartment." My parents knew me well enough to realize it was my idea, but Robert nevertheless felt embarrassed.

The next time they came to visit me they brought me a gift. Dad always handed me some cash before he left, but this time my parents had a beautifully wrapped package. I thought perhaps it was a small TV, but it wasn't. My mom, always the practical one, was worried that I wouldn't get enough air in the closet. The package was a fan, with a note that said, "We don't always understand why you do the things you do, but we support you fully. Hope this fan keeps your closet cool on the hot summer nights. Always know that we are your biggest fans forever. Go after your dreams, sweetheart. Love, Mom and Dad."

I will also never forget one Saturday afternoon when the landlord paid a visit to Schimmel. We were late on our rent, and he was in the neighbor-hood. Since we'd all performed late the night before, we were all still asleep when he came to the door. Robert let him in, and he sat on the sofa while waiting for Robert to bring him a check. Robert came up short, so, right in front of the landlord, Robert knocked on the closet door and said that he needed the rent. I turned on the light, wrote him a check, and slid it under the door. Robert enjoyed the priceless look on the landlord's face.

I continued to do stand-up and even found the courage to return to the Improv. Even though a part of me never wanted to go back to that place, I knew I had to at some point because I needed the work and the practice. That is the only way comics get better at their craft. Besides, it was a pop-ular club, and I had always enjoyed working there. About two and a half months after the horrible incident with Jack, I finally called in for a spot. I thought that I was emotionally ready, but as I performed I began to stutter, and I even forgot a punch line. I just looked lost as the audience waited patiently for the funny to happen. The sad reality is, it never did. I was off the mark and off the stage as quickly as I could be. You could almost hear Dorothy Gale saying, "My, people come and go so quickly here!"

Comedians are always going to have bad nights. For whatever reason, the best of us will bomb at one time or another. That is one absolute guar-antee. If a comic says they've never bombed, they're either lying or they've never performed. However, this night was more than just being off the mark. I was terrified of being on that stage. I kept looking for Jack in the shadows and the darkness of the audience, waiting with raw anxiety for him to appear. Was he standing in the back of the room waiting to humiliate me further? It's not like he'd have to do much: I did a great job of embarrassing myself by allowing the fear to affect my ability to be in the moment onstage.

As the emcee scrambled to the stage, covering for an extremely short and confusing comedy routine, I was met by Budd Friedman in the hallway. My heart raced when he spoke to me. I remember him asking, "What kind of shit was that? You weren't funny, and you don't stutter! What is that stut-tering shit and forgetting your material?" I just looked at him, not sure of what to say. He continued to scold me, "I don't want that shit on my stage! Do you understand?" Of course I did, since I didn't want that shit on his stage either. I apologized for doing such a poor performance and simply said that I got scared.

He told me that all comedians are scared; that's why you have to be funny, so the stage won't be so scary. I knew that he was right. I apologized again and said that I was scared of someone being in the audience. Budd humored me by saying something like, "That's why they are called an audience . . . because someone is watching you." I smiled weakly, still sensing he was not happy with me. Then he surprised me, by adding, "Who were you so afraid of? Is it Jack?"

My mouth fell open. "You know?"

"Geri, of course I know. Nothing goes on here that I don't know about." That shouldn't have been so surprising, as Jack did work at the Improv in some capacity. At this point, I was half expecting him to say, "I'm so sorry, what I can do to help you?" But anyone who knows Budd knows that is not his style, and, besides, I truly doubt that Jack told him what *really* happened. When I told him that he hurt me badly, Budd's response was that people get hurt in life, that I had to grow up and move on. As insensitive as he sounded, he was right.

I never ran into Jack at the Improv again. I do not know the circumstances of his disappearance from the club, or if it had anything to do with our conflict, but I do know that, in the end, Budd respected me. He was always kind when we saw each other in the following years, and much later when he produced *An Evening at the Improv* on A&E, he had me on the program. He also raised money for United Cerebral Palsy by partnering with the telethon, filming segments of stand-up acts from the Improv. I have always felt that that was Budd's way of acknowledging me. I have the utmost respect for Budd because, regardless of whatever happened, he was right. If I was going to continue in show business, I had to be strong and keep moving forward.

During this time I got cast in my first movie, the Cheech and Chong film *Nice Dreams*. I don't recall the actual audition, only that the following day I got the role. I worked three weeks on this film and got my Screen Actors Guild card as a result. My role was that of a mental patient who dresses as a waitress and walks around with a pen and notepad taking orders from all the other mental patients. The role was actually inspired by one of my own jokes: "I used to be a waitress, but they didn't like the way I tossed salads. . . . I was fired, but I'm thinking of applying for a job at Shakey's."

It was a wonderful experience working on this cult film. In fact, my friend Alex Valdez was in the film as well. They filmed a hysterical scene where Cheech Marin was given LSD by Timothy Leary and on his acid trip he saw me onstage doing stand-up comedy, instead of walking around in a delusional state taking orders as a waitress. It was an obvious showcase for my act, and it would have remained in the film had I not had an unfortunate mishap.

When I signed the contract to do the film, I also had to sign an additional contract that prevented me from "walking" anywhere. The insurance company felt that because I had poor coordination, it would be best if I not be allowed to walk anywhere. They felt that I might trip and become a liability. (The only trips allowed on set were acid trips.) It was only under these conditions that the insurance company would allow me to do the film. I even had to use an electric cart to go to the restroom. I wasn't happy with it, but I was working, so I didn't complain. (Even though there were many other people in this film who walked a hell of a lot worse than I did!)

I was well into the third week of filming when I had a 5:30 a.m. call. I had been up late the night before, and I pressed the snooze button one too many times. When I finally realized what time it was, I quickly headed for the set on Sunset Boulevard. I was late and half asleep. I pulled into the parking lot and started walking up the hill to the actual set where we were filming. I was quickly reprimanded by a production assistant, who reminded me that I was not allowed to "walk" up the hill. I protested, saying that I was late. He didn't care.

He radioed to another assistant that I needed a cart sent down the hill to transport me to the set. They were scrambling to find one. None were available at the moment, and there was precious time being wasted by me waiting for one. I knew I could be up that hill in a couple of minutes if they'd just let me walk. As fate would have it, a small pickup truck came by on its way to the set. I was asked if I minded hitching a ride on the back. The driver said that he would go slow, and for me to just hang on.

As he put his foot on the gas, I was startled by the quick jolt, let go, and fell off the truck. Well, that certainly woke me up! Of course, everyone was in a panic, forming a small entourage around me. With all the attention I was getting that morning, you'd think I was the star of the film. The doctor on the set (besides Timothy Leary) thought that I should be taken to the emergency room of Cedars-Sinai. I've always hated emergency rooms and wished they could have just taken me to an urgent care center instead, but at that hour there were none open.

It turned out I had broken a thumb and one finger and sprained my wrist. They put a cast halfway up my arm so that I couldn't move anything. Because my body makes so many involuntary movements, limiting motion in any part of my body causes me a lot of pain. By the time I got back to the movie set, they were already serving lunch. I had been at the hospital for the entire morning and was starving. Eating was difficult, though, as my dominant hand was the one I had fallen on.

I was sitting at the lunch table trying to eat with my right hand, when Tommy Chong sat down across from me. He was concerned about me, asking how I was doing. I told him that I was fine, but could he please cut my steak for me. He did so and felt horrible about what had happened. "Jeez, Jewell, had the insurance company only let you walk, I wouldn't be sitting here cutting your meat!" We both laughed. What I didn't understand was that because my arm was in a cast, I was about to be axed from the film.

They tried their best to keep me in it, but my new cast made it really difficult, so every bit of my footage ended up on the cutting room floor. However, I've never been one to believe that there are accidents in life. There is a reason for everything, and had I actually made the cut, it would have been a nightmare for the producers of *The Facts of Life*, a squeaky clean G-rated show. So, maybe an angel *gently* pushed me off the truck to save me from embarrassment later on. Overall, it was a wonderful experience. I got my SAG card, got paid (or rather, George did), got film credit, and eventually my left hand healed.

Even though I lost my job working on *Nice Dreams*, I had another audition that same week, even with the cast on my arm. Burt Reynolds was specifically looking for actors with disabilities to star in a play that he was producing in his theater in Jupiter, Florida. It was an open audition for all actors, but I remember there being a significant number of those us with disabilities. The audition took place in a large auditorium in Los Angeles, so of course I was lucky enough to be in the right place at the right time.

I chose to wear my famous T-shirt for the audition, thinking that if Reynolds was reading what it said, he wouldn't notice the cast on my arm. Truthfully, I had never been asked to do a cold reading before. Even when I auditioned for the Cheech and Chong film, there was no script to read. I was nervous, but anxiously waited for my name to be called. Finally, my scene partner and I walked onstage. I had the first line and waited patiently for Burt Reynolds to say "action." It felt as though 15 minutes had elapsed, but it was actually only about five. Still, what was taking him so long to yell "action"? I was beginning to feel like an idiot just standing there, so I finally took the initiative to ask Burt Reynolds what the problem was. I looked right at him, inquiring what on earth he was waiting for! Everyone started laughing.

"What am *I* waiting for?"

"Yeah, I've been waiting for you to say 'action,' so I can start saying my lines." Everyone in the auditorium howled. Laughter to any comic feels like a good thing, so I smiled . . . that is, until Mr. Reynolds explained to me that he had said "action" almost five minutes earlier. And he wasn't willing to repeat it. Instead, he said, "Next." Needless to say, I was not asked to come to Jupiter, or any other planet for that matter.

Afterward, Reynolds told those of us who didn't get a role that we shouldn't feel as though we had failed. "No audition is a failure. The fact that you showed up is a success in itself. There are going to be a lot of auditions in your career, and each one is as important as the next. All it takes is one yes, no matter how many noes, so you must never give up trying. You all did a terrific job, even Geri Jewell, who kept us waiting in total suspense as to what she was going to do. She had all of us on the edge of our seats, waiting with genuine anticipation for her performance. Too bad we never got to see it. If it was intentional, Geri, you did get all our attention. I, for one, will never forget you."

It was genuinely *not* intentional. I was not wearing my hearing aids and had no idea that he had said action. I was so pissed at myself, but not enough to start wearing my hearing aids. My hearing loss had been problematic for my entire life, and I stubbornly refused to wear my hearing aids because the feedback was worse than the hearing loss itself.

There are times when hearing loss can work to one's advantage. Freeway traffic, electric lawn mowers, annoying neighbors throwing loud parties, and children screaming are just a few sounds that I take pleasure in missing. In 1980, Howard Rosenberg did an article on me for the Calendar section of the *Los Angeles Times*. In reviewing my act, I was particularly surprised by his comment about how much self-confidence I had onstage. "When heckled repeatedly, she acted as if she didn't even hear them!" I laughed, because had Howard not pointed this out, I wouldn't have even known I had any hecklers. I could hear the occasional chatter, but never was able to hear the mean remarks that were said. So my impaired hearing can be a blessing in disguise.

Granted, I did have a tremendous amount of self-confidence, although there were definite holes in it from time to time. Think of my self-confidence as a beautifully crocheted blanket. As a whole, it looks great and offers warmth and security. However, if you were to look at the same blanket stitch by stitch, you'd become aware of each individual hole between the patches of yarn. From afar, it looks like a strongly woven item. Up close, you see the cracks.

There were many things that happened in 1980 that reinforced the beautifully crocheted blanket as a whole. One of the producers of the Second Annual Media Access Awards, Fern Field Brooks, had heard about me, and came to see me perform. She then hired me to do stand-up comedy at the awards banquet in Beverly Hills. To dress up a little, instead of wearing my typical blue denim overalls, I bought a pair of blue satin overalls with my famous T-shirt underneath. I ended up receiving a standing ovation, and this performance is literally what changed my life.

After my performance, Fern's husband, Norman Brooks, took my hand and brought me over to his table to introduce me to Norman Lear. Mr. Lear congratulated me on a wonderful comedy routine and told me he was thrilled to meet me personally. Because I was hearing impaired, I didn't hear who I was being introduced to. I thanked him for the compliment and quickly excused myself to go find George.

As fate would have it, I ran into Mr. Lear a second time that evening, this time in a crowded elevator. Norman smiled when George and I stepped onto the elevator. I turned to George and said "This is the man I met earlier," and then turned toward Norman and said, "I'm sorry, what's your name again?" George rolled his eyes, and Norman laughed, repeating his name and adding, "Don't forget it, kid. You'll be hearing from me again real soon!" A few months later I *did* hear from Norman Lear again, when he offered me the role of Cousin Geri on the NBC sitcom *The Facts of Life*.

Lear asked me to set up a meeting with Al Burton, one of the executive producers of the show. My dear friends, Fern Field Brooks and her husband, had had several discussions with Norman Lear about what he could do to secure a showcase for me on one of his shows. Among the list of shows that either he created or produced were *Archie Bunker's Place*, *Diff'rent Strokes*, and *The Facts of Life*.

Out of all the shows, *Facts* seemed like the one best suited to me at the time. Al Burton was more than delighted to create a showcase for me. The show was struggling and NBC had reservations about its future. It had been canceled, and then brought back with a smaller cast. Cutting the cast in half was done to allow greater character development for those who remained. This second season of the show was going to determine whether it would succeed or fail. The almighty Nielsen ratings were monitored each week for approval from viewers.

My very first episode, "Cousin Geri," written by Ann Gibbs and Joel Kimmel, was taped about two weeks before Christmas in 1980, and actually aired on Christmas Eve. I played the role of Geri Warner, Blair Warner's cousin. I felt as though I was on cloud nine, believing that I had "made it." I was vaguely familiar with the show and was looking forward to joining the cast members — Charlotte Rae, Lisa Whelchel, Kim Fields, Mindy Cohn, and Nancy McKeon. Everyone — the cast members, crew, and the producers — was extremely supportive of me. We rehearsed for four days and then taped on the fifth day, twice, in front of a live audience. I had to laugh when the wardrobe department reproduced my infamous cerebral palsy T-shirt for the episode (and this time with correct spelling).

There has always been the assumption that I was friends with all the girls, but in reality there was a huge age gap that set us apart. I was 23, whereas Mindy, Kim, and Nancy were between the ages of 11 and 14 in 1980. When the girls weren't rehearsing lines, they were primarily studying with a teacher in another room. Lisa, on the other hand, already had her high school diploma, so naturally I was able to socialize with her more frequently, and we did develop a close friendship fairly quickly.

Charlotte Rae was also very supportive. I can recall her giving me a small book about love. In it she had written that she was delighted I was on the show, and if I ever needed anything, to feel free to call her. "Love, Charlotte Rae." I was touched by the kind gesture, but knew because of our age difference that she was not going to be someone I would be able to hang out with; she became more a parent figure than a friend.

It was an extremely exciting week, and even though I only signed a contract for one episode, depending on how well the "Cousin Geri" episode did in the Nielson ratings and how the public responded, I was told I might be asked back. I can recall George telling me that this was just the beginning, but I was truly only living in the moment. If there was more of this "dream" to come, I couldn't fully visualize it, as I felt it was remarkable that I had achieved as much as I had already. The "Cousin Geri" episode in itself was a dream come true, and nobody was more grateful or amazed than I was.

Because it was taped right around the Christmas holidays, it made the week feel even more magical and exciting. When I opened my dressing room door, I was stunned to see a huge gift basket from the executive producers and NBC. It was as if Santa had come early. I had a little Walkman, and when I wasn't working on my lines, I listened to Christmas music on cassettes. To this day, whenever I hear John Denver's version of "O Holy Night," I immediately associate the music with filming that episode. For me, that song holds the memory of the joy that I felt.

I was a quick study, but there was one part of that episode that was a bit difficult and took more takes than usual. It was the last part of the scene where I had to do a song and dance with Blair called "Tea for Two." Because of my cerebral palsy, dancing was always difficult. I find it strange that not only did I have a dance scene in my first episode of *Facts*, but years later I also had a memorable dance scene in the HBO series, *Deadwood*. Strange, because I absolutely *loathe* dancing. In the '80s, when friends would take me to discos, I never enjoyed myself and always wanted to leave early.

I remember knocking on Lisa Whelchel's dressing room door, feeling embarrassed that I needed some additional rehearsal time to get the dialogue and dance steps in sync. It felt as though one part of my brain memorized the lines, and another part of my brain tried to memorize the dance steps. Both parts of the brain having to work together was stressful and quite difficult. The part of the brain that memorized lines could function at an incredibly fast pace, but when the other part of my brain that was affected by CP had to tag along, it would cause the faster part of my brain functioning to slow down so the physical part could catch up.

I learned a long time ago that the fewer things I have to do physically onstage the easier it is to recite lines — it's 100 times easier. Most actors do not have a hard time with this because they are not trying to juggle a neurological impairment. Years later when I observed Michael J. Fox performing with the additional challenge of Parkinson's disease, my heart went out to him, and I applaud him for what he has been able to achieve. He became an acquaintance of mine during my *Facts of Life* days, as we were both on NBC shows at the same time. We saw each other at many of the same functions. He also dated Nancy McKeon the following season, so often he would be at the tapings of the show.

Lisa Whelchel couldn't have been any sweeter in her willingness to rehearse the song and dance sequence over and over again until I could finally get the two parts of my brain fairly compatible. When I watch that episode on DVD today, I can see the struggle: desperately trying to deliver the lines while keeping my torso, arms, and legs moving. When we taped the show the second time in front of the live audience, I ad-libbed "I love you, Blair." It wasn't in the script, and I never said it in any of the rehearsals or the live taping earlier that afternoon. It was out of sheer raw gratefulness for many things: the incredible opportunity to be on the show, the total appreciation for Lisa for rehearsing that part of the script so many times with me, and out of absolute relief that it was a wrap and I would not have to do that song and dance ever again. I believe the reason it was kept in the final cut was because even the executive producers knew it was genuinely powerful and sincere. It added two seconds of compassion that were not there previously.

Mom and Dad didn't come to very many of my stand-up performances, as it was a long haul to drive from Orange County to L.A. Truthfully I didn't invite them that many times, and the times that I did, I remember well. I didn't want them in my audiences at the nightclubs, not until I honed my craft. I was nervous enough already without having the additional anxiety of my parents being in the audience. What if I bombed? I knew instinctively that if Mom and Dad had ever witnessed me bombing onstage, it would have been a lot more painful for them than it would ever be for me. So it was with some trepidation that I invited them to the live taping of my first *Facts of Life* episode.

I remember when they arrived and knocked on my dressing room door. They were very excited about the gold star with my name on it that was on the door. Mom was always very shy, but she said hello to everyone. Both my parents were beaming from ear to ear. They were so proud of me, and I knew it. Now I had to do a good show. When the episode aired on Christmas Eve in 1980, it had the highest Nielsen ratings the show had ever gotten to date. Between that fact of life and the fan mail that followed, it looked like I was going to return the following season.

I remember watching the episode when it first aired with Mom, Dad, Gloria, and her husband Skip. My parents both wiped tears from their eyes and laughed in all the right places. For Christmas that year, they gave me a gold necklace with the comedy and tragedy masks. They couldn't have given me a more special gift. When the credits rolled at the end of the show and my name flashed on the television screen, I knew that this was the beginning of something big. I had no way of knowing it yet, but I would forever go down in history as the first person with a visible disability to earn a regular role on a prime-time television series. No matter what would happen next, that part was written in stone.

It felt as though my life had become very surreal overnight. As a lonely teenager, I procrastinated doing my homework and lived vicariously through television. Now I had stepped into the television and merged with the images that I had previously enjoyed only from a distance.

My dreams were unfolding right before my eyes, but "real life" does not occur in neat, 30-minute segments. With every dream that comes true, there is a lot of life experience that happens at the same time. There was a tremendous amount of work, pain, and growth that ran parallel with the instant magic of my overnight success. My life was about to become more public, which in turn made me become intensely private. I was about to move out of Schimmel's closet. But, symbolically, I was about to move into another one.

Chapter Twelve

Out of the Closet, Onto a Pedestal

I remember hearing Carole King singing the song "Tapestry" when I was in high school. My life had definitely echoed those lyrics, as it had been quite a tapestry, unfolding right before my eyes. Some of the most amazing and difficult years to write about are 1980 through 1985. My life seemed to take one surreal turn after another, ultimately plunging me into depression. I have battled depression since my teens and know positively that it had nothing to do with cerebral palsy, but with my isolation and lack of social skills.

Because my life during this time was such a roller coaster, I have wondered whether my mood swings were the result of what was happening outside of me, or were reflecting outwardly what was happening on the inside. Spiritually, I tend to believe the latter. One of my strongest traits since I was a child has always been my sense of humor. Without it, I wouldn't have taken the road to stand-up comedy. My creative mind and sense of humor are what carried me to rarely experienced highs, and what heightened my ability to cope with shadowy lows as well.

I will never forget meeting my next roommate and friend, Laurel Dann, just before I filmed my first episode of *The Facts of Life*. I was booked at an awards dinner for ADEPT, a nonprofit organization that created employment for persons with disabilities. It was one of my first comedy/motivational speaking gigs. For whatever reason, I wasn't comfortable driving myself there and asked the contractor if someone could please give me a ride. Laurel offered to pick me up in Hollywood and take me to the dinner. We were the same age and we both had cerebral palsy.

We hit it off instantly and were surprised to discover that we had known each other as kids when we both went to Camp Paivika. When Laurel found out that I was renting a closet, she was more horrified than my parents were and offered to let me live with her in Hermosa Beach. I knew intuitively it would be a good move, and we became fast friends. Schimmel was a bit irritated that he was losing a roommate, but he also knew that living at the beach was much better than living in a closet, and he couldn't stay mad at me for long. Besides, Schimmel needed more closet space. I was forever grateful for the time that I lived with Robert. We followed each other's careers, and I was deeply saddened when he died in September 2010. Robert was one of the great unsung comics of our time, a genius who offered profound insights into the absurdities of the human experience. I am truly blessed to have known him.

Laurel had a small one-bedroom apartment above a garage right on the strand, the cement version of a boardwalk. I believe our total rent was $375 a month. Today if we were to rent the same place, it would be at least $2,000 a month. We were literally 20 feet from the ocean. I used to roller-skate on the strand all the way to Manhattan beach and back, and, in a case of perfect timing, I had a bike again so I could ride along the beach too. I had done a show for Dick Clark and they were going to film me skating, but Clark felt I handled a ten-speed bike better and had me ride that in the segment. He was right of course, as years later Big Bird would attest when I roller-skated with him on *Sesame Street*. As a gift, Dick Clark gave me the bike when we finished filming.

Life at the beach was such a wonderful time. Laurel and I loved to toss a football or a Frisbee in the sand. Sometimes we would sit outside and watch the sunset together. We even enjoyed some of the same music, like Jane Olivor, Christopher Cross, Joan Baez, and Judy Collins. We laughed a lot and were the best of friends. Laurel sometimes accompanied me to the comedy clubs to watch me perform. It used to crack us up when some people would come up to *her* after *I* performed and comment on how funny she was, thinking she was me!

Laurel and I had so much in common that I used to refer to her as "my astro-twin," possibly separated at birth. She was employed as a rehab counselor for the California State Department of Rehabilitation. She also knew sign language and was surprised that I didn't know it, being as hearing impaired as I am. She tried teaching it to me, but realized quickly that I just didn't have the patience to learn it. To this day, I do not know sign language.

Laurel wasn't only astonished that I didn't know sign language, but she was also surprised when I told her I wasn't gay. She was and thought that I was as well. I felt totally comfortable with the idea of it, but I just wasn't sure who I was yet. Deep down I knew my true orientation, but I was in denial about it. At the same time, because I associated sex with trauma, whatever natural leanings I may have felt were met with emotional and psychological barriers.

My identity was quickly solidifying as a "comedienne." The more well known I became, the more I was perceived as an inspirational, funny, "special" person. My sexuality was basically a nonissue, which I reinforced. Because I was in such deep denial, I had a hard time recognizing sexual energy when it was being expressed. Being a comedian created a safe place for me to go in my mind, pushing my sexuality aside altogether. I longed for intimacy, but truly did not know how to attain it. So, I retreated into the safety net of the stage, consciously wanting to be loved and accepted, and subconsciously wanting to be held.

Before the episode "Cousin Geri" had even aired, Lisa Whelchel invited me to have dinner with her. Lisa was living in a small apartment in Studio City. I still was driving from Hermosa Beach to either the San Fernando Valley or Hollywood/Westwood, where most of the comedy clubs were located. Lisa was driving a gold Trans Am at the time, so after I got to her place we decided we'd use her car. I was a little surprised how modest her apartment was and that she lived by herself. I thought for sure she would still be living with her parents. She told me that her family lived in Texas, and she tried to get home as much as possible. Lisa was only 18 at the time, but because she had been a working actress since she was 12, she was very mature in a lot of ways, as if her childhood had been taken from her prematurely. Like me, she was young and old at the same time, trying to find her way in the world.

We had a lovely dinner and got back around 10 at night. Lisa was genuinely concerned about me driving all the way to Hermosa Beach so late, not realizing that making that drive at least four nights a week was routine for me. It really wasn't a big deal to me; it was only a big deal to my clunker that was looking forward to retiring at some comfortable junkyard soon. Lisa insisted that I stay the night. I reluctantly said no, but she handed me a spare key, explaining that she was leaving for a red-eye flight to a John Denver Celebrity Ski Tournament. She would be spending the holidays with her family in Texas and would be away for about a three and a half weeks. She said I was welcome to stay at her place until she returned from Texas. In a moment, she was out the door and I was left standing alone in Lisa Whelchel's apartment on Bluffside Drive.

By the time Lisa returned, it was 1981, my episode of *Facts* had aired, and

I was beginning to get a little taste of the notoriety that Lisa had experienced for quite some time. After my debut on the show, I was recognized everywhere I went. People were responding to me in ways that ranged from smiling as I walked by to mobbing me for an autograph. I wondered if that was how David Cassidy felt. After all, *Facts of Life* was a popular teenybopper show, and I was even interviewed by *Tiger Beat* and *Teen Beat* magazines.

When Lisa returned from Texas, she surprised me once again. This time, instead of asking me to house-sit while she was away, she asked me to move in with her. I thought she was joking, but she wasn't. She explained that she could really use the company. My heart ached for her a little, realizing that she'd been famous for so long that she didn't know who loved her for just her, and who loved her because she was on television. It was this side of Lisa that I empathized with, the child/adult struggle. I wanted to protect her, when everyone else was enamored by her "Blair" persona. I felt touched that I was someone she felt she could trust.

Now, not only was I going to tell Laurel that I wasn't going to be coming home for a while, but that I wasn't coming home at all. I explained that Lisa had asked me to move in with her, and that it might not be a bad idea, considering how many miles I was already putting on my car.

Laurel was just as surprised as I was. She asked, "Is Lisa gay?"

Shocked, I yelled, "Of course not!"

"Then why are *you* moving in with her?"

"For the same reason I'm living with you: we are just friends."

"But Geri, what are you going to tell her when she finds out you're gay?"

Slightly irritated, I said, "Well, *I* haven't even found out I'm gay yet." I don't think denial gets much deeper than this. I wanted to go deep into a walk-in closet and stay there for the rest of my life. On the one hand, I had accomplished so much, so young, and should have felt the joy of having done so, but each moment of joy was followed by guilt, pain, and shame.

People tend to believe that gay men and women cannot have friendships with straight men or women because either they will fall in love with them or "make" them gay. No one can make anyone gay, and I have always had straight girlfriends who I have never been attracted to sexually. Lisa was one of those friends. There was no fantasy, lust, or longing. I was dealing with the opposite problem that Nancy McKeon was going through — while I was gay and almost everyone thought I was straight, she was straight but assumed to be gay because of her butch tomboy character. Thank God I was Lisa's roommate and not Nancy's. The rumor mill would have never stopped.

As it was, I ended up living with Lisa for about seven months, up until she purchased her first condo in Westwood. Although I didn't make that move with her, we both enjoyed our time together, and I felt we were very supportive of one another. Lisa had a social life that I understandably was not a part of, and I was doing my nightly stand-up gigs. We did see a lot of movies together and loved frequenting a fun frozen yogurt place in Studio City called Snacks.

I will never forget the time when we went to Westwood for dinner and a movie. The waiter was so excited to meet both of us and couldn't stop gushing about how much he loved *The Facts of Life*. We gave him our autographs, and he was so thrilled he almost forgot to take our orders. After he brought our check to the table, we took turns going to the restroom, and then we both left together, driving to a theater nearby.

Reaching for her wallet to pay for the movie, Lisa said, "That was so sweet of you to pay for dinner. I'll get the movie." I thought she was being sarcastic, because I had forgotten to thank her for the dinner. I said, "Very funny, Lisa. Since *you* paid for dinner, *I* will pay for the movie." We both looked at each other, shocked that neither one of us paid for dinner, stiffing that poor waiter who was so excited about meeting us. We couldn't stop laughing, but we did return later to pay for our dinner.

Lisa was lonely a lot of the time, and once she woke me up in the middle of the night to tell me that she was going to get a dog.

"You're kidding, right?"

"No, I really want a dog."

"But Lisa, we're living in a building that says no pets allowed."

"Well, it'll be a little dog; nobody will even see it."

"But the neighbors will hear it bark."

"We'll teach it not to bark."

I told her I thought it was a bad idea, and that she should think about it further.

Two days later, she brought home a tiny, white Maltese puppy under her jacket. I know that these are a much sought-after breed, but when I saw it for the first time, it looked like the end of a mop. Shortly after, Lisa had to leave for three weeks and left me to care for the mop with the shrill, high-pitched bark. I don't remember what the circumstances were behind her leaving so unexpectedly, but I was very worried about my ability to care for her puppy, which meant taking it outside to do its business without anyone seeing it!

The first time I tried to do what Lisa had done, hiding it in my jacket until I was safely out of sight, I was so panicked about getting caught that I didn't think it was worth it. Instead, I laid newspaper down inside the apartment, hoping it would know what it was for. When I got home each day, it was a horrible mess to clean up, and Lisa's puppy was lonely and crying. Insanity breeds insanity. I bought a kitten to keep Lisa's puppy company during the day. I gated the puppy in the kitchen with a chair from the living area, and the kitten used the cat box.

One evening, in the middle of a heat wave, the air conditioner broke. I opened the windows, but without the air conditioner, the place was unbearably hot. I decided to sleep on a neighbor's sofa next door. At about one in the morning, my neighbor was awakened by a dog barking. I bolted up and went to our apartment door, but the manager was at the door already.

"Do you have a dog in there?"

"Nooo . . ." As if on cue, Lisa's bog barked again. Our manager opened the door and was horrified! Not only was there a dog, but dog poop on the carpet, a cat, and a chair propped against the kitchenette with a hole chewed all the way through it!

I called Lisa the next day with the news of our eviction. I explained to her what had happened and promised her I would return the kitten. "What kitten?" Lisa flew home the next day to tend to our little crisis. She called everyone she knew until someone finally adopted her puppy. The kitten was returned, and the carpet was professionally cleaned.

However, there was still the problem of the chair with the hole in it. None of the furniture was Lisa's. It was a fully furnished apartment, with cheap, ugly, identical '70s-style furniture in each apartment. It occurred to us that there were several chairs in the recreation room that matched. So at about two in the morning, Lisa and I hauled the "holy" chair down the stairs and into the rec room, grabbing an "unholy" chair and lugging it up to the apartment. The next day when the manager inspected our apartment, it looked immaculate. The manager was very confused and rescinded our eviction. We knew we were very lucky. Deviously so.

No one can say that Lisa didn't have a sense of humor, because she did. I remember one time when she came to pick me up at LAX airport. We were laughing and so I elected to try to humor Lisa further. I asked her if she had heard the news of the producers doing a spin-off of *Facts of Life* for us to have our own series. She actually fell for it momentarily, "When did you hear that?"

"My manager told me yesterday."

"I think you heard him wrong."

"No, I didn't. He even told me that they were going to call it *The Gimp and the Blimp*." I was laughing at my own joke, but was surprised that Lisa wasn't. She swiftly pulled over to the side of the road and told me to get out of the car. I looked at her, stunned. "You're joking?" But she was very serious. I got out of the car, and she drove away! I knew that she was sensitive about her weight, but I thought that having made myself a part of my joke too, that it was okay. I stood there for about five minutes before she returned to get me. She was laughing. "Scared you, didn't I?"

Lisa and I remained friends for quite some time afterward, and I was one of her bridesmaids in her wedding to Steve Cauble in 1988. I still love her dearly, but the one area where we do not see eye to eye is religion. Lisa is a devout, born-again Christian and she made a very sincere effort to convert me. I was raised Catholic and was confused as to why that wasn't just as valid as her own religion. I knew her heart was in the right place and sincerely tried to embrace this fundamental kind of thinking, but to this day organized religion does not resonate with me. I am spiritually grounded and have respect for all religious paths. It is not for me to judge anyone else's beliefs. I have found peace in the teachings of Ernest Holmes, who founded the Religious Science movement, better known as Science of Mind.

I wish that Lisa and I could have remained close friends, and that I could have had more time to get to know her as an adult, but we grew worlds apart. I always enjoyed her Christmas cards and seeing her children grow up in pictures. I am proud of Lisa for all of her accomplishments. Even though we differ in our beliefs, I cannot find fault with her strong convictions. She walks her talk, and she lives the life that she always intended to. Even when we were roommates, she used to express how much she wanted to be a wife and a mother someday. I think that was always more important to her than any television show. For Lisa to survive the trappings of being a child star and find stability and happiness as an adult is truly remarkable.

I had to strive for that as well. Even though I was not technically a "child star," as I was chronologically and legally an adult, emotionally I felt like one. However, because I was 23 years old when I became famous, there was no Jackie Coogan Law to protect my assets. I was a sitting duck for anyone to take advantage of me financially, and by the time I became aware of the enormity of what my manager had done, I barely had enough money to hire an attorney to fight back. Emotionally, I was 12 and was facing what most 12-year-olds would never face in their lifetime.

Facts offered me a contract for the following season, guaranteeing four episodes. I was ecstatic! I was fast becoming a bigger part of the show. The producers were considering grooming me for my own series, and I signed a contract giving them the option to do so. Lisa threw a birthday party for me in September 1981 on the set of *Facts*. It was dubbed a "surprise" party, but I was aware of it, as I had to give Lisa a list of all my friends and family to invite. I still have a couple of photos from the party, taken by a photojournalist and my dear friend Michael Jacobs. Looking at one photo years later, it struck me as kind of eerie. It was a picture within a picture. My manager, George, is standing in front of a framed picture of Sherman Hemsley as George Jefferson from *The Jeffersons*. It was a fitting scene, seeing as both men would have screwed their own mother out of a dime. For my birthday that year, my manager gave me a gold necklace with a diamond-encrusted letter "G" — the G was for Geri and the diamond for Jewell. Looking back, I wouldn't be surprised if I paid for it myself with my own money.

When Lisa moved to Westwood, I found another roommate, Keith Jennings. Keith was one of Lisa's neighbors, and we met one day in the laundry room. We became fast friends. He was very sweet, and we are still friends today. When I met Keith, he was extremely vulnerable and unsure of himself. His dear friend, Claudia Jennings, who had taken Keith under her wing when he was only 13 and treated him like an adopted brother, had died fairly recently in an auto accident, which left a huge hole in Keith's life and psyche. In fact, he had even changed his last name to Jennings in her honor.

When he was only eight, Keith had lost his father in a plane crash, so Claudia's death was a second wound without closure. His pain was palpable, and I could relate to it, identifying with his feelings of isolation and loneliness. We were mirrors for one another, reflecting our need to be loved and seeking the companionship we both craved in each other. We also shared an infatuation with the entertainment industry.

From the time Keith was 14, he spent much of his time with his uncle Barry, and his uncle's best friends, Bobby Hart (of Boyce and Hart fame) and Claudia Jennings. Keith wanted to follow in their footsteps into show business. Claudia was well known as a centerfold model for *Playboy* and for doing many B movies. From knowing Barry and Bobby, Keith had a rare glimpse of fame, and at an impressionable age, he was enamored with Claudia's life. Now he was about to have yet another glimpse of fame through my life.

I looked all over for an apartment for the two of us. Oddly enough, I never took Keith along to find a place for *us*. In fact, I don't even think Keith knew we were going to be roommates. He was living in a studio apartment and was struggling to just pay for that. He was working as a waiter at a restaurant near Universal Studios called Whompoppers. It occurred to me that if I could find a big one-bedroom apartment that we could share, it would be cheaper than for each of us to rent a studio separately. I thought I had found the perfect apartment for us and was so excited to show it to him. In hindsight, it was far less than "perfect," but the extremely low rent is what caught my attention more than any little details that I chose to ignore.

One of the little details was its overall appearance. It looked like it hadn't had a facelift since 1970. It had dark green and rust shag carpeting, all the kitchen appliances were ugly olive green, and the countertops were bright yellow. Neither one of us drank alcohol or did drugs, so we were never quite able to numb our senses to such an ugly sight every time we opened the door. When Keith saw it for the first time he was aghast, but when I reminded him how cheap it was ($495 per month), he sighed and moved in.

The second little detail came in the form of an eviction notice five months later. When I signed the lease, I only mentioned myself as the sole occupant. I didn't think it was that big a deal and didn't think it would be a problem with Keith living there as long as he parked on the street. There was no manager on the premises, so in my mind, nobody could ever possibly know that I had a roommate. However, a neighbor complained about the noise, and I was red-flagged. The landlord knocked loudly on my door. Even though Keith was at work at the time, it was obvious that I was not the only one living there, and we got an eviction notice. It was the first Keith knew that he wasn't supposed to be living there. Okay, so I forgot to mention one teeny tiny little detail. . . .

During this period, a lot of things were happening. I had bought my first car, a brown 1981 Honda Civic. I was able to get $200 for the old 1969 Chevy, selling it to one of the studios to use in films. I became involved in an acting class called PATH (Performing Arts Theater of the Handicapped). This was the effort of Bob Cole, who passionately wanted to promote talented and gifted artists with disabilities, to create awareness and employment. Bob was able to get many celebrities on board to support the initiative. Classes were taught by Al Valletta on the Paramount Studios lot. I was also involved with the Media Access project of the California Governor's Committee, which tries to promote employment of qualified persons with disabilities in the entertainment industry. To this day, we face a higher rate of unemployment and lack of opportunity than any other minority group.

Shortly after getting involved with PATH, I had the pleasure of meeting Anson Williams (Potsie on *Happy Days*), who was producing a movie for television called *Skyward*, starring Bette Davis. It was a story about a young wheelchair-bound girl who wanted to learn to fly a plane. Anson wanted to hire an "authentic" person with a disability. Just about every actress with a disability auditioned for this role. It was an incredible opportunity, not to mention being able to say, "I worked with the great Bette Davis!" Unfortunately, I wasn't the one who got to say it. A wonderful young actress, Suzy Gilstrap, was the lucky one. She really was paralyzed, and even though I was a tad envious of her getting the role, I could not have done a better job myself.

Even though I didn't get the role, I did become friends with Anson. We would meet for lunch, and he was always supportive of me. Once he surprised me with two tickets to a formal dinner honoring Carol Burnett in her victory against the *National Enquirer*, which had wrongly accused her of public drunkenness. (She donated the money to journalism schools to warn future journalists against libel.) I was stunned. I had tears in my eyes when he handed me the tickets over lunch in the commissary at Paramount. However, sweet as it was, I told Anson I couldn't accept them.

"Why not?"

I was so embarrassed to tell him the real reason I couldn't accept his gift, but even to this day, Anson always expects to be told only the truth. I explained that it was a formal dinner in Beverly Hills, and I didn't own anything that could even remotely pass as a formal gown. I pushed the tickets back over to him and thanked him for the kind gesture.

Then Anson's sense of humor came into play. He took out his wallet and pretended to put the tickets inside it, but instead took out a credit card and handed it to me with the tickets. I was floored. "You're kidding?"

"Nope, I'm not. You, Geri Jewell, are going to that dinner whether you like it or not." After we walked back to his office, he placed a call to Western Costumes and told them that I would be coming in to rent a beautiful evening gown. He told them to take good care of me and to help me find the most beautiful, perfect dress. Tears streamed down my cheeks. Now I just had to find a date! Anson laughed, "Don't push it Jewell, I'm married. . . ."

I ended up taking Keith to the dinner. It wound up being one of many magical evenings that I would experience again and again throughout my career. When I asked Keith to be my date, he hesitated for the same reason

I did. He needed a tuxedo to go to something like that. However, somehow he was able to come up with enough money in the nick of time. Since he only owned a motorcycle, we took my car.

Although it was a Honda, to me it felt like a Rolls-Royce. That is, until Keith and I got to the Century Plaza Hotel in Beverly Hills. We got in line to valet park, and there were limousines after limousines, Bentleys, Mercedes, and real Rolls-Royces. I was so embarrassed by my little brown Honda. It was Keith who reminded me what was really important. "The only people who know you drive a Honda are you, me, and the parking attendant. I won't tell anyone, and I doubt that he will either. All he cares about is if you tip him. So be generous."

As we walked into the lobby of the Century Plaza Hotel, the paparazzi were everywhere. I was amused thinking Carol's victory against the *National Enquirer* was being covered by the tabloid media. Cameras were flashing, and everyone was excited for Carol, who was graciously meeting and greeting all who came in her honor. I took notice of her husband, Joe Hamilton, and was thrilled that he recognized me. He nudged Carol, alerting her to my arrival. Of course, panic set in, and I was struggling to find the right words to say to her. A woman behind me jumped in and began talking to Carol. I was surprised when Carol politely told her that she was speaking to me and to please wait. I only wish I could have said what I wanted to, but I was so star struck, that I just said something like, "Anson Williams gave me the tickets!" At least I remembered to introduce Keith in my state of tunnel vision.

Next, Keith and I made our way to our table in the huge grand ballroom. As fate would have it, we were seated right next to Dave Madden, who had played Mr. Kincaid on *The Partridge Family*. We were able to strike up a conversation with him, as he was actually an acquaintance of Keith's. It wasn't David Cassidy, but it was one degree of separation from David! I'm sure Dave Madden was used to people like me only wanting to talk about David, but I'm also sure he was tired of it as well. Nevertheless, Dave Madden couldn't have been a nicer gentleman. Like Anson, he was down-to-earth and had a wonderful sense of humor. At one point, I was so excited about discussing David Cassidy that when I picked up my water, I had involuntary movement and flung the glass toward Madden. He grabbed it in midair, commenting that he had his own water, but thank you.

CHAPTER THIRTEEN

Big Dreams, Dark Shadows, and Frolicking in Between

While I was still living with Keith on Vineland, I made a new friend, Jaymie Sloane, whom I met on the set of *The Facts of Life*. Jaymie was employed as Charlotte Rae's assistant, so naturally Jaymie was in the circle of trust of the other actors on the show. Both Charlotte and I believed that Jaymie was intelligent, charming, and trustworthy. The two of us hit it off instantly. Jaymie filled a void in me on many levels. At the time, I didn't feel accepted by, or was unable to form friendships with, other comediennes (with the exception of Lotus Weinstock), and I was limited in my friendship with Lisa Whelchel because of our different beliefs. With Jaymie, I felt a mutual bond. We were both creative and intelligent, and we had a lot in common. We would hang out regularly, which was a form of socialization that I craved. I may have even been physically attracted to her, but I never acted on it, as I valued her friendship too much. We always had so much fun when we were together and even collaborated on several scripts.

I will never forget the time Jaymie treated me to a midnight showing of *The Rocky Horror Picture Show*. The theater was completely full, with more than half the audience dressed like the characters in the movie. Some people had squirt guns, lighters, and umbrellas (it reminded me a little bit of my high school graduation). Everyone knew all the lines by heart and said them out loud in sync with the dialogue on the screen. I got drenched by the squirt guns, because I didn't have an umbrella. It felt like Halloween in April.

Because Jaymie was my new best friend, I confided in her completely. Looking back, I realize that Jaymie was selective about her own confidences, and I only knew what she chose to tell me. What she did share about herself was mostly glowing, with hardly a flaw in her character. I only met her sister and one other friend of hers. Other than that, I had no idea of any other relationships that she may have engaged in, except her friendship with Charlotte. She also told me a lot of stories, and I never questioned whether they were true or not. I always believed that if I were honest with someone that I would be met with equal honesty in return. This faulty belief system would come back to haunt me.

For now, though, I was simply enjoying our friendship and never questioned any other motive for it other than mutual respect, commonality, and love for one another. Jaymie even helped Lisa plan the birthday party for me. In my mind, if Charlotte and Lisa both "approved" of Jaymie, then I thought I had a pretty good friend in her. What I did not understand was that some individuals can fool a lot of people, and for long periods of time. We hear stories all the time of people being taken for fools by these charming sociopaths; even the smartest are duped from time to time. I was one of them.

Long before I saw her true colors, I trusted Jaymie completely, but I believe now that she may have instigated a monumental character assassination of me in the eyes of others, primarily Charlotte. As Jaymie was filling my head with things that Charlotte had purportedly said about me, I can only assume that she was filling Charlotte's head with lies as well. Neither one of us confronted the other, and instead became more annoyed with each other as we continued believing what Jaymie was telling us. By the time both Charlotte and I figured out who Jaymie Sloane really was, Charlotte and I were no longer on the show and the damage was done. Unfortunately, if I am correct about Jaymie's part in my declining role on *Facts*, I also acknowledge that I probably fed into any negative perception of me without even being aware of it.

Because I was thrown into such emotional turmoil from the end of 1981 to well into 1984, I was conveying to the producers without saying so that I was unstable and incapable of handling "stardom." If only one of the producers had actually talked to me at length and given me the guidance that I so desperately needed, they would have discovered that I was gifted and needed protection instead of being judged without question. In telling this part of my story, I can only present it as I experienced it from my own perspective. I will never know everything that happened, so even in writing this today, many open-ended questions remain.

Around the same time that I was enjoying my friendship with Jaymie, another person walked into my life, Daria Fellner. On some level, as much as I attracted wonderful people into my life, I also seemed to attract those people whose greatest talent in life was to lie.

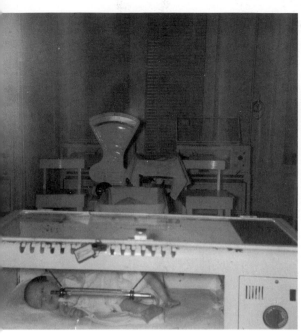

For the first three months of my life,
I was a precious jewel in a glass case.

Occupational therapy: Which hand
would I use to grab my first pack of
cigarettes?

Mom and Dad were a knockout
couple, and their love for one
another always radiated from
any snapshots taken of them.

The Jewell family in 1958: Fred, me, Dad, Mom, and David. I look like a deer caught in headlights.

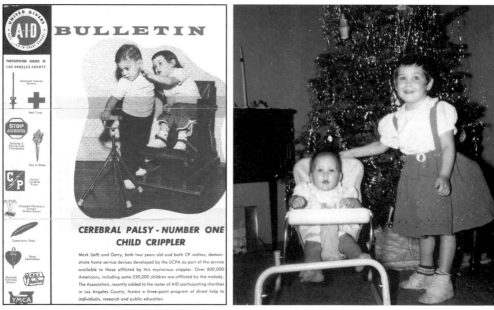

I was briefly a poster child. Notice my feet are buckled to the chair, preventing my legs from involuntarily flying everywhere.

Me in 1960 with my new baby sister, Gloria. The dress I am wearing was handmade by my mom.

In 1980 at the Comedy Store. I had just ended my impression of a Q-Tip.

(Photo courtesy Michael Jacobs)

Keith and I ready to go on "our date" to the dinner honoring Carol Burnett. I am wearing the dress that Anson rented me, and the comedy and tragedy necklace I got for Christmas that year from Mom and Dad.

A scene from my first episode of *The Facts of Life*, with Charlotte Rae, Kim Fields, and Mindy Cohn. (Photo courtesy NBC)

1981. This was taken at the birthday party that Lisa Whelchel threw for me on *The Facts of Life* set.

With my mentor and friend, Norman Lear. (Photo courtesy Michael Jacobs)

Playing tennis with
John McEnroe

Riding the bike that Dick
Clark gave me, following an
appearance on one of his shows.

One of my favorite pictures: me with Big Bird. Carrol Spinney is the man inside Big Bird, and his heart is as big as the character he plays. I am honored to have worked with him.

Performing in *I Love Liberty* in 1982.

This photo was taken at Lisa Whelchel's 1988 wedding to Steve Cauble. I was thrilled to be one of her bridesmaids.

This photo was taken in 1987 in Charlotte, N.C., when Liza graciously did a fundraising concert for my friend Deborah McKeithan.

Kathy Buckley and I are more like sisters than friends, and this photo shows that clearly.

At the White House in 1985.

Meeting my idol David Cassidy for the first time in the greenroom at ABC studios.

In 1990, trying to look sexy. Ironically the leather jacket was a Christmas
gift from my fiancé, Richard Pimentel. I loved the jacket . . . and Richard.

(Photo courtesy Richard Armas)

This was taken shortly after I moved to Vancouver, Washington, to live with Richard. My love for him was genuine.

My wedding to Richard on June 27, 1992. That night the earth moved!

Even though I didn't have the confidence to pose for a picture with Patty Duke in 1982, I did in 2007 at the Hollywood Autograph Show.

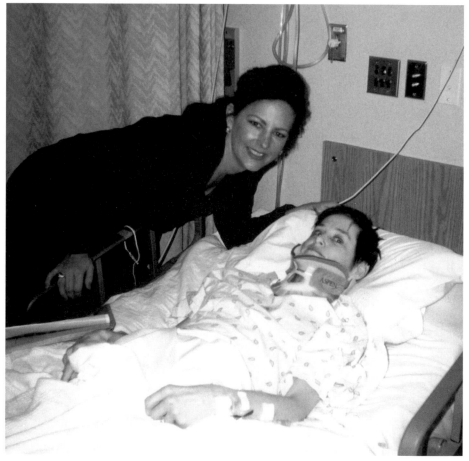

In 1999 at UCLA, following neck surgery. My loving sister, Gloria, was looking after me.

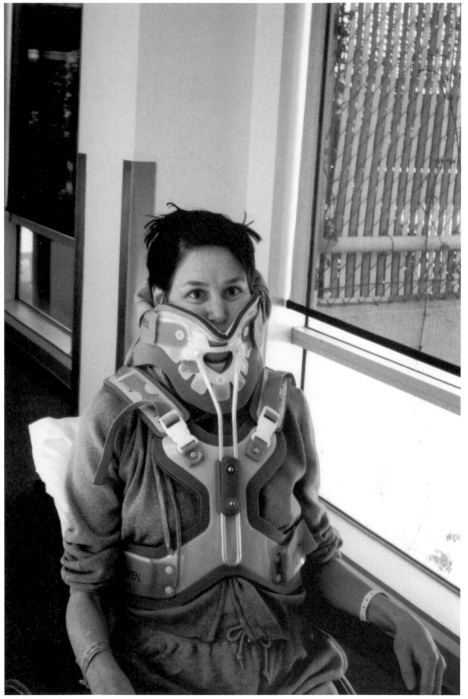

I was transferred to a rehabilitation hospital from UCLA and began rigorous physical therapy, fighting to gain mobility again. Personally, this picture always cracked me up, as I hated my hair!

This was taken during the first season of HBO's *Deadwood*. I loved this picture of my character, Jewel.

Here's another candid picture of me on the set of *Deadwood*, dressed as Jewel. My teeth were rotten, and I was filthy, but Jewel's beauty still radiated from within.

I enjoyed working with Ian McShane on set, and also enjoyed his company at a wrap party following the second season of *Deadwood*.

This photo of me and David Milch was taken at the dinner honoring me in Santa Rosa, California. I will never forget David's sincere gesture in being there on my behalf. He even wore a tie! He never wears a tie.

This photo was a part of the NOH8 campaign to support gay marriage. I decided to stand up for what I believe in. I posed with my dear friends David Zimmerman and Tony Benge Johnson, all of us coming together in unity and supporting one another.

(Photo by Adam Bouska)

I met Daria in late 1981 in the studio audience of *The Facts of Life*. Jaymie and I often sat in the audience to watch tapings of episodes that I wasn't in. It was always a fun thing to do on a Friday evening. At the beginning of the show, I was introduced from the stage as the newest member of the cast. I stood up, and the audience applauded. Jaymie was sitting on my left, and Daria was to my right. I could not have known it at the time, but I was sandwiched between two people who were both going to play mind games, and I didn't know the rules. Daria made small talk when the cameras weren't rolling. Before we left the studio, she gave me her phone number and asked if I would be willing to go for coffee or something.

I had a very strange feeling, and I didn't know the best way to handle it. This was brand new territory for me, being approached by total strangers who would give me their phone numbers, write long letters, and send gifts. Even if I had better "boundary skills," this kind of attention is completely alien to the average person. I tend to not want to hurt someone's feelings, even at the cost of hurting myself.

When Daria asked me to call her, I didn't want to hurt her feelings or for her to think I was stuck up. Today, I simply would have recognized that I didn't know this person and would have politely declined her number. In setting proper boundaries with people, we protect ourselves and honor what is best for us. I ignored my intuition about Daria. When I called her the following week, she seemed delighted that I had done so. I don't remember why I did, but instead of meeting her in a public setting, I drove to her home. I believe that that action in itself told Daria how naive I was, giving her a glimpse of how trusting I could be.

I have spent countless years kicking myself for every foolish choice I had made, from signing with George, to becoming friends with Jaymie, to calling Daria. However, wisdom tells me that there are no accidents in life; these people came into my life for a reason, and perhaps the pain and agony I went through was necessary for me to grow and evolve.

Nineteen eighty-two was an amazing year in many ways, and although I could fully appreciate the magical and dreamlike events that occurred, I seemed to be pulled down by one drama after another. My dad was never a man of many words, but if there was ever one thing that he said that held enormous truth, it was when he told me to forget the sideshow and keep my eye on the main event. He didn't say that to me until many years later when I was on *Deadwood*. However, if there was ever a time when his wisdom applied, it was in the '80s.

Sometimes there was so much overlapping that I didn't know where the "main event" ended and where the "sideshow" began. Naturally, the main event was my role on *The Facts of Life*, followed by another big event: being cast in the ABC star-studded special *I Love Liberty*. This was followed by yet another big event: being cast in the CBS television movie *Two of a Kind* with Robby Benson, George Burns, and Cliff Robertson. In less than one year, I had appeared on all three major networks. It looked like I was riding a huge wave of success. However, all waves crash eventually and the bigger the wave, the harder the crash.

Because of appearances on *Facts*, it looked as though I was actually going to enjoy financial security. I'd bought my first car and was also finally able to live in a cute little bungalow without needing a roommate. Toward the end of 1982, I also convinced George to let me have a little more of my actual income, so that I didn't have to remain dependent on supplementary security income. I will never forget how proud I was to stop collecting disability. I actually drove to the local social security office and handed them the unopened envelope with the last check they had mailed to me.

The spectacular *I Love Liberty* was Norman Lear's launch of human rights organization People for the American Way. In a way, it was Lear's response to Jerry Falwell. *Liberty* was a creative effort to honor the values of all Americans, not just the religious right, who were claiming that their values were the only ones that mattered. In fact, looking at how the world is today, with America polarized once again, I would love to see an *I Love Liberty II*.

Lear created yet another showcase for me with *Liberty*, as I played the role of the American Disabled Person. *Liberty* was a huge production where I was working alongside many celebrities that I had grown up with and was in awe of. Among them were Mary Tyler Moore, Martin Sheen, Shirley MacLaine, Patty Duke, Barbra Streisand, Robin Williams, Christopher Reeve, and Big Bird.

Most of the cast didn't even know who I was at the time, and why should they? I was virtually unknown, unless you happened to catch my nightclub act or see my few appearances on *Facts*. Many people just didn't know what to say to me. My being a newcomer set me apart, and the cerebral palsy created an awkwardness that was almost embarrassing.

No one saw me perform until the actual production — onstage in front of 25,000 people at the Los Angeles Coliseum. However, there were a few who actually took the time to talk to me when they weren't rehearsing.

Robin Williams knew me from the Comedy Store, and I was absolutely thrilled when Desi Arnaz Jr. said hello and told me that his mom loved my work and was a huge fan. That floored me, and as much as I wanted to meet Lucille Ball, and even had an opportunity to do so, I never had the confidence to pursue it.

Because *Liberty* was such a star-studded cast, they had to double up dressing room trailers, with two celebrities in each. When the production assistant brought me to my trailer, the actress refused to share it with me. It could have been for any reason. I didn't know what the reason was, nor could I hear well enough to try to figure it out, but the argument continued for several minutes and it became embarrassing for me to stand there, knowing that I was not welcome. Patty Duke rescued me from the awkward situation. She had overheard the argument and came over. We had actually met earlier when Desi took the time to introduce us. I had always been fond of Duke, and discovering that she was such a sensitive soul was icing on the cake.

She grabbed my hand, and, loud enough to make a point, she said, "Geri, why don't you come with me. Jane Fonda and I are sharing a trailer, but there's no reason we can't make room for you, too." I walked into the trailer, and Jane Fonda was sitting there going over her lines. I truly don't think Jane Fonda knew who I was, but if Duke brought me in, then I guess I was welcome. Jane Fonda was scheduled to go on first, before Duke or me, and I remember Jane being quite nervous about her role. At one point, she asked me if I could follow her script and make sure she said her lines correctly. I was running lines with Jane Fonda, and Patty Duke just gleamed at the sight of it.

Before I knew it, the time had arrived for my performance. In this show, I elected to use a pair of Canadian crutches (ones that support the forearms rather than go in the armpits) so that I could look more like the role I was playing. They did not specifically ask me to look "more disabled," but when I made the suggestion, they loved it. My reason for wanting to use the canes was because, even at that time, I knew that I was going to be asked to play "me" again and again, and I wanted to prove in some way that I could act by playing a character other than myself. I thought the crutches would give me more credibility as an actress, as a way to distance myself from "Geri."

I walked up several long platforms onstage with a spotlight following me with each step that I took. It was quite dramatic and effective. When I finally reached center stage, I went into my comedic monologue. One joke after another was met with a deafening silence. I was not wearing my hearing aids that evening, again because I was afraid of the feedback, and didn't want to risk screwing up the sound. At first I speculated that perhaps they were laughing, and I just couldn't hear it, but I quickly concluded that my career was over. I was bombing in front of 25,000 people, not to mention in front of Patty Duke, Desi Arnaz Jr., and Norman Lear. My heart sank, and I went into sheer panic from the perceived humiliation. I dropped the crutches on the stage and said that I needed help badly. I closed my eyes tightly for a few seconds, hoping that when I opened them, it would have all been a dream.

But when I opened them, I saw Norman Lear standing onstage next to me. When I looked beyond him, I saw both of our images on the widescreen TV. Norman was visibly upset and genuinely concerned. He hugged me in front of all those people, and then asked me if I was okay. I can remember having tears in my eyes and apologizing to him for bombing. He smiled, put his hands on my shoulders, and said, "Geri, look at me. Read my lips, your mike wasn't on sweetheart. If you did bomb, nobody could hear you anyway!" He then asked me if I could pull myself together to do the routine again with a microphone that worked. I told him I could and was wired with a new mike.

What happened next was amazing. He put his arm around me and explained to the audience that there was a sound malfunction, but that I was willing to perform again. He asked the audience, "How many people out there want to give Geri Jewell a second chance?" Twenty-five thousand people stood up and gave me a standing ovation. There are no words to even describe my gratitude for a second chance to do it right. I performed again and got another standing ovation. It was easily one of the greatest moments of my life.

When I walked backstage afterward, I was immediately greeted by Patty Duke, who had tears in her eyes as she hugged me. She explained that everyone was on the edge of their seats, not knowing what I was doing up there. Patty, however, knew intuitively that I didn't know my mike had malfunctioned. When Norman went up onstage, many people thought that he was going to quietly walk me off the stage and my part would be cut from the show. Patty held my hands tightly and said, "I knew you could do it!"

Liberty was a "main event" that occurred simultaneously with the Daria "sideshow." The first time I went over to Daria's house, she revealed that she was gay. I was panicked that, again, I found myself with another gay woman.

When she asked me if I would like to get together, I was thinking she was reacting as a fan. I was very poor at recognizing sexual energy. I could never comprehend someone making an advance: it was a mental process that had to go through two locked doors, a safe-deposit box, and a brick wall before I "got it." In hindsight, I believe that subconsciously I wanted a relationship with a woman, so my own energy attracted Daria into my life.

The conflict was so great within that I shut down out of shame, and not having the emotional maturity to know exactly how to handle all of my feelings, I left her home in a full-blown panic. I fought the panic, thinking that perhaps I was overreacting, that maybe we could just be friends, but intuitively came to the conclusion that I couldn't embrace this friendship, and the next day I told her so. Even though we had not known each other long, she acted crushed, and I felt guilty. But I had the "main event" to think about. I couldn't even imagine what the producers of *Facts* would think if I allowed myself to have a relationship with a woman. No, it wasn't going to happen.

Even though in my mind I had said goodbye to Daria, she wasn't going anywhere. It seemed as though everywhere I looked, she was in my face. I was always running into her in the studio audience of *Facts* and she was even bold enough to strike up a friendship with my roommate, Keith. I was so angry and tried to explain to him that she was just using him to get to me. He, in return, was upset with me for not believing that her intentions were genuine and that she was a nice person. I understood his argument, but I knew he was wrong. But Keith also thought that I would get over my paranoia in time, come to like Daria, and possibly find love and happiness. Years later, Keith admitted to me that he was wrong, but at the time he didn't see how manipulative she was.

The best way I can describe why I was so afraid of Daria is because of her persistence. She was tenacious in continuing to see me, not accepting no for an answer. For weeks, every time I opened our apartment door, not only did I have to look at the godawful yellow Formica countertop, but I had to look at Daria as well. She would be in the living room with Keith watching TV or eating dinner. I would repeat my pattern of ignoring her completely, going into my bedroom, and slamming the door.

Then one night, she came into my room to talk. I cannot recall most of the conversation, but I do know that we talked well into the wee hours of the morning. We ended up having sex, and afterward I cried softly, feeling only shame and despair. I was terrified of engaging in a relationship that felt insincere. Even though I finally gave in, I hated it. I can remember lying there, feeling as though I had lost the war. It was pleasurable only in the sense that I was aware of her physical beauty, but intuitively I felt as though I was in a bad dream that I kept trying to wake up from but couldn't.

I had only about two hours of sleep that night, as I was awakened by the phone at about 7:30 in the morning. It was Lisa Whelchel phoning me from the racquet club, asking me if she could stop by to use my shower. In a panicked state, I said no. She asked me if I had forgotten that we were going to go to a department store to sign autographs that day. I told her that I did remember, but that I didn't think we were going to connect until at least 9:30. Sensing something was wrong in my voice, she asked me if I was okay. I told her that I was, and to please just wait at least an hour before she came over. I hung up the phone and showered. I told Daria to please leave. She wouldn't. She just sat there, amused at my frenzy over Lisa's call. Before I could say another word, there was a knock on the front door, and Keith let Lisa into the apartment.

Lisa knocked on the bedroom door. I told her I would be right out, but before I could button my jeans, Lisa opened the door and walked in. The next moment was surreal, and I felt I no longer lived on Vineland Street, but that now I was living on Elm Street and the nightmare had just begun. Very protectively, Lisa walked over to Daria, introduced herself, and calmly asked her to get out of my bed.

Daria was stunned and insulted, looking at me for validation that she had every right to be in my bed. "Are you going to let her talk to me that way?" I nodded my head yes. Daria was furious with me, saying that I had no backbone, and that I was a total wimp. She was right, I didn't, because if I did, I would have said no to her the night before. "Why don't you just tell Lisa that you're gay?" I couldn't and I wouldn't.

Daria got out of bed and left the apartment in anger and disgust. I wanted to leave the apartment too. I was mortified and wanted to go into a dark cave and hibernate. All I can say is that I was experiencing an acute case of shock and humiliation. I told both Keith and Lisa to go to the autograph show without me. I then curled up in a corner of my room, facing the wall. My hands covered my face, and I just wanted to die.

Lisa and Keith both insisted that I keep my commitment to sign autographs that afternoon. As much as I didn't want to be there, it was probably the wisest thing for me to do, because it kept me from going deeper within myself and being swallowed up by humiliation. Lisa's willingness to stay with me was more than most people would have shown. I was never completely able to let go of my embarrassment of the situation with Lisa, but I knew that to the best of her ability she did not reject me.

After that night with Daria, I was never the same. I felt shamed, paranoid, and angry. However, that old cliché "The show must go on" drove me to keep performing. My safe happy place onstage and the healing effect of laughter kept me sane. I had a long road ahead, and if I thought that the worst was behind me, I had no idea how many potholes and detours were lying in wait. If there was such a thing as a GPS system to our lives, mine would have been rerouting every five minutes or so.

Again, I continued my nomadic pattern of moving. This time I went to George and asked for his help in finding an affordable place to live on my own. I was angry with Keith for befriending Daria, but eventually I did forgive him and today he is one of my closest friends. George was able to find me an adorable, small one-bedroom bungalow from the 1940s in Studio City. It was owned by a friend of his who managed it and had an apartment across the street. It was the first time I had a place to live without being dependent on a roommate. George even educated me about establishing credit. He explained that I could buy furniture and only pay a little at a time. So now I was truly living the American dream by the way of plastic.

Unfortunately, I did not live alone for long. Shortly after I moved, I got a call one evening from Daria in tears. She was upset and urgently needed me to come pick her up at the Palomino Club in North Hollywood, claiming that somehow her life was being threatened. Daria also exclaimed that her partner threw her out of their home because of her "affair" with me. My naiveté and guilt forced me to drive to North Hollywood to rescue her. I told her she could stay at my place for a couple of days, and before I knew it, I had a new roommate.

I felt emotionally blackmailed. Daria did not contribute anything toward the rent, food, or anything else. I resented this, but complied to keep her placated. In essence, she was living life as a kept woman, and I was living life with a kept secret. I seriously believed my career would be over if my secret life got out, and I worried that if I kicked her out, she'd go straight to the tabloids. I was experiencing full-blown paranoia, checking the tabloids each week for the "untold story." I became more withdrawn from casual social situations than usual. I just couldn't imagine what I could say to anyone.

To the outside world, emotional entrapment seems easy to escape. It's not like Daria threatened to kill me, but when I thought of the death of my reputation and my career, it felt as though I had a gun to my head. I tried to make the most of the situation, and there were even some things that I came to like about her. For example, we went to a shelter and adopted a kitty named Lady. Daria loved animals, and having a cat to love was something that drew us together. I believe Daria may have even genuinely loved me in some way, but she had total disregard for what was in my best interest.

Ironically, one of the writers for *I Love Liberty* was Rita Mae Brown. She was a pioneering gay novelist. I did not know that she had recently broken up with tennis champion Martina Navratilova, and had no idea that Rita Mae Brown was gay. I was so touched when she invited me to a dinner party at her home. I had absolutely no gaydar and, as usual, did not realize I was giving off signals that were picked up by others.

I went to the dinner party without ever letting Daria know; the gathering was a little window of a social opportunity away from someone I felt emotionally and psychologically held to by Velcro and SuperGlue. I did not become aware of who Rita Mae Brown was until that evening. I had assumed it was a gathering of talented professional writers, and it was — *gay* talented professional writers.

I remember there were about 10 of us at the table. Everyone was talking, and I was quietly eating my salad, trying to smile and laugh in the right places to look like I was following the conversation. As usual, I was slow to grasp the entire conversation that was going on because of being hearing impaired. All of a sudden, a question was specifically directed at me. I don't remember who asked it, whether it was Rita or someone else, but the question took me completely by surprise. "So, Geri, are you aware of the percentage of people with disabilities who are gay?"

Before I could even think of an answer, I had involuntary movement, and the salad that was on my fork flew across the table. To cover up what just happened, I replied, "Oh, I wouldn't know. I've only known one person with a disability who was gay." Then I continued to listen to their theories as to what the actual numbers were. I went home that night feeling as though I had missed an opportunity to be completely honest, and maybe even receiving the support and acceptance that I wanted.

The next day I called Rita and asked her if she would like to meet somewhere for lunch. I wanted to open up to her, taking the opportunity for whatever it was worth. She picked me up in her black Mercedes and drove us to a quiet deli in Studio City. She commented that she was surprised I would want to be seen with her publicly, meaning that she was openly gay, and I wasn't. I retreated within myself once more, not revealing much of anything. I think Rita became aware of how young I truly was and felt empathy for my struggle.

She drove me home afterward, and in the car she asked me point-blank if I was gay. I had tears in my eyes, as if she was asking me if I had cancer or leprosy. I wanted to answer yes, but I could only give the answer that was the easiest: "I don't know." She kissed my cheek and told me when I figured it out, to call her. I never did call, but have not forgotten her sensitivity and kindness.

Meanwhile, my life continued moving forward. I stayed in that loveless relationship for about seven months. When I was cast in the CBS television movie *Two of a Kind* with Robby Benson, it was another surreal moment, as I had always thought Robby Benson was adorable, and in this film I was playing his girlfriend. I remembered that time in college when I sat alone in the theater watching *One on One* while my family thought I was pitching a script to CBS. Now I was appearing in a movie with him on CBS.

I absolutely adored Robby. He was a joy to work with. He did an absolutely phenomenal job portraying Noel, who was developmentally challenged. My role as Irene was no match for Benson's portrayal, but it was cute. I also got to meet George Burns and Cliff Robertson. I had seen an elderly bald man on the set for a couple of days and said hello, but didn't know who he was. I asked Robby when I was going to meet George Burns, and he laughed, saying I already had. When I filmed a scene with him the next day, I realized he was the elderly man I'd seen on set; I didn't know Burns was actually bald and wore a hairpiece on-screen.

One thing I never forgot about *Two of a Kind* was filming a birthday party scene with Noel and his friends sitting at the dining room table having cake and ice cream. We had to do take after take, since all of the actors were off target. There was a foul odor in the air. We were all a little nauseated. Finally, Robby Benson couldn't stand it anymore and asked who farted. The next thing I knew, everyone was looking at me. I knew I didn't pass gas, but the odor was definitely coming from me. That's when we realized I had stepped in dog poop on the way to the set and was now sharing it with everyone. Symbolically, that poop may have represented what was overwhelming my life at that moment — however, my bigger problems couldn't just be scraped away by a wardrobe assistant.

The stench of my life lingered, but my director's chair, presented as a gift from the producers of *Two of a Kind* with my name on it, will forever represent a glimmer of hope in the midst of despair.

CHAPTER FOURTEEN

Breaking Up
Is Hard to Do

After completing *Two of a Kind*, I continued to do stand-up comedy and was offered a contract to appear in the third season of *Facts of Life*. I was also embarking on a new path as a motivational speaker, because I was considered a role model for millions of people across the country with disabilities. I received a vast amount of fan mail at NBC. The irony was, while so many people were looking to me for guidance, I was looking up clinical psychologists in the Yellow Pages, seeking guidance of my own.

I was uncomfortable being a role model because of how tumultuous my own life had become. I felt as though I was living multiple lives, each one dancing to different music. Even the best DJs in the world couldn't rotate songs fast enough to keep up with the ever-changing tempo of my life-dance. My main confidante during this time was Jaymie. I told her everything about me, and I naturally believed she could be trusted. She gave me no reason to believe otherwise.

I was seeing a therapist whom I used as a sounding board, trying to make sense of my life circumstances, which were becoming increasingly complex. I was having tremendous difficulty balancing my emotions and sorting through what continued to be a maze of puzzles and lies. Hollywood had become Hollyweird for me. I sought the comfort and support of former teachers such as Blaine Moss, Jerry Hershey, and Kaleta Brown. I turned to these people over my own parents because I didn't want to worry them. However, as with all parents, they worried anyway.

My mom especially carried the burden of worrying over my finances, because she had been the one who balanced the books, keeping our family on a very tight middle-class budget. My father was never good with money and depended on my mom's practical sense of it. Mom was *always* practical and would give a set of pots and pans as a gift rather than something more personal. Mom never forgot growing up poor during the Great Depression and never wanted to go there again.

Mom knew better than anyone that there were huge gaps in my development, especially in the area of money. Ever since I was on my own, Mom collected receipts from me and helped file my taxes. When I was hurting financially, she often paid some of my monthly bills. She even opened a separate savings account at the Postal Credit Union and put a little of her own money away for me. She became frustrated by the end of 1982, when George forbade me from giving her any more information regarding my finances. I knew nothing about the full scope of my situation, so when George told me I couldn't talk to her anymore about it, I, like his obedient child, complied. Quite frankly, my dear, George didn't give a damn about alienating my mom in the process. Years later, I found a couple of letters Mom had written him (either she didn't mail them or she'd made copies) expressing her anguish over his "hold" on me. By the end of 1983, Mom could no longer help me, and I now needed Perry Mason. I probably could have used an attorney long before then, but was not aware that I actually had any legal rights.

Even when I did retain an attorney, I never sued anyone. Someone else beat me to it.

George went to prison sometime in 1985 on charges that were totally unrelated to me. One of the main reasons I never sued him was because there were so *many* charges against him. I was the low tomboy on the totem pole, and all I could recoup was basically nothing. I spent most of my young adult life paying for the damage that was done to me, and being compensated by no one. How much of my money was accounted for? All I know is that it was in the amount of thousands of dollars. Not to mention the thousands of dollars on top of that it was costing me to retain my attorney. It was even discovered that my money had paid thousands of dollars on three separate credit cards that I didn't even know existed. George danced his way through one CPA after another, trying to make legal sense of my finances. A seasoned choreographer couldn't even follow the steps that were taken in dancing with his little star.

I hired new managers in late 1983. My chaotic life was a mess, and Richard Lippin and his then management firm, Lippin and Grant, did everything possible to try to prevent a train wreck. They were the ones who helped me find the attorney and wrote hundreds of letters to producers and casting directors on my behalf. They were able to continue to book me on the road and tried their damnedest to build a new foundation based on integrity and honor.

For every letter that was sent out, we'd receive a nice letter back telling us how much they loved me, but they'd already done an "affliction" story. To my disappointment, I couldn't even get on a *Love Boat* or a *Fantasy Island*. It seemed to Richard Lippin that Hollywood was finished with the excitement of 1981 being the International Year of the Disabled and had moved on to something new. There were even rumors that I had been blacklisted. To this day, I do not know how much truth there was behind this rumor, but from an employment perspective, it certainly seemed like I had.

Personally, I was still limping along, but more because of emotional issues rather than cerebral palsy ones. Toward the end of 1982, another incident threw me off balance big time. I had just finished a day's work on *Facts* and had reached my car in the parking lot at KTTV Studios on Sunset Boulevard where *Facts* was still filming (before they moved to Universal Studios the following season). On my windshield, I discovered a note that said: *Dear Geri, please come up and see me on the* One Day at a Time *set. I would love to see you. Jack.*

The note seemed odd, as the only Jacks that came to mind were my dad and Jack Elinson, one of the producers of *Facts of Life*. I wondered why Jack left a note on my car, rather than just contact me on the *Facts* set. Perhaps I was in trouble for something, so like an obedient child I hurried off to the *One Day at a Time* set. Reaching the long corridor of dressing rooms of *One Day at a Time*, I took notice of the nameplate on one of the doors. There was no need to go any further. Jack King was a guest actor on *One Day at a Time* the very same week that I was doing an episode of *Facts*. I even caught a glimpse of him, as the door was ajar. I couldn't believe it was Jack be nimble, Jack be quick, the Jack that loved me to fondle his dick. Despite my ardent wishes, he obviously hadn't died of some mysterious disease.

I was relieved that it wasn't Jack Elinson, but nevertheless horrified about which Jack had left that note on my windshield. I did an about-face and walked as swiftly as I could back down the hall. Very loudly, I heard my name called from behind me. For a second, I felt as though I were frozen in my tracks. I knew that voice, and it derailed me instantly. I was still fearful of him even so many years later. I turned around, not sure what to expect.

He was smiling, clearly taking delight in recognizing the emotional hold he still had over me. Why he chose to seek me out at this time, I have no idea. I had done nothing to bring him down earlier, but maybe that night had haunted him, and he had to find out for sure that I would never say anything to anyone. He said, "Geri, I warned you that if you stayed in this industry that we would run into each other again. Remember, Hollywood is a very small town." I don't know what he was thinking, but his words were menacing, enough to emotionally send me back to that night in 1980.

I angrily asked him what he wanted with me. He laughed, asking me if I had any more dental work done lately. "Would you like to go out for some ice cream?" He was enjoying his power, and I gave him more power by still not being able to stand up to him. I wanted to tell him to fuck off, but instead I allowed the very sight of him to eat away at my self-confidence. That night, I couldn't fall asleep. Every scenario played in my mind, from the possibility of him being in the studio audience to him telling my bosses at *Facts* that I was an idiot. I simply didn't comprehend that all his bravado was masking the fact that he was more afraid of me than I was of him. I had the upper hand and didn't know it.

When I returned to work on *Facts* the next day, I was depressed and had trouble memorizing my lines in my exhaustion. Jaymie told me to snap out of it, that I was not being professional, and I knew she was right, but I just didn't know how to turn my emotions on and off like a light switch. My inner life was an emotional roller coaster, dealing with all the highs and lows that circumstance kept throwing at me.

I just wanted to make all the pain go away so I could sleep at night. I wasn't getting much rest while Daria was living with me, but didn't have the courage to break my ties with her. Anyone who has ever been to a psychologist knows that they will not tell you *what* to do, but rather guide you and allow you to see for yourself what you *need* to do. Day after day, week after week, month after month, I knew I had to break from Daria, but I had to arrive at that place on my own. After all, I was an adult, or so my birth certificate said.

By the time I finally had the courage to tell Daria to move out, my life was in full-blown chaos. My manager, George, had been arrested for security fraud and embezzling $1.3 million. I was into my third season on *Facts* and performing all over the country, which fueled the perception of my success. Yet until he was actually arrested, I was still being paid through George. By that time he had moved all my money into another account, leaving a total of $125 in the Jewel Productions account. I was entitled to the *entire* amount without a legal fight. (Hooray.)

Shortly after his arrest, I bolted into his office and went right past his secretary's desk to see if there were any checks that were made out to me on his desk. She told me I had no right to barge into his office and that I would have to wait until George came into the office. He was out on bail, but I ignored her stupidity as I spotted an unopened envelope from Tandem Productions, which produced *Facts*. I grabbed the check as she scolded me, saying that George would be mad at me. George would be mad at *me*? As usual, I was treated like a misbehaving child, but for the first time, I was not buying into it. I drove home and opened my paycheck from *Facts*, which I had filmed two weeks earlier. Thinking I was going to at least have a net amount of something with three zeros, I was shocked to discover the only zeros were in the cents portion of the number. The whole amount was $45.

I thought it was an error and called the accounting office at Tandem to inform them of their mistake. It was the first time I had ever called them to question anything. I explained that I needed them to issue me another check, that they obviously owed me a lot more money than $45. The woman on the other end of the line calmly informed me that there was no mistake, that $45 was the correct amount.

"How can that be?"

"Well, Geri, you cannot repeatedly take out advances toward your future work and expect your paychecks to remain the same."

"What advances?"

The poor woman hardly knew what to say.

She calmly told me that I had given power of attorney to my manager, and that he had the legal right to any approved advance payment. The only thing that I was aware of by way of an advance was that I had signed a promissory note of $6,000 that George said he would return to me when he was able. I never did collect on that note and still have that piece of useless paper in a box in storage.

Knowing that I now only had $45 to live on, I was desperate. I called Al Burton, one of the executive producers of *Facts*, and requested a meeting. I have always loved Al, and from the beginning, when Norman Lear introduced us, I felt like he was in my corner. If anyone had big plans for me, it was Al. Norman would have done anything in the world for me, but he was out of the loop by this point. Many producers fulfill a parental role while an actor becomes the child. This is a tricky psychology for actors. The producer is at once our boss, our parent, and, for some, our God. Luckily for me, Al was not like Louis B. Mayer of MGM, and he genuinely cared for me.

Walking into his office that afternoon felt as safe as going to Dad.

Al Burton is a good man and admired by many. He has had a long career, and I have only appreciation and gratitude for him being in my life. When I sat down in his office that day, it felt as though I were sitting with a beloved uncle. I explained what was happening, and that I needed his advice. He was already aware of the situation with my manager because he had read about his arrest in the trades. However, George had not been tried yet, so he was innocent until proven guilty.

As I mentioned earlier, though, it really didn't matter whether George was guilty of those charges. None of the charges against him had anything to do with me. I was the *only* talent he managed. He was primarily a producer and saw the prospect of managing me as a way to make a quick buck on the side. Al admitted to me that he did not like George from the moment he first met him, but often an actor's rep does not rub well with producers when it comes to the demands made on behalf of the actor.

Al told me George was not someone to be trusted, and that I needed to get rid of him as soon as possible. He wrote me a personal check for $2,000 and told me to open a bank account with it. I was not to give a cent of it to George, and that I needed to get new representation very quickly. Any association with George could hurt my chances of getting further work. He told me that Hollywood was a small town and I needed to distance myself from someone who had affected my ability to get work.

I asked him if I was going to come back for another season of *Facts*. He said that he had no way of knowing the answer to that question, but that if it was within his power, he would look after me. Unfortunately, all the big plans he had for me went out the window when his position with *Facts* ended not long after that afternoon I met with him in 1982.

When it was time to determine what would happen in the following season of *Facts*, Al Burton, like Norman Lear, was out of the loop. Regardless of what came into play, the two men that I trusted completely, and still do, were no longer a part of any decision-making for *The Facts of Life*. Before I left Al's office that afternoon, he hugged me and told me to be strong. I knew I had to break all ties with George . . . and Daria.

Daria's manipulations were wreaking havoc on my self-esteem. Between her and George, there was very little peace. Both manipulated me in different ways, each playing on my youth and naiveté.

Daria additionally toyed with my Catholic upbringing, playing on my guilt and fear. I remember one night, for whatever reason, the conversation turned into her taunting me, telling me that everyone in my life was a Satan worshiper, and that Satan wanted me because I was such a sweet Goody Two-shoes. A part of me knew she was playing a game, but the Catholic girl inside me secretly wondered if my soul hung in the balance of good and evil. My life, after all, was becoming a huge "unholy" mess.

Daria even started wearing a small cross and attending Lisa Whelchel's church. I think her motive was to win Lisa's approval about her being in my life. Lisa never bought into it, thank God. Daria even admitted to me that it was a joke, and she enjoyed the game. Had I been more mature at the time, I would have realized that pretty much everything was a game to her. She had such low self-esteem herself that she didn't think twice about how she affected those around her.

For example, one afternoon Daria showed me several items from NBC that she had gotten for us: some NBC pens, sweaters, T-shirts, and a couple of other things with the NBC logo on them. I was stunned, as she was unemployed, and here I worked on an NBC show and wasn't given such things. Daria didn't work for NBC, so how did she get her hands on those things? She smiled and told me that she forgot to tell me what she did for a living before she met me. She told me that she was a professional call girl, and that some of her best customers worked for NBC. She told me that all she had to do was tell these men what she wanted, and she got it. One of her "regulars," she said, was one of the producers of *The Facts of Life*. It didn't even cross my mind that she was probably lying, and I begged her to tell me which producer she was referring to. She wouldn't tell me, saying that it was more fun watching me guess who it was, and knowing I'd never know for sure.

These were the kinds of mind games I was dealing with, and I couldn't take much more. The damage was already done, but I had hoped that I could move forward. I took a short trip to New York City with Jaymie. I was absolutely thrilled that Jaymie was going with me. Before I left, I even told Daria that I wanted her out of my home by the time I came back. Somehow we both agreed it was easier if she moved out while I was away. I think whenever we break up with anyone, be it a spouse, business partner, or friend, it is always a "process" that involves emotions that are difficult to understand. We know we need to make the break, but we are also letting go of someone we are familiar with. Even in some of the most destructive relationships, we are not apart from it, but rather a part of it. In ending that relationship, we are also breaking up with a part of ourselves that engaged in the relationship.

Jaymie and I stayed at the Milford Plaza Hotel, sharing a room. We had a great time, catching a couple of shows, going to Little Italy to have what Jaymie said was the best Italian food in the world, and visiting some of my relatives on Long Island. The trip to New York with Jaymie was a much-needed vacation, with me trying to clear my head and gain a new perspective on my mounting troubles. George had contacted me and told me that everything was a big mistake, and that he would make good on any money he owed me. In fact, we paid for the room with a credit card that belonged to George. I felt it was the *least* he could do. But at the same time, it made me feel even more beholden to him, which was a problem.

Jaymie and I had a great time until just before we returned to Los Angeles, when we got in a huge argument about George. She reminded me of everything that George had done for me, and said I should reconsider standing by him in his time of need. I couldn't figure out why she was trying to make George the good guy after everything he'd taken from me. That is when she told me that he had asked her to talk to me, saying that I would listen to *her*. *That* was why he was letting us use his card. I was furious with Jaymie, but forgave her quickly. She was my best friend, and I didn't want to lose her too.

I arrived in Los Angeles a day earlier than Daria had expected. I didn't think one day would make any difference, as she had had almost the whole week to move her things out of my bungalow. Not only was she still there, she was in my bed with another woman. Again, I felt violated and couldn't believe that Daria was sleeping with someone else in *my* bed. I spent the night at the Beverly Garland Hotel a couple of blocks away. The only lady I wanted to find in my bed when I returned was my cat. I loved Lady and was glad that Daria let me keep her when she finally left.

It's not like Daria would never see her again. She and her girlfriend moved into the apartment *across the street*, in a building that was also managed by George's friend who managed my building. Daria explained that she took the apartment because it was such a great deal, and that I was selfish to expect her to move elsewhere simply because I lived across the street.

Even though I often walked across the street to give our manager my rent check, I never once stepped inside Daria's apartment. I spoke with her once through the screen door, asking her if she would return some clothes that were mine. She said no and told me not to come over again. As awful as the relationship was, it was my first intimate one, and it was nevertheless painful knowing she was right across the street in a relationship with someone else, who was wearing *my* clothes from time to time.

I remember asking her why she did the things that she did, desperately wanting to understand the psychology of such dysfunction. Her response actually took me by surprise. She said that she really did love me and had to work through a lot of things herself and come to terms with having hurt me the way she did. "Although, Geri, the person you should really be looking at more closely is Jaymie. She is a piece of work, and if anyone was playing anyone, it is Jaymie." She told me that Jaymie was as gay as they come, and that she probably had even Charlotte fooled. I repeated the statement to Jaymie, and she laughed at the ludicrousness of the words, reminding me that she had a boyfriend and was a devout Catholic.

All of this drama was often broken up by events that took me to happier places. One such event was Tim Conway's Celebrity Golf Tournament. I didn't play golf and wisely declined to. I am sure that I could probably find a way to play if I really wanted, but all I could envision was having involuntary movement, hitting someone in the head before accidentally tossing the club in the air, and hitting someone again. I was asked to come for the day, hang out, and do a comedy routine at the dinner. A car picked me up early in the morning to take me to Westlake Village.

My Honda was left parked in the driveway the entire day, and to anyone who noticed, it looked as though I were home. That evening I was paid a visit by a police officer, who said I'd been accused of breaking into Daria's apartment across the street. I needed to provide a handwritten alibi from the Tim Conway Golf Tournament, proving that I was in Westlake Village from the time I was picked up in the morning until I got home, which was about 9 p.m. Whether it was a setup by Daria, her girlfriend, or both, I will never know, but I am grateful that I was with Tim Conway on that particular day.

Meanwhile, I was getting more signs that perhaps it was time to move again. One morning, George's friend, my apartment manager, was working in the little garden outside my bedroom. He called me to the window and said he had more information about what was going on with George. I was beginning to feel as though I were in a bad B movie with each subplot growing thicker. Rather than chatting over a cup of coffee, he was outside my bedroom window with a rake in his hand, covertly talking to me through a window where I stood holding my electric toothbrush.

He told me that George was in the process of liquidating his assets, primarily his diamonds. Maybe it's because of my last name, but I found it amusing that he specifically mentioned the liquidation of diamonds. Also, when I was a kid, I had a reoccurring dream that I was being chased by a diamond man. It was the same dream every time. This faceless figure covered with diamonds would chase me until I woke up. The apartment manager suggested that I demand George give me some of his diamonds, because if I didn't I would never see a penny of any money he owed me. I asked him if he thought George was guilty. He wouldn't say one way or the other, but told me I was a good kid and I needed to look out for myself.

Could things get worse? Yes. One afternoon I received an urgent call from Charlotte Rae, warning me about Jaymie. She told me that Jaymie wasn't who I thought she was, that she had forged her handwriting and had stolen $7,000 of Charlotte's money. I didn't want to believe Charlotte. Jaymie had managed to convince me over time that Charlotte couldn't stand me and had filled my head with all sorts of bald-faced lies. Looking back, I just think it was too painful for me to face the fact that someone I trusted so completely was playing me. It was easier to accept that Charlotte didn't like me, because I didn't have the same closeness and trust with her that I had invested in Jaymie. I was so lost and confused and couldn't bear the fact that yet another "friend" was not a friend at all.

Shortly after Charlotte's call, I got a frenzied call from Jaymie. She was hysterical, telling me how crazy Charlotte was. She was crying and said she needed to see me in person. She came over, telling me the whole ugly tale of how Charlotte was trying to ruin her life. When she finally stopped sobbing about Charlotte, she asked me if she could borrow $400. I explained that I didn't have much money myself, and could not afford to lend her any, but she promised me she'd have it back to me by the end of the week. When she walked out the front door with my money, she left me with the *exact* thought that she wanted to leave me with. If she needed $400, then she obviously didn't have Charlotte's $7,000. I'm only guessing, but I can imagine her thinking, "What a sucker."

She did give a check to me by the end of the week for $400. It bounced. She apologized and gave me a second one. It bounced. She apologized and wrote me another one. It bounced. When I complained about all the rubber checks, she told me how selfish I was, and that I didn't know what real friendship was. If money was more important to me than our friendship, she said, then our friendship was over. She bounced all the way down the driveway, while I tried to bounce back emotionally, not fully understanding what had just happened.

Chapter Fifteen

The Three Faces of Geri:
Jewell, Warner, and Tyler

My next residence was a cute one-bedroom apartment across from the Jerry Gardner Training Stables in Burbank. It was not that far from NBC Studios, yet far enough away to feel like a retreat. There was grass, flowers, a small family-owned liquor store, and it smelled of sycamore trees and horses. My building was white brick with red doors and trimmings. My cat, Lady, loved living there just as much as I did. Sometimes I would walk across the street to feed the horses carrots, and I would notice Lady observing from the curb.

There were a lot of cowboys at the stables, real as well as actors. I became very good friends with Chad Everett, and he used to invite me to the set of his short-lived series, *The Rousters*, which was actually filmed at the stables. When I was a teenager, I had my crush on David Cassidy, but I also loved Chad Everett from *Medical Center*. I remember the day we met. It was at the beginning of the fall season in 1983. NBC did their annual "new fall season" celebration in which all the NBC stars would mingle with the affiliates, touting the new season lineup. I was standing next to Lisa Whelchel, when I noticed Chad from across the room. I squealed like a schoolgirl, "Lisa, it's Chad Everett!"

"Well, go say hello to him!"

"What could I possibly say to him?"

"You'd better think of something fast, because he's coming over here!" I looked up, and there was Dr. Joe Gannon right in front of me. Chad and I remained friends, and I was so thrilled when he invited me to celebrate his star on the Hollywood Walk of Fame.

In 1982, Daria was behind me, but even though I had new management and an attorney, I was not totally free from George yet. I was told to stay away from him, but was determined to collect on the promissory note I had. What I failed to understand was that no matter how smart I thought I was, George was smarter. I was convinced that there was something I could say to him that would cause him to have a change of heart, but like the old saying goes, a zebra doesn't change its stripes.

George asked me if I would testify on his behalf as a character witness. I told him that there was no way I would do that, that my attorney — and my new management — would kill me. He reminded me of everything that he had done for me and said that it was the least I could do in return. He added that I wouldn't have to make an actual court appearance, but could be tape-recorded with his attorney present. That way, *my* attorney would never know that I actually testified. If I was willing to do that, then he would make good on the promissory note when he was able to. (I cringe at my own stupidity as I am writing about this now.)

I showed up at his office, and just as he described, a tape recorder was set up to record my statements. I cannot recall if there was only one attorney present or more, but I do remember George being especially sweet to me that afternoon. I almost backed out and should have, but didn't. Every time an attorney would ask me a leading question about George, it always reinforced how wonderful and kindhearted he was. They had to stop the tape recorder several times and said my answers were not satisfactory enough. They would rephrase the question, hoping to get a different answer (which they recorded over the previous one), but if I were hooked up to a lie detector test, I would have failed miserably each time I said how wonderful George was. When I left that afternoon, I had lost a part of my self-respect. I couldn't believe that I was such a wimp, and I was grateful later, knowing that my testimony didn't help get him off in a court of law. I don't even know if it was admissible. According to court records, with or without my words, George was rightfully convicted of what he was tried for. He never did make good on that damned promissory note.

When I returned to *The Facts of Life* in 1982 for the fourth season, I was getting mixed messages. On the one hand, I was a part of several NBC functions, including being given the usual NBC gifts celebrating the new fall season. To open the show's fourth season, NBC aired a special *Facts of Life Goes to Paris* TV movie, and while I assumed at first I wouldn't be going, I was thrilled to realize I'd be part of this episode when I got several telegrams from different departments at NBC (including one from Brandon Tartikoff himself). Each welcomed me back to the show and wished me a wonderful trip to Paris! With each telegram, I got more and more excited about the anticipated trip to France, waiting for the producers of *Facts* to send me my script. However, I soon found out that for whatever reason, NBC was mistaken and had just assumed I was going to Paris. I went from one emotional extreme to another . . . but at least I didn't have to get a passport.

Also, for no apparent reason, the producers decided to change my character's name. I was no longer Geri Warner, as I was originally, but now my name was changed to Geri Tyler. There was no explanation for the name change, and even Lisa was annoyed by it. She took it upon herself to stand up for me. She stopped in the middle of taping a scene in front of a live studio audience and asked the producers if there was a mistake in my name, and could we say "Warner" instead of "Tyler"? You could hear a pin drop. After a beat, over the microphone, everyone could hear one of the producers say, "We are leaving the name Tyler, Lisa." I don't know which producer actually answered Lisa that day, as all of them were in the control booth. My character's name was now officially Geri Tyler.

The name change drove me nuts, as I couldn't figure out why they would choose to do that. I basically accepted it as their way of distancing me from the show (unless Geri Warner had had a quickie wedding they'd never talked about). At no point did they ever sit me down and say, "By the way, we're changing your name, and this is the logic behind it." Had I not been as fragile as I was, maybe it wouldn't have bothered me so much, but it was starting to feel like my days with the show were numbered. I filmed two episodes — "Sound of Silence" in October 1982 and "Teacher's Pet" in January 1983 — which made me wonder if I was just overreacting. Then, in January, I met with two of the show's writers, Stuart and Dee Wolpert, for lunch several afternoons and they tape-recorded talks about my life. They said my comments on tape were going to be used to help create and develop a very special Cousin Geri episode called "Here's Geri."

On the Friday before we were to begin rehearsing the episode, instead of receiving a script I received a call from the *Facts* production office telling me the episode had been nixed, and that it had nothing to do with them, but rather everything to do with NBC. The caller explained that because there were exterior scenes to film, like doing comedy at the Comedy Store and additional footage of Cousin Geri's apartment, NBC felt that it was not within their budget to do such an expensive episode. "We all love you here at *Facts* and are terribly disappointed in *their* decision." I sensed insincerity and had a hard time believing that NBC had budget concerns when they had just filmed *Facts of Life Goes to Paris*. Why couldn't anyone tell me the truth about anything?

When I was called to work again, the episodes that were rehearsed and filmed over a two-week period were the two parts of the "Graduation" season finale. Both scripts were read at the table reading at one time. In the first 25 minutes or so, I had a total of three lines, no more than a couple of words each. I didn't think too much of it, as it was not a story about Cousin Geri, but after we read through the second script, I only had one line, which was basically four lines in an hour. Looking back, it felt like a *s-l-o-w* death. However, I tried not to show my true feelings, and instead humored myself out of feeling so sad. At one point, I went up to my director, Asaad Kelada, and parodied a song from *The Wizard of Oz*, singing, "I could entertain the children, and entertain the women, and entertain the men . . . I could say something funny, and a chance I might be witty, if I only had a line!" Asaad laughed and let me know how much he loved and respected me. I felt the same about him.

It was terribly obvious that something was wrong, though. In fact, Stuart Wolpert (whom I respect completely for being one of the few people who was totally honest with me) approached me and briefly expressed how sorry he was for the nixing of the "Here's Geri" script. I asked him about the tapes that he promised to return to me, and he sadly said that he had no choice but to hand them over to one of the executive producers. He actually had tears in his eyes, because the tapes contained very personal conversations, and he had broken his promise to me that the tapes would go nowhere. I hadn't said anything earth-shattering, but I felt like a teenager whose diary had just been read. I was crushed.

After lunch, when we were finished with the table reading, I went and sat out in the hall. I didn't have a lot of lines to memorize, but instead I had to digest one blow after another and tried not to show my overwhelming disappointment. I wasn't sitting there long before Charlotte Rae came over. She crouched down to speak with me. The first thing she said was "How are you handling it?"

"Excuse me? Handling what?" I knew exactly what she was talking about, but didn't dare admit it.

"Geri, I know it hurts, but you can read the writing on the wall. They don't want you on the show anymore." She didn't realize what I had already learned from Stuart about the audio tapes, and I didn't tell her. She went on to explain how wrong it was for the producers to do this to me, saying that I had contributed so much to the show. She also said that she herself was powerless to do anything about it, but that perhaps if I went to Norman Lear, maybe he could help me.

Because I had been lied to by so many people, I actually thought that perhaps Charlotte was really just setting me up, since going over the producers' heads to Norman Lear could have landed me in hot water. Because Jaymie had filled my head with so much crap about Charlotte, I was always second-guessing her intentions. But I decided to take her advice; after all, what did I have to lose? With everything I had learned that afternoon, I'm surprised I didn't just walk into Norman's office and bawl. In hindsight, I believe that Charlotte was sincere in her effort to help me that afternoon.

Arriving unannounced at Lear's office that very afternoon, I met with him for no longer than about 10 minutes, and I downplayed what was really going on. I simply stated that I was confused about what the producers of *Facts* were doing with my character. I did not repeat anything that Stuart or Charlotte had said to me, because I didn't want to get either of them in any trouble. Even though Lear did place a call to the producers, telling them they needed to be clear with me about the future of my character, I didn't tell him the half of it, so I'm not sure if his phone call made any difference. One thing I do know, though, is that Norman Lear cared enough to pick up the phone on my behalf. That in itself meant the world to me.

I knew I had at least one more episode to film to fulfill my contract, but after being told by Charlotte that "they" didn't want me on the show anymore, I didn't quite know what to expect. However, halfheartedly, I was hoping that perhaps Norman's influence would create a change of attitude, and perhaps a renewed appreciation for my worth. I would have to wait and see.

Life went on. I moved again. (Surprised? I think by now, if I *didn't* move, you'd be more surprised.) Keith needed to move in with me once again because his roommate at the time dropped the ball and Keith did not have enough money to go it alone. Truthfully, I still had resentment toward him for befriending Daria, but I forgave him, instead honoring the friendship that we had. He needed me, and I was his friend. He slept in the living room, and the quarters were quite cramped.

One night when Keith and I came home together, we unlocked the front door, but found it chained from the inside. We knew someone was inside our apartment, since Lady hadn't figured out how to chain the door herself.

When Keith busted open the door, whoever was in our apartment had gotten away through the bedroom window. Everything was ransacked. Dresser drawers were left open; everything was strewn everywhere. If someone had hoped to find valuables, they were in the wrong apartment. They did, however, steal the valuable part of a motivational speaking award I had received, unscrewing the gold-plated figure, but leaving the marble base with my nameplate on it. It was the first time that I had ever been robbed, and it left me feeling scared to be in my own home. It was time to move. Besides, we needed a bigger place.

In spite of the ransacking of my apartment, I did miss living there. It was very peaceful, and I missed not only the horses across the street, but the Pickwick Bowl a half a mile away. I would go there frequently to play Ms. Pac-Man. I think Ms. Pac-Man was my drug of choice at the time. God only knows how many quarters I shoveled into those video arcade machines, but it had the same numbing effect of any drug. As I gobbled up the dots and dancing fruit, I didn't have to think about how unhappy I was. It seemed as though I had the talent to create happiness for others, but did not know how to attain it for myself.

However, I just didn't have it in my genetic makeup to give up. Keith, Lady, and I quickly set up our new home together. Keith was still working as a waiter, and although he was often late with the bills, he always paid. He was never one to take advantage of me financially. Although we were good friends, the roommate situation only lasted about six months. Without much thought, Keith invited a friend of his from San Jose, Tony, to move in with us. Upon his arrival, Keith realized that it was unrealistic to think that he could help Tony be situated in L.A. and told him that he needed to find another place to live even before he unpacked his suitcase.

As much as I loved Keith, I empathized with Tony. He was only 18 and had taken a huge risk to move all the way to Los Angeles to live with Keith, only to be told upon his arrival that he had to find another place to live. Looking back, I am certain that Tony would have figured out how to survive. However, I felt the need to protect him and take him under my wing. I think I was also fulfilling my own desire to be protected. It ended up working out for all of us. Keith found another roommate, and Tony and I found a friendship that lasted a lifetime.

True to my pattern, Tony and I became fast friends. At first he had a fannish reaction to me, only knowing me from television, but he quickly moved past that and has always loved me for me. Tony was like the little brother I never had. We found an apartment together in the same building Lisa, Keith, and I had lived in previously. I also taught Tony how to drive — as a result, to this day he is a shitty driver. He found employment immediately, and when that seasonal job was over, he became employed again. We had mutual respect for one another, and both helped each other grow up.

Tony was gay, and he was totally at ease with his sexuality, which helped me become more accepting of my own.

What was wonderful about having Tony as a roommate and friend was that he accepted me without question and never lied to me about anything. I actually had a sweet, kind girlfriend not long after, and Tony was there on every level, becoming friends with her as well. I met Sue at a gay bar that I reluctantly went to with my old roommate Laurel. Women wanted to dance with me, but I kept refusing. I was absolutely *not* going to dance, but Sue slipped me her phone number and asked me to call her.

Sue was beautiful inside and out. She had long, naturally blond hair, and a gorgeous body, toned from years of surfing. Sue was 21, and I was almost 30, but we felt like we were the same age. We had fun together and spent a lot of time at the beach. She moved in with me, and Tony moved in with another roommate. I even introduced Sue to my family, not saying she was my *girlfriend*, but rather my roommate. I was enjoying my relationship with Sue, but I still had "Geri Jewell" to think about, and my career wasn't exactly flying. What I discovered over time was that Sue was not as mature as I was, and she had a lot of growing up to do. At the time, she was a party girl and didn't have any ambition to further her growth. We went our separate ways, but always remained friends. In fact, she told me years later that because I used "tough love" with her, it changed the course of her life, and she would forever be grateful for the impact I had on her.

Even though my union with Sue was short-lived, it taught me that there could be happiness in a relationship, and she helped me move toward being more comfortable in my own skin. However, I was not courageous enough to be *out*. Interestingly, I did receive at least two postcards delivered to my home address, simply stating in bold print on the back, "We know you're gay!" I never knew who sent me these postcards, but I do remember each one fueling my state of panic, sometimes keeping me in bed for days.

I was offered another contract for the fifth season of *The Facts of Life*. Richard Lippin was disappointed that instead of offering more episodes than the previous season, they offered me less. It was hardly surprising though, when you consider what I went through in the fourth season. It felt as though I were being strung along for the sake of appearances. Out of 26 episodes for the entire season, I was guaranteed three. The first one I worked on was in October, "What Price Glory," in which I had a couple of lines. I didn't work again until February, in the episode called "Star at Langley." Again, my inclusion in it was only to fulfil a contract. I was hardly in a position to complain, as I was grateful for at least a week of employment.

Then, in February I was offered my third contractual episode of the season. It was actually a Cousin Geri storyline, but because I was so confused about what the producer's intentions were, I didn't know what to make of it. The episode was titled "All by Herself," and the storyline was about how Geri Tyler screws up a dinner for charity because she wants to run the whole show "all by herself." There seemed to be hidden references in the dialogue of the episode, which could have been subliminal messages to me without saying anything to me directly. For example, in a scene when Blair and I are trying to come up with a theme for the evening, Blair interrupts me: "Why don't we do like the gay '90s?" If that were the only *gay* reference, I probably wouldn't have given it a second thought, but it wasn't. Later, there was a scene where an obviously gay florist delivers tons of flowers to Mrs. Garrett's store and claims that he is looking for Geri Tyler (to sign the receipt). Noticing Tootie, Jo, and Natalie, he says, "Boy, *he* must like one of you girls a lot!" Tootie replies, "He is a she!" to which he responds, "Well, that's none of my business."

Was it all a coincidence, or did the dialogue run much deeper than that? Charlotte told me point-blank that I was no longer wanted on the show, I had a mysterious new last name, and now I was leaving on an episode about Geri Tyler screwing up a big charity dinner. I believed that the dialogue was completely intentional. Funny thing is, had any one of the producers talked to me privately about any concerns that they had about me, it wouldn't have been nearly as painful as living with the inner shame of constantly being off balance, never knowing for sure what was going to happen next.

In not knowing what exactly the issues were regarding me, I do not know if it was one thing or several things that played into my obvious decline on the show. There were so many interconnected dramas going on that one could have simply fed into the next one. Could my choice in attire have sent a message without me even being aware of it? I was never out of the closet, nor did I flaunt my sexuality. But thinking back, I did wear clothing that could have suggested that I was gay.

The '80s was an offbeat era in fashion. I also hung out with many people who were gay. So, I imitated what I thought was just "cool and funky," not realizing that perhaps it was "hot and dykey." Oftentimes, I wore rainbow patches on my jeans and jackets, but I had no idea that the rainbow symbolized the gay population. For me, it just was my way of quietly showing my affection for Judy Garland. I also wore a leather cock ring as a bracelet, because I saw so many people wearing them. I honestly thought it was just a cool bracelet, never realizing what I was actually wearing until long after the fact. I wore different colored bandanas tied around my jean legs, or my wrists, and discovered later that each color symbolized what your sexual preferences were. I wore metal and plastic clothespins on my jacket lapels because I thought they were cute. I was advertising that I liked rough sex — which was false advertising indeed! While all of these fashion choices may have been misconstrued as me flaunting my sexual orientation, all I was really doing was showing off my naiveté.

When Richard Lippin got the call that I was being offered another contract for the sixth season of *Facts*, he was ecstatic! That is, until he realized that they only offered me a guarantee of *one* episode for the entire season. He fought for more, but *Facts* was not willing to even match the previous season's guarantee of three episodes. I actually *wanted* to do that one episode, but Richard Lippin advised me not to accept it. I was so sad and torn at the same time. On the one hand, my manager was right when he told me it was a slap in the face, and that I had to maintain a certain amount of selfrespect. However, there is also an unspoken law in Hollywood that you never turn down anything unless you truly have negotiating power.

Maybe Richard Lippin believed that they would counter the offer. As it was, they didn't return with a counter offer, and I never returned to the show. I believe that they probably knew the contract would be rejected, and thus they could wash their hands of any more commitments to Geri Warner, Geri Tyler, and Geri Jewell. I was never *fired*, rather, I turned down employment, and my actions could easily have been perceived as a case of being too big for my britches. How my life would have played out if I had signed that contract for a guarantee of one more episode, I will never know. But I do know that the way my life *did* play out was never a mistake. As painful as it was, I still believe there are no accidents in the grand scheme of things.

CHAPTER SIXTEEN

Touring with "Geri"

In 1984, I came to the end of my run on *The Facts of Life*, but spiritually, I believe that whenever a door closes, a window is opened. Not necessarily a huge bay window, sometimes just a little window of hope and opportunity. I was *exactly* where I needed to be whether I believed it or not.

I was in so much emotional pain in the spring of 1984 because of having come through so much in such a short period of time. Also, I believe that one of the reasons I have allowed myself to become so emotionally derailed at times is because, even to this day, the most difficult emotion for me to express is anger. Rather than feeling anger toward someone else, I tend to direct the emotion inward onto myself. After so much self-loathing, all I wanted to do was numb the pain.

I was also dealing with unbearable back pain, neck pain, and overall joint pain, which had begun in college, secondary symptoms of cerebral palsy. Being as mobile as I am with CP, my body has endured overuse. This is seen in professional dancers or athletes, where the body becomes somewhat battered over time, developing other conditions such as arthritis, bone spurs, herniated discs, and sciatic nerve issues. I have developed a very high threshold to pain, but there are times when the pain has been so severe I've reached for remedies outside of myself, like using moist heat and prescription meds.

I've never used recreational drugs, except for trying marijuana a few times. I did drink alcohol in the '80s, but not regularly, so it never became a problem. However, there was one drug that was prescribed to me in 1984 that I became addicted to, and it wasn't prescribed for any of the physical pain that I suffered from. Because I was going through so many emotional problems, getting to sleep became more difficult than usual. Most people with cerebral palsy have problems getting to sleep because it is so hard to turn the mind and body off.

My psychologist had sent me to a psychiatrist whose specialty was sleep disorders. I never even questioned the fact that I was seeing a psychiatrist, because, in my mind, he was a "sleep doctor." In fact, this part of my story, I'll just refer to him as Dr. Sleeper. Dr. Sleeper introduced me to a drug called Restoril, and it became my downfall; I became an addict for life. Even when I was prescribed other pain meds, I never abused them like I did Restoril. It *magically* put me to sleep at night, and what was even more fascinating about it was that it temporarily relieved me from involuntary and spastic movement. The relief was threefold. One, it gave me a brief window of being CP-free; two, it allowed me to have a good night's rest; and three (the most powerful), it numbed emotional pain.

Unfortunately, like with any feel-good drug, the user does not realize at first how something so good could be so bad. Very quickly, Restoril became my answer to everything: I am no longer on *Facts of Life*, but it's okay, I've got Restoril. I don't have very much money to live on; not a problem, I can afford Restoril. I am gay, but I can't be true to myself; so what, Restoril is my truth. The unfortunate reality is that the longer we stay in a relationship with a drug, the less is healed, and it simply prolongs unnecessary suffering.

In this same period, I was in the midst of having my autobiography, *Geri,* published. George had agreed to the book deal when he still managed me. In the wake of everything that was happening on a personal level, I didn't believe it would actually be published. Initially I was excited about it, but as the writing progressed, my life began falling apart and it was no longer the same story. Lippin and Grant tried to help me stop publication, but it was an iron-clad contract, and I had to follow through with it.

In fact, my last episode of *Facts* aired at the exact time that *Geri* was published, in the spring of 1984. I know that *Geri* had a place in the world, and it was a good book for kids to read, but even though I was listed as the author of the book, I had very little to do with the writing of it. The author of the book turned my life into some happy-go-lucky fantasy story of success, whereas, in reality, my manager was on his way to prison and I was in tremendous emotional pain. What this book did was force me to wear a "happy face" when I was only "coping." There aren't even any words to describe the anguish of having a book published about your own life, that you supposedly wrote but instead loathed.

I had a top-of-the-line publisher, William Morrow, and a top-of-the-line book tour that authors dream about, yet I dreaded every talk show, interview, and book signing, and didn't even want some of my friends and family members to read it. When I was sent the galleys in overnight mail to peruse before the book went to print, I couldn't even force myself to read the whole thing. Not only had I very little to do with the writing of that book, but I didn't have much to do with the reading of it either. Maybe if I had, I would have discovered the "revelations" and insider gossip about *The Facts of Life* that would instigate most of the questions during the interviews I had on the book tour.

I left on my two-week book tour immediately following the book's publication, zigzagging all over the country touting the sale of my "auto-biography," *Geri*. The cover of the book had a photo of my smiling face beneath the words, "A warm, funny, and moving account of a courageous young woman's rise to stardom and her triumph over cerebral palsy." To me, it felt like a bad punch line, and I certainly hadn't triumphed over cerebral palsy, nor will I ever. In fact, spiritually, it is not about overcoming the disability, but instead learning to accept it so you can live life to its fullest.

My brother Fred, who was going through a divorce at the time, was trying to figure out what he wanted to do with his life. He had thought about starting a limo service, and I thought it would be a good idea to take him with me on my book tour, actually meeting one limo driver after another, and soaking up kernels of information he would need to start his own company. After the tour was over, he ended up not wanting to go in that direction, but I had a wonderful bonding experience with him, and it also gave him some time away to think about what he really wanted to do at this stage in his life. He wasn't the only one looking to get away from his life for a bit.

So Fred followed me to bookings on practically all the major talk shows across the United States. I was flying from city to city almost nightly. I was booked on *Larry King Live*, but he had the flu so I was interviewed by Geraldo Rivera instead.

The book tour was grueling, flying all night and getting up at the crack of dawn to do all the "good morning" shows. I was using Restoril to sleep and cope with the stress of promoting a book that I didn't believe in. One day in New York City, I had finished doing all the morning shows and early afternoon shows. Fred and Debra, my publicist from William Morrow, were both starving, wanting lunch. I was hungry too, but for no apparent reason this diva-like energy gripped me, and I let everyone know that I wanted to go shopping in the theater district, and not take the time to have lunch.

Fred couldn't believe my behavior. Both he and Debra explained that I could go shopping anytime, but that I needed to eat. I understood their logic, but I wasn't going to change my mind. Besides, I hated my book, and as much as I was obligated to keeping my contractual commitment with the publisher, emotionally I was still a child. It was equivalent to being in high school and wanting to cut class. The rationale being, "I'm just cutting one class; it's not like I'm dropping out of school . . . jeez!"

Now that baby diva Geri got her way, I actually had to buy something. I spotted a theater poster that I loved and purchased it under the disapproving and glaring looks from Fred and Debra. They got hot dogs from a vender, both wondering why it was so damned important that I go shopping. Not that I had an answer to the question, because truthfully I didn't understand my attitude either. It honestly felt as though I had left my body, and someone else had entered it and was making me act strangely. Considering that I didn't want to be connected to my own autobiography, however, it makes sense that I would begin to act differently than the Geri Jewell whose face graced the cover of that book.

We were now battling rush hour traffic in New York City, slowly making our way toward NBC to do another interview on *Live at Five*. The producers were not happy that we were late to arrive and no one would dare say that we were late because Princess Geri had to go shopping. After the show, we had several more interviews to get to. Both Fred and Debra were determined to get me something to eat before I fainted, but before we left the studio, a production assistant asked me if I could spare a few minutes, that a fan of mine really wanted to meet me. So, I followed the PA into a small dressing room. I was absolutely stunned to discover that my fan was Liza Minnelli.

Liza and Chita Rivera were there that afternoon, both being interviewed about the Broadway musical they were doing together called *The Rink*. Liza was thrilled to meet me, and the feeling was mutual. She gave me a warm hug, telling me that she had followed my career and couldn't believe that she was finally meeting me. *She* was thrilled to meet *me?* Fred and Debra were even shocked! I also had the pleasure of meeting Chita Rivera, but unfortunately did not ask her for an autograph. I did ask Liza, who graciously agreed, but only if I autographed a copy of my book for her. I didn't want her to read my book, but autographed one for her anyway. I then pulled out the theater poster that I was still carrying in a bag under my arm for Liza to sign.

Funny thing is, when we arrived at NBC, the limo driver told me I could leave the poster in the car, but as if it were a crown jewel, I wouldn't leave it, taking it into the studio with me. Neither Debra nor Fred had seen the actual poster until I removed it from the bag in front of Liza. Upon seeing it, she turned white. The poster was of Judy Garland at Carnegie Hall! Stunned, she asked, "How did you know I was going to be here today?"

"I didn't; I just bought this on the way over here this afternoon." She signed the poster as everyone in the room took in the magic, as if Judy herself was in the room too. I believe she may have been. After Liza signed the poster to me, she made the comment that it was the only poster that she didn't have of Mama's. Everyone in the tiny dressing was stunned. It was kind of spooky, but a good spooky.

But almost as if I couldn't allow myself to fully enjoy the moment, my insecurities gripped me once again and ruined the whole meeting. Liza was so sweet and asked if she could have my home phone number and address, saying that she would love to get to know me, maybe get together, have popcorn and ice cream, and watch movies. I told her that I didn't have a home phone number. Fred and Debra looked at me as if I had lost my mind. For a moment, I agreed with them. Liza thought I was joking, and said, "Why, you don't have a home?" To which I said, "No, I don't. I don't actually live anywhere really. If you want to find me badly enough, you'll know where to find me." Even as the words were coming out of my mouth, I didn't understand what I was doing. When we got to the car, both Debra and Fred asked me why I was so arrogant. I didn't know. It could have been the lack of food, the exhaustion, the Restoril, or the belief that Liza would never be my friend. It was almost easier to reject her than to risk her rejecting me. I went back to my hotel room that night, took a Restoril, and cried until I fell asleep.

The following day I was still bummed about how I had reacted to Liza. I was booked on *The Howard Stern Show*, and at the time I had no idea who Howard Stern was. Very quickly, I realized that he was edgy and thoroughly enjoyed the power of embarrassing his guests if he could find a weak spot. I knew he would have had the last laugh with me, because he was ahead of me in witty remarks. However, I was able to get him in the very last segment of the interview, when he asked me what it felt like to have CP. Trying to be just as hip and shocking as he was, I replied, "It feels like having a continuous orgasm, only my partners never know when I'm coming or going!" Taken totally off guard, Howard was speechless for a few seconds before he burst out laughing. That line earned a certain respect from Howard. Over the years, he has made a dozen references to me on his radio and television shows. As with all good lines, I remembered it too and told it many times after, making it a staple of my act.

After *The Howard Stern Show*, Fred and I boarded a plane to Detroit to follow the same routine, starting with *Good Morning Detroit*. Unfortunately, due to a snowstorm, our flight was five hours late on arrival. We didn't get there until 4 a.m., and our limo hadn't waited for us. Fred and I were finally able to find a cab to take us to our hotel, having barely enough time to change clothes for my appearance on the show. They sent a car to take me to the studio. I was exhausted and had been up for more than 24 hours. I got makeup and was wired, ready to tape in front of a live audience.

The last thing I remember was someone placing a copy of my book on the table in front of me, and the host of the show sitting down next to me. In the next instant I was sound asleep. I didn't even hear the audience applaud as the host introduced me. On the air, in the middle of my own interview, I was asleep! The host shook my shoulders trying to wake me up. When I woke up, the audience was laughing, and my host was trying to make light of the situation saying something like, "Well, I certainly hope your book is more interesting than you are." I wanted to say that it actually wasn't, but even when I was half asleep, I knew better than to be a smart-ass.

My next stop was Chicago, and I had another amusing appearance, this one on *The Phil Donahue Show*. Most talk shows are filmed in front of a live audience. If I thought Howard Stern was challenging, I was in for an eye-opener with Donahue. Some talk show hosts didn't even read my book. Of course that never bothered me — the less *Geri* was read, the happier I was. To my astonishment, not only had Phil *read* my book, but the book itself was highlighted and the pages had been marked up; he wanted me to elaborate on what I had written. This wouldn't have been a problem . . . had I actually written my own book! But because I only skimmed through my own book, I didn't recognize what Donahue was referring to by a phrase or a paragraph.

Within minutes, the interview started out on the wrong foot (it could have been my left foot or my right). On the air, he read a quote from my book. "Geri, you wrote early on in your book, that 'cerebral palsy' are the two ugliest words in the English language. That statement sounds almost hypocritical to what you represent. Why would you write something like that?" Of course I wanted to say it was because I didn't write the damn book! However, I worried that if I said that I'd be in trouble with my pub-lisher, so I bullshitted about how it was really a metaphorical statement . . . blah, blah, blah, blah. It just got worse from there.

Next, he asked me to elaborate on the story that I wrote about a certain teacher who greatly influenced my life. When the camera panned back to my face, my expression was completely blank. At least it looked that way, as I was actually trying to do a mental search in the archives of my mind for the teacher he was referring to. He did mention which chapter it was in, but how would I know what was in each chapter? I smiled, kind of embarrassed, and asked him to give me a bigger hint as to which teacher he was talking about. Donahue hit himself in the forehead three times with his microphone (something he often did when he was frustrated by a guest), almost bewildered, saying, "I could swear her name is on this book, and she wrote it!"

A little later in 1984, I was also booked in Alaska for an interview about the book. I had missed my plane from Anchorage to Juneau and had to sit in the airport for almost seven hours. Thank God I always had at least three books with me to read on the road. I had just bought the autobiography of Sid Caesar called *Where Have I Been?* I had a lot of time to kill in Alaska, and was able to finish this fascinating book in a couple of days.

After my gig in Alaska, I flew to New York. I was going to do some club work and bebop in the city for a few days, but upon arrival I got an urgent message from Richard Lippin. He informed me that there was a change of plans and that I was booked on a flight the next morning back to Los Angeles. I was slightly annoyed and asked what could be so important that I would have to fly home so soon. I hadn't even eaten the chocolate mints on my pillow yet! I was informed that Sid Caesar had seen me perform and wanted to meet with me, possibly to do a series with him.

"You've got to be kidding! I just finished reading his autobiography!"

Richard was pleased. "Good, you're prepared." It seemed as though I was indeed prepared. Like the situation with Liza, my angels had guided me again, knowing that Sid was coming into my life.

I flew home and met with Sid Caesar at his house. One of the writers who I also met with that afternoon was Emmy-winner Ed Simmons, one of the head writers on *The Carol Burnett Show* and later on *Mama's Family*. Ed wrote a wonderful pilot for Sid and me called *Sid's Kid*. It was a half-hour sitcom, with Sid as an old-time vaudeville performer who lives in New York City. I played his daughter, who was conceived during a one-night stand and showed up on his doorstep at 22 because she wanted to know her dad. So, not only does Sid become an instant father, but he also discovers that his daughter has cerebral palsy, has inherited his love of show business, and wants to move in with him. It was well written, and Ed, Sid, Richard Lippin and our agents, and I tried to sell this show to all three networks. Sadly, after trying for almost three months, the project was dropped, much to the disappointment of everyone.

Truthfully, I felt that the greater sadness was for Sid. He was so ready to be back on top after successfully beating his demons with drugs and alcohol. It was a shame that no one in Hollywood would embrace him again, or appreciate the magic that Sid and I could have brought to the small screen. Sid and I had great chemistry, and my disability didn't faze him in the least. He had nothing but love and admiration for me, and held the same standard of work ethic for me as he did for any other actress. I remember him telling me that he didn't like the way some actors had become lazy and were not always quick on their feet. I said, "I'm quick on my feet?" He laughed and handed me about five books to read, two of which were about Albert Einstein. Giving me my homework, he said that one must have a tremendous knowledge and understanding about life in order to interpret life as an artist. Sid was a genius, and I was more than willing to learn whatever I could from him.

One afternoon when we were sitting by his pool, he came out and put about 20 scripts from *Your Show of Shows* on my lap. This was his pride and joy and a part of the history of television, and now it was right in front of me to peruse. I could feel his genuine excitement in being able to share his "baby" with me. These scripts were gold, and it was a dream come true to be able to look at these originals. In his excitement of sharing them with me, he dived in the pool, doing not less than 25 laps (I lost count after that). I didn't know what was more impressive: the scripts in my hand or Sid's phenomenal physical shape at age 63!

When he finished his daily workout in the pool, he came over and sat down, anxiously waiting for me to say something. Truthfully, I hadn't gotten that far into the stack of scripts, as I was distracted by something that was bothering me the entire time Sid was in the pool. He finally asked me, "Well, what do you think?"

Without even realizing the absurdity of my remark, I said "I was thinking, while you were swimming . . . is your watch waterproof?" Of all the things I could have said, that was the last thing he expected.

He laughed, thinking I was humoring him. "Now . . . what do you *really* think?"

"I really think you shouldn't swim with that Rolex!" That's when my youth shined in splendor, and he seemed to adore me for it.

Even though we were not able to launch *Sid's Kid*, I did make a new friend in the writer, Ed Simmons. We spoke on the phone every so often, and we got together several times thereafter. I loved Ed, and he was always honest with me. One thing that bothered him early on in developing our project was that I seemed to be missing a lot. He picked up very quickly that I was hearing impaired. He asked me why I didn't wear hearing aids, and although I didn't tell him all the reasons, I told him the easiest reason — that they were too expensive. I promised that if we sold the series, I would buy them.

The following week when we met at Sid's home, Ed placed an envelope in front of me, telling me to open it. He had written on it "Now hear this!" Inside was $1,500, all in $100 bills. The note inside read, "You will not wait until we sell the series. You are going to hear everything *now*! Love, Ed." Well, I certainly wasn't going to tell him all the other reasons I didn't want to wear hearing aids after such a kind gesture. The least I could do was buy a pair of hearing aids, hoping that the technology was good enough now that maybe I could actually benefit from better hearing. I bought a pair two weeks later. Ed was delighted when I walked in wearing them: I didn't say "What?" the entire afternoon.

That gift of hearing from Ed was the beginning of me wearing hearing aids from that point on. Shortly after my meetings with Sid and Ed, I met Bill Austin in Palm Springs. Bill is the owner of Starkey Hearing Instruments, and if anyone understood the frustrations and problems that some people have with hearing aids, it was Bill. One of the main reasons I was so resistant to wearing hearing aids was not because I didn't want to hear, but because I didn't want to hear the feedback. It took Bill Austin's tireless engineers at Starkey Hearing Labs years, through trial and error, to finally develop the technology to build me a pair of totally "feedback free" hearing aids, which I began wearing in the mid-'80s. Because of my cerebral palsy and tiny ear canals, this was quite a challenge. Bill has always had passion and drive throughout his life, and demands the best quality in all of his hearing instruments. His company has helped millions of people worldwide to have better hearing. I am grateful to be one of them. Starkey has built me at least 18 pairs of hearing aids over the years, and today I not only wear my hearing aids, but I love them.

CHAPTER SEVENTEEN

From Sesame Street to
1600 Pennsylvania Avenue

After my book tour, I continued to do stand-up comedy and motivational speaking, but because I was no longer on *The Facts of Life*, the work only trickled in. Lippin and Grant tried vigorously to get me work in Hollywood, but it was almost impossible. However, there were those like Dick Clark who never forgot me, and when Richard Lippin approached him for me to be on his series *On Stage America* I was booked. I did a comedy routine and was eager to tell my new orgasm joke that was inspired by *The Howard Stern Show*. It never occurred to me that it might be too "blue" to tell on national television, but it was left in the broadcast.

After it aired, I received hundreds of letters complaining of my usage of the word "orgasm." The complaint wasn't really about the word itself as much as the fact that I was supposed to be a role model for people with disabilities, and joking about sex was offensive. A lot of the letters came from concerned parents and the religious right. A couple of my presentations on the road were even picketed by people with disabilities and disability advocates. I had no idea that one little orgasm joke would cause so much outrage. But truthfully, neither the joke about an orgasm nor the fact I actually didn't have one in 1985 seemed to concern me at the time.

Nineteen eighty-five was an interesting year, because I was barely scraping by financially, paying attorney fees. On top of that I received a bill from the government for $9,999.99. The Department of Health and Human Services wanted all the supplementary security income back that was paid to me while in college and throughout 1981. They even seized the little Postal Credit Union account that Mom had put aside for me in my name. I was terrified, heartbroken, and didn't know how to fight back. Again, even though George was in prison by this time, I was still paying for what he once said would be "a drop in the bucket." All I can say is that it was one *big* drop! I knew on a technicality I owed it to them and paid them monthly until it was finally paid in full.

Every month I felt strangled by back taxes, attorney fees, credit card debt, and now my ssi bill. I worked as much as I could on the road, and once in a while I would get a television appearance, thanks to Richard Lippin. However, it was also at this time that Lippin made the painful decision to let me go as a client. He recognized that, for whatever reason, he was unable to secure work for me in Hollywood. He had put all of his efforts into helping me break through the barriers and put me back on the map where he believed I rightfully belonged.

I will never forget the last time I met with him at his office. He explained to me that he was unable to break through the high walls of Hollywood or repair whatever damage had been done in the past. He told me that he believed in me, but that he was not the right manager to put me back on the map. He gave me several boxes of videotapes, and all the correspondence he had done over the years on my behalf. Tears streamed down my cheeks, but I knew that he was right, and it was painful enough for him without me collapsing in despair.

However, the meeting wasn't quite over yet. Before I left his office, he handed me an envelope containing a savings and loan document from Merrill Lynch for $9,800. He told me that the entire time he managed me he had put his fees for managing me away in a savings account. He told me that he felt it was unethical to be paid for turning my career around when in fact that hadn't happened. I hugged him, and to this day I don't believe that he "failed" me.

I probably should have left the money in savings and let it gain interest, but instead I paid a chunk of the ssi bill, put a down payment on a new Honda Accord, and paid off some credit card debt. Driving around in my new car that I couldn't really afford was sort of an escape from reality, making it look like I had some power and confidence, when in fact I felt powerless, and my self-esteem waned.

Lisa Whelchel came to my aid more than once, giving me jobs like house-sitting when she was out of town. Lisa was a good friend, and I have never forgotten what she did for me. We still went out occasionally, and I came to the set of *Facts* with her many times, with both of us hoping that seeing me there would get me back on the show. Alas, it never worked. For whatever reason, they were absolutely finished with me. Even when Cloris Leachman replaced Charlotte Rae, it still didn't make a difference. I felt like the black sheep of the cast and could not shake the feeling. I was devastated that what I was most famous for would no longer embrace me. The series hadn't been canceled — just me.

By this time, I had so much anger that I didn't know what to do with it. From 1983 on, I dealt with anger in a private, quiet manner that very few people were aware of, outside of my psychologist and Dr. Sleeper. I felt so helpless in not being able to solve my problems constructively that the only thing that gave me any kind of relief was to repeatedly burn myself. The behavior was never life-threatening, but it was disturbing. I was depressed much of the time and became more and more dependent on Restoril.

Sometime in 1985, I had to find another doctor to prescribe it to me as well. Not because Dr. Sleeper wouldn't, but because I loathed him. During one visit, I was crying and telling him how depressed I was, yet he never once considered prescribing me an antidepressant and never paid much attention to a clear warning on the Restoril bottle, "Do not take if you are depressed." Dr. Sleeper told me point-blank that the reason I was so depressed was because I didn't know Jesus Christ. I told him that he was wrong, that I did know Jesus, and that I was baptized and raised Catholic. I went on to say that Christ was inside of me, in my heart. Dr. Sleeper just looked at me smugly and said that that was one of Satan's biggest lies. I was stunned! I just took the prescription for Restoril and walked out of his office in a state of despair.

I went home, took Restoril, and lay down on the floor with a pillow and blanket in a dark closet. It was as if that tiny dark closet was the only place I felt safe, but it was only symbolic of the bigger closet I was hiding in. No matter how much pain I was in, I never attempted to commit suicide. I could have easily taken a whole bottle of Restoril or driven off the famous Mulholland Drive cliff, but quite honestly, I never wanted to die. I just wanted help. There was *always* a pilot light on in my will to live.

Part of my anguish was that I was always in dire financial straits, never able to work regularly enough to make ends meet. I had to move again because I could no longer afford the monthly rent of $735 for a one-bedroom place. I ended up moving to a studio apartment on Courtney Avenue, right off Hollywood Boulevard, for only $400 per month, still barely making it. Because I was so determined to live independently, it didn't even occur to me to move back home with Mom and Dad, even though they both would have welcomed me with open arms. It was my pride that kept me from allowing my parents to know how desperate I really was.

I have learned over the years that desperation can be a direct result of having lack of faith. I didn't trust that my needs could be met and therefore unwisely sought help from a limited, faulty reservoir. In my desperate frame of mind I tried to think of where I could get the money I needed. George? I don't think so. Jaymie? It had been over a year since I had seen her, and she owed *me* money. Maybe she was a different person now. And besides, I did miss her. True to my nature, I clung to the memory of what was, rather than the reality of what is. I called Jaymie out of the blue, and to my surprise, she seemed pleased to hear from me. Before I could ask her for any money she brought it up, saying she wanted to make good on the loan.

Jaymie picked me up to take me to dinner the following evening. It was a little awkward, but she apologized for the way she had treated me and said that now that Charlotte was out of her life, she was happy and stable (I'm sure Charlotte felt the same way). Because Jaymie *wasn't* in jail, though, I wondered if Charlotte may have been mistaken about the stolen money and had decided not to press charges. I *needed* to believe that. It was as if my mind was forcing me to see a pretty landscape, when in fact I was staring at a landfill.

Before we went to dinner she drove me to a studio in Hollywood where she was now employed. She told me that she had a little more work to do before we left for dinner. No problem. "Geri, would you mind taking some boxes out to my car? It will save time, as I have to deliver them to another studio in the morning." I said sure. While she worked at the word processor, I carried one box after another out of the studio, down Sunset Boulevard, and around the corner on Gower to her parked car.

I was getting a little winded, as some of the boxes were quite heavy, but Jaymie explained that it would be impossible to drive the car onto the lot. After I was finished, she was too, and we finally had dinner. It was a nice evening, reminiscing about the past and catching up on the present. She paid for dinner, but had forgotten her checkbook to pay me any money. Oddly, before she left my apartment, she asked if she could borrow my VHS copy of *Sunset Boulevard*. I hesitated, but she laughed, asking me if I didn't believe she'd return it. I felt small, so I let her take the movie.

I really didn't give it another thought or even suspect anything other than perhaps I wouldn't see the money (or the movie). About four days later, I got a call from the West Hollywood Sheriff's Department. I spoke to Detective Bob Piper. He explained that I was a possible suspect involving grand theft, and would I please come in for questioning. I laughed, and asked him if he was joking, to which he very seriously said no. He said that he knew I was that comedian from *Facts of Life*, and that it would be a lot easier if I just cooperated and came down to the station rather than have a squad car come to my apartment and get me. I was scared and called my sister to take me to the Sheriff's Department. Gloria asked me what I had done, and I truthfully told her I'd done nothing, that someone had probably confused me with some other person with CP who was suspected of grand theft.

We were met by Detective Piper. Gloria was furious; I was confused. Here I was being interrogated and I had no idea what I had done. Piper's little office reminded me of the television show *Barney Miller*, but there were no actors, no scripts, and definitely no laugh tracks. In fact, Detective Piper had no sense of humor at all. He questioned me for what seemed like two hours, and Gloria was ready to put her fist through a wall. Piper told her to pipe down, or she would be asked to leave the room.

I honestly thought it was a big mistake, until the address of the studio was given to me. Slowly I came to realize that it was where Jaymie had taken me earlier in the week, and what I had carried out to her car was actually $45,000 worth of video equipment. As I became aware that I was the person Piper was looking for, Piper realized that I had been set up for the fall. He was enraged, and apologized to both Gloria and me, and said that if it was the last thing he did, he would arrest Jaymie Sloane. He also made me promise that after he made the arrest I would testify in court to make sure that she got a conviction. I *would* keep my promise to Detective Bob Piper.

A couple of months later, I arrived early to the Los Angeles Superior Court downtown. I quietly slipped into the courtroom, sitting in the last row. I was extremely nervous, but I knew I had to keep my promise to Detective Piper. When Jaymie walked in, she spotted me instantly, coming over to me as if I were a long lost friend. "Geri, I was hoping I'd see you, as I have so much to explain to you." I calmly told her that there was nothing more to discuss, that she had set me up for grand theft, period. She continued to explain that it was all a misunderstanding. Before she could go any further, her name was called and she had to go to the front of the courtroom. As if I was there to support her, she asked me if I would please hold her purse until she returned. Of course I refused, wondering what kind of a game she was playing, or if she was a complete sociopath. She ended up plea bargaining, so I never got to testify against her.

Before we left the courthouse, Jaymie once again asked to talk to me. I agreed, out of sheer curiosity. I felt I was "safe" because, after all, I was at the county courthouse. What could she possibly do to me? We were on the ninth floor of the building, and there was a glass door that led out to a patio deck next to the cafeteria. She was very casual and was even laughing about the whole thing. She explained that someone else had set her up, using me as a way to hurt *her*. I didn't believe her and told her so. She propped herself up on the ledge, and offered to give me a hand to come sit next to her. I declined, keeping my feet planted on the concrete as I turned and walked away. I never saw her again and I still don't have another copy of *Sunset Boulevard*.

During this same time, I did a special with John Ritter on CBS called *The Secret World of the Very Young*, about children with disabilities. I was a disability icon, so any work that I got in Hollywood always had a disability theme. As much as I welcomed every job that came my way, I resented that I was never able to be mainstreamed into other roles that were not disability related. Even today, I haven't successfully crossed that barrier, but am certainly moving closer.

Nineteen eighty-five was interesting in that I was doing television shows back to back that revolved around children: *Secret World*, *The Great Space Coaster*, and, of course, my now famous appearance on *Sesame Street*. The producers of the show were always proactive about hiring people with disabilities. They had tremendous success with Linda Bove, an actress who is deaf, so it didn't take much to convince them to have me on the show as well. They asked me if I had any hobbies other than stand-up comedy that would appeal to children. I told them that I loved Ms. Pac-Man, and that I knew how to roller-skate. Both were true, except that I could ride a skateboard far better than I ever managed skates. I knew how to skate, I just had problems stopping. Why I never mentioned my skill at skateboarding is a mystery to me, except perhaps in the '80s skateboarding was out and roller-skating was in.

On this particular episode of *Sesame Street*, I appeared in one scene playing a video game with Elmo, and I roller-skated with Big Bird. We did a couple of rehearsals, but the actual roller skates were not put on me until we were filming in front of a live audience of three- and four-year-olds with their parents. I was excited about working with Caroll Spinney again, as he was the puppeteer inside of the Big Bird costume. He remembered me from *I Love Liberty* and was equally thrilled. Had he known what a headache it was going to be, he probably would have called in sick that day. As it was, we *both* roller-skated that afternoon, and I don't think either one of us were roller derby material.

Misjudging my speed, I came flying onto the stage from the wings. I was going so fast that I had missed my mark by at least by two feet. Within seconds, I knew I couldn't slow down. Depending on which way I shifted my body weight (with CP it was always unpredictable) I was either going to roll off the stage and into the studio audience or hit the camera, or slam into Big Bird. As it was, I hit Big Bird so hard that his head fell off and dramatically rolled across the stage. The kids were screaming and crying, Carroll Spinney was a bit dazed, and the producers were horrified. Luckily, no one was seriously hurt and we were able to film a second take.

After filming the string of children's shows, including another one in Canada called *Polka Dot Door*, in which I sang and danced with another big puppet named Polkaroo, I filmed an adult show, *Good Sex with Dr. Ruth*. It was so weird going from one extreme to the other, but I knew that I had an opportunity to shatter the myth that people with disabilities are asexual.

Dr. Ruth Westheimer couldn't have been a kinder soul. She is extremely intelligent and intuitive as well. She has a doctorate in psychology, and within five minutes of the 30-minute segment of her show, she must have picked up on my vulnerability and knew that I was much too fragile to talk about sex. So, even though the show was called *Good Sex with Dr. Ruth*, she led me into topics that had absolutely nothing to do with sex. She even went as far as saying on the air, "Let's hope that there are producers out there who will hire you in Hollywood. You need a sitcom!" For a split second, it felt as though I was on *This Is Your Life* with Ralph Edwards, and I was Frances Farmer.

However, without question, there were always angels along my path, guiding me when I least expected it. Lyle Gregory was one such earth angel. In fact, everything about Lyle carried angelic themes. Lyle was one of the producers of the KABC radio talk show with host Michael Jackson. After Lyle booked me on the show, Lyle and I were friends for life.

Lyle introduced me to Science of Mind and took me to the famous Agape Church in Culver City and to his own Science of Mind Church in North Hollywood. It was through Lyle that I had the pleasure of meeting Ray Bolger, who played the Scarecrow in *The Wizard of Oz*. Like me, Lyle was a huge fan of Judy Garland and thought that it would be cool if he could book me and Bolger back to back on the Michael Jackson show. It *was* cool, and Ray Bolger couldn't have been nicer.

Slowly, through Science of Mind, I came to understand how everything in life is what we make it. In some ways, because I had such low self-esteem, life reflected more hardship than usual. In other words, if I believed that I couldn't have something, I wouldn't. I had always had a strong mind and understood the power of visualization, which is why I have accomplished as much as I have. However, what is even more powerful is what we believe about ourselves subconsciously. Subconscious thought often overrides conscious thought. For example, I believed I could be an actress and a comedian, but deep down, I had bought into the belief that I would never be accepted in mainstream society because that idea had been reflected back to me since I was a child.

I originally wanted to be famous so that my cerebral palsy would take a backseat to my fame. However, the opposite happened, putting cerebral palsy at the forefront of everything I did. Though many doors slammed in my face as a direct result of having CP, there were some doors that opened *because* of it. One such door was that of the White House. I was asked to be a part of Inspire '85. This was a huge disability gala put on by the President's Committee on Employment of People with Disabilities. That year they decided to honor disability and the arts, showcasing various talented people with disabilities, inviting celebrities and politicians alike.

Even though I was not able to get work in Hollywood, I had been successful enough to make a name for myself representing people with disabilities nationally. I had become acquainted with many influential people in the disability community and made many connections in the Disability/ADA (American with Disabilities Act) movement in America. It took many years to be fully embraced and taken seriously by this powerful minority group, but in 1985, I had enough recognition to be asked to do stand-up comedy at the White House. I was initially excited, and I knew several people that were part of planning of this show. All of my friends were thrilled for me. How many people get the opportunity to appear at the White House? It was quite an honor, but at the last minute, it almost didn't happen.

When I was first approached, I was asked to do 10 minutes of stand-up comedy, but then they called me back the next day to tell me that I could only do two minutes. I asked why and was told that they had so many performers in the lineup that there just wasn't enough time to give me the original 10 minutes that I had been offered. I was disappointed, but agreed to do it anyway. That is, until I got a phone call shortly after from a friend of mine who was on the planning committee.

My friend told me in confidence that there were a couple of people on the committee who absolutely did not want me at the White House, or any other house for that matter. It seemed as though I had gained a reputation for being vulgar because I had told an orgasm joke on national television. I was not a good role model for people with disabilities; I was a loose cannon and could not be trusted. At first I laughed, and then I was furious. I was so sick of being unfairly judged. I told my friend, through tears, that I would "just say no" to the White House! My friend laughed and said, "It's funny that you would quote Nancy Reagan, because it was Nancy who fought for you yesterday!"

I was floored. I was not a Republican and couldn't understand why the First Lady had come to my defense. Apparently she had argued that in spite of my questionable jokes, I was still the most recognizable person with a disability in the entertainment industry, and that it would simply be wrong not to acknowledge my contribution to the arts. The others agreed that she had a point, but there was still concern about that damned orgasm joke. It was decided that they would give me only two minutes of stage time so that I would not have time to tell the one joke that everyone was so afraid of. Truthfully, had someone just asked me not to tell the joke, I would not have. But once again I was being talked *about*, like a child, rather than being talked *to*, like an adult. It's as if they thought I was breakable and could not handle reality.

Even after I became aware that people had fought for me, it took a lot of arm twisting to finally agree to do it. My friends basically said that if I turned down the gig I'd be cutting off my nose to spite my face, and that I was being foolish to turn down an opportunity to perform at the White House. I knew my friends were right, and I agreed to fly to Washington to do the show. However, my ego had been bruised, and I wanted to be respected, not just tolerated. I decided to let my real feelings be known. I felt I was being shut down and on a very raw, deep level, I wanted my voice to be heard.

I arrived in Washington, D.C., the day before the event. I was met by a town car, which took me directly to a production office where I met with the producer of the show. He wanted me to tell him what jokes I intended to tell, so that they could be approved and then put into the teleprompter at the White House. I told him that he didn't have to worry about getting approval, because I wasn't going to tell *any* jokes at all. He looked at me, knowing I was serious, and asked what kind of a game I was playing. "If you are not going to appear at the White House tomorrow, then why on earth did we fly you all the way from Los Angeles?" I smiled and said that I didn't say I wasn't going to appear at the White House, I said that I wasn't going to tell any jokes.

I felt for him and knew that he didn't need any more stress than he probably already had, but I was on a mission and I wasn't willing to back down. I could tell he was trying desperately to control his anger when he asked me what I planned to do instead. I told him that I wanted to tell the audience what I really felt, and that I was sick of being censored and silenced. Without revealing my friend's name, I told him what was told to me about how I could not be trusted. Then I smiled and said, "Well, I guess I'm feeding into that perception of me by pulling this with you." He said yes, I was.

I made a deal with him. I asked him if he could let me type what I wanted to say the following day, and if he didn't like it, then I would give him two minutes of stand-up comedy. He said that was fair and led me to an office to write my speech. It didn't actually take me that long to write, as it was only two minutes in length. When I finished, I read it to him and his entire staff:

> Love and fear cannot exist at the same time; the two conflict. One cannot exist in the presence of the other. Now, think for a moment. How do we react to fear? We attack it, deny it, alienate or avoid it. As a result this leads to prejudice and discrimination. We are not born into the world with feelings of prejudice. Prejudice is a learned behavior, and as I stressed before, fear is what stops us from loving and accepting genuinely. I firmly believe that in order to begin to deal with accepting and loving people, we have to learn to deal with our own fears, within all of us. Only then can we begin to accept others as whole. I would only hope that I heightened awareness and insight of that self-acceptance and self-love. The acceptance of our own inadequacies will give us the freedom to see the humor and the beauty that flows through all of us.

The entire room was silent. Some people had tears in their eyes. The producer was speechless for a moment, searching for the right words to say to me. He smiled, then told me to go back into the other room and type two minutes of stand-up comedy. I felt dejected, but I knew he had me. I had made a promise to him and I had to keep it. He followed me into the room and told me that what I had written was extremely powerful and moving, but that if I chose to stick with that speech, I would have to take responsibility for it.

"The only thing that I know about is the two-minute comedy routine that you are going to write now. Do you understand?"

I did and knew that what he was allowing was phenomenal. My jokes would be in the teleprompter, and he could pretend he didn't know I was going to switch gears and do my speech instead. I also would have to type my speech on index cards and discreetly carry them in. To say I was nervous was an understatement.

Standing outside my hotel the next morning, I didn't know that each celebrity had their own limo and would arrive at the White House one at a time. When Jermaine Jackson and his wife got in their limo, I climbed in, too. It was awkward, and Jermaine just smiled. We started talking, and within minutes, someone from the secret service stuck his head in the car, trying not to embarrass me. "Miss Jewell, you are planning to take your own limo, are you not?" Not wanting to admit that I had made a stupid mistake, I replied, "Oh yes, of course I am. I just wanted to tell Jermaine to break a leg!" I patted him on the knee and was escorted to my own car.

When I got to the White House, I had to pee. Years later when I saw *Forrest Gump*, I realized that we had a lot in common. While in the restroom, my lipstick fell onto the floor, rolling across several stalls. At least I didn't drop my index cards in the toilet!

Several celebrities were a part of the gala, including the Gatlin Brothers, Cliff Robertson, and Jermaine Jackson. I had previously worked with Robertson in *Two of a Kind* and with Jackson when he did an episode of *Facts of Life*. Not everybody actually had a disability, but we all shared a passion and cared about performers with disabilities. I only regret not being able to be in the moment fully, because I was so preoccupied and anxious about my upcoming surprise speech. I was also self-conscious because of my shoes. After I wrote my speech the day before, my escort decided that I needed a more conservative outfit than what I had brought with me. I went shopping with my escort, but I forgot to buy new shoes to match. The only shoes I had with me were a funky pair of Madonna ankle-high boots with a little silver chain that roped across. I wore a simple pink blouse, a plaid burgundy skirt, a burgundy angora vest, a string of pearls, and a pair of wild boots!

Next, we all proceeded to the room where we were going to perform. Nancy Reagan greeted each of us as we entered. I noticed immediately how tiny she was. She was very petite, with fine delicate features. When I shook her hand, I gripped it too hard and could hear and feel her knuckles crack. She just smiled, until she glanced at my boots. She was still smiling, but had sort of a pained expression on her face. It could have been the sight of my boots, or the pain of my handshake, but either way, I became even more anxious than I was previously, especially since she'd been the one who'd fought for me.

By the time I was finally introduced by Cliff Robertson, I was petrified. I looked up from the podium and saw my jokes reflecting back at me from the teleprompter. I had a split-second thought of going with the jokes that were in front of me rather than doing my speech from the now sweat-soaked index cards under my vest. I went with my notes. I started my speech by saying, "I'd like to share with you something that means a lot to me, a philosophy that I've come to understand over the years." You could hear a pin drop. Although I probably could have said something far better had I not written it only the day before, I made my point and was well received. About a month later I received an invitation to perform at the Kennedy Center — a direct result of what I had said at the White House.

CHAPTER EIGHTEEN

The People You Meet
on the Way Down

It was actually through hearing-aid specialist Bill Austin that I got to meet another entertainment icon, Robert Goulet. The Austins often invited me to celebrity functions that they held to raise money for the Starkey Hearing Foundation and as result, I met many wonderful people. It was always a lot of fun driving to Palm Springs. I even went hot air ballooning one time and was amused when our "pilot" mentioned that we were now flying over the Betty Ford Center. Little did I know that years later I would enter a rehab facility myself. For now, I was high in the sky in a hot air balloon that was much too slow of a sport for me to thoroughly enjoy.

I did enjoy performing at one of the Austins' big galas. Bill's wife bought me a glamorous dress and shoes and arranged for my nails and hair to be done. I wasn't totally comfortable dressed like that to perform, but it was a black-tie event, and they wanted me to shine. After my performance, I was approached by Robert Goulet's manager, who informed me that Mr. Goulet loved my act and wanted to hire me down the road to open for him. About three months later, he brought me to Tulsa, Oklahoma. He was truly one of the most easygoing, fun people you would ever want to be around.

He knocked on my dressing room door shortly after I arrived at the theater, wanting to personally welcome me. When he looked at my dressing room, he laughed. "Sorry about the dressing room . . . it looks more like a closet!" I laughed and told him that it did, but I was accustomed to closets, and it made me feel secure. I am positive he had no idea what the hell I was talking about and thought I was just being polite. Then he came back 10 minutes later, saying that he was moving me to his dressing room (with his wife, of course). He said his was big enough for a whole orchestra, had a lot of good food, and great company. He was right — it had all of that and more. Most importantly, it brought me into his world. My little dressing room was equivalent to special ed, whereas being able to hang out in his dressing room was the acceptance I always longed for.

As I stood behind the curtain waiting for my name to be announced, panic began to set in. Robert walked over to me on the dark stage and asked if I was okay. I told him I had never opened for anyone before. "If I bomb, I'll ruin your show!"

He laughed and said, "No Geri, you can only ruin your show, not mine . . . and besides, they are going to love you. You must believe right now that you already have them in the palm of your hands." He cupped his hands to give me the visualization, and then started laughing again, waving his hands in a jerking motion. "Okay, maybe you have the audience more like this . . . but nevertheless, you still have them!" When the curtain opened, Robert beamed, waving his arms jerkily from the wings. The beauty of that story illustrated how comfortable he was around me, no phoniness or bullshit. I appreciated his kindness more than he ever knew.

I finally met my idol, David Cassidy, in 1985. My friend Keith found out that he was going to be on *Good Morning L.A.* He called the producer and said that I was a huge fan of his and asked if I could possibly come watch the show and meet David. No problem. My name was left at the gate and we were told to come straight to the greenroom to meet David beforehand. It was another dream come true, but as usual, I was an anxious mess over it. I changed my clothes at least six times that morning, and when we got to the gate at ABC studios, I told Keith I didn't want to go through with it. If Keith had not fought me, I probably would have chickened out. But Keith knew how long I had wanted to meet David, and he refused to allow me to sabotage my opportunity.

We arrived before David, so it gave me a little time to relax. Whatever composure I was able to conjure up in the 15 minutes of waiting for him went out the window when he walked in the room. Keith leaned over and whispered for me to introduce myself to him, but before I could even think of what to say, David extended his hand to me and said he loved my comedy. I was floored that he knew who I was! I thanked him and said that I loved his work as well. Then he asked me if I wanted to get makeup first. I told him thank you, but he could go first, as he was at the top of the show. He thanked me and left the room.

Keith was furious with me. "Why did you let him believe that you were doing the show too? You're not doing it, and he's obviously going to figure it out!"

"Okay, then let's just leave now. I met him, c'mon, let's go."

"Geri, why are you acting like this? You've wanted to meet him since 1971!"

"He'll think I'm a groupie!"

"You have to *be* a groupie for him to *think* you're a groupie! When he comes back, I want you to tell him the truth!"

When David returned, he thanked me for allowing him to go first, but before he could continue, I interrupted him. "David, I lied . . . I mean, I may *need* makeup, but I'm not doing the show this morning. My friend Keith found out that you were going to be here today and arranged for me to be here to meet you."

David smiled sweetly, and said it was okay.

"No, you don't understand . . . I have been in love with you since 1971! When I was in high school I didn't have a boyfriend or go on dates or anything, I was so lonely. But I had this crush on you, and sometimes that gave me a reason not to give up." By this point, tears were trickling down my cheeks. He grabbed both of my hands and held them in his own. He told me to calm down, that he wasn't Jesus Christ. At this point I was feeling so embarrassed that I had emotionally melted in front of him.

Still holding my hands, David said, "Geri, I have beaten my head against the wall time and again wondering why I ever did *The Partridge Family* in the first place, and then I meet people like you. You remind me of the good things that came out of it. If I was able to give you hope and joy, then I am grateful for that. Thank you for being honest with me. You are so sweet, don't lose that quality." He kissed me on the cheek and was rushed onto the stage by a production assistant. Unbeknownst to both of us, a part of that little talk went over the airways before David went onstage. He was pre-miked, and somehow while the host, Christina Delorean, was talking about David, her mike turned off, and David's mike was on. I never did find out if it was done intentionally, or by accident, or through some sort of cosmic interference, but I do have a copy of the show on a VHS tape, and David and my voices are heard very clearly while Delorean moves her lips.

Even though I was just barely scraping by in 1985 and 1986, they were years of one amazing connection after another. But I felt like Moses, allowed to see the Promised Land, but not allowed to enter it. Celebrities, wealth, and privilege were all around me, yet all those perks were just beyond my grasp. Because my insecurities gripped me, I had a difficult time believing that I was intelligent enough, talented enough, or socially skilled enough to ever be fully included and accepted completely by my colleagues. Every actor has these insecurities — it is what makes us actors in the first place — but when you add a disability to it, these insecurities can be insurmountable. What we believe about ourselves is very powerful, and until we become completely aware of it, we will be unable to shift it and create a different reality for ourselves. So for most of my adult life, I continued to live on the fringes of the world that I desired so much to be a part of, believing that I would always be in special education, or seated at the children's table at holiday dinners.

Speaking of holiday dinners, there is one that I will never forget as long as I live. I had the distinct pleasure of meeting Steve Allen and Jayne Meadows at a conference about healing through laughter. I had reunited onstage with Sid Caesar, as he and his son Rick were also a part of this fabulous gathering. It was my old friend C. W. Metcalf who gave me this wonderful opportunity. We had lost track of one another, and he had since become a bigwig in the field of humor and health. C.W. was thrilled to reconnect and introduced me to Dr. Gerald Jampolsky and the people who were booking the laughter conference. I did 15 minutes of stand-up comedy to an audience of over 1,500 health care workers. I got a standing ovation and was booked sporadically at similar events like this, including performing for people who were infected with HIV and AIDS.

Steve Allen Jr. and I were booked at the same conference in Toronto. His famous father was also in town at this time, and Steve Jr. invited me to join his dad and him for dinner. Steve lived in Ithaca, New York, was a doctor, and had his own private practice. Even though Steve Jr. went into medicine instead of entertainment like his father, he still inherited his dad's sense of humor. He combined his medical profession with the field of laughter and play. He juggled, laughed, and healed in more ways than most doctors ever will. I love him and his family dearly.

The three of us had dinner at a nice quiet Chinese restaurant. We laughed a lot and got to know each other a little better. When the food arrived and chopsticks were placed in front of me, Steve Allen Sr. couldn't stop laughing. He was laughing so hard, he was crying. Soon all three of us were laughing (I was praying I wouldn't pee). Then it suddenly occurred to me, I didn't know what was so funny, as Steve was just laughing hysterically, but never said why. So, through tears and laughter, I asked, "What's so funny?"

"The chopsticks! When you asked the waitress to bring you a fork and a straw, the look she gave you was priceless. She was unable to hide her discomfort with you. Then I kept seeing this image of you trying to eat with chopsticks. I imagined you being born in China. You'd starve!"

Then Steve Jr. chimed in. "Dad, she wouldn't have starved. She's a girl and has CP. She probably would have been adopted by an American and would have skipped the chopstick challenge altogether!"

It was an evening I will never forget, and less than a year later, in 1986, Steve Sr. and Jayne Meadows invited me to their annual Christmas dinner at their home in Beverly Hills. Steve Allen Jr. called me to tell me how excited he was that Jayne and his dad had welcomed me into the family, and that he couldn't wait to see me on Christmas Eve.

During this time in my life, I was falling deeper and deeper into depression and loneliness. I just wasn't able to work enough to support myself, and Hollywood continued to be something in my distant past. There was no work to carry me between sporadic speaking gigs. I always tried hiding my struggles and pain from people like Steve, fearing rejection. I was living a double life as usual: inspiring others through laughter, and going home alone, still using Restoril to numb my pain.

Because I wasn't working much, I often lost track of time, like what day of the week it was. My life had very little structure, and all the days blurred into a continuously long day's journey into night, and long night's journey into day. I was able to keep it together enough to perform when I had to, but beyond that I was coping and doping. The Christmas season of '86 was depressing for me because I had no money to buy gifts for family and friends and felt isolated. I usually went to shopping malls, which only exacerbated my feelings of despondence. I was so deeply entrenched in a rut of despair that I missed a lot of the gifts that were right in front of me, including Christmas Eve dinner at Jayne and Steve's house.

I had told Mom and Dad that I was not going to come home on Christmas Eve and that I would drive to Fullerton on Christmas Day instead. They both understood, and my mom was very excited to hear I would be having dinner with the Allen family. She couldn't wait to hear all about it. However, because I was so depressed and slept much of the week away, I didn't realize that the day I chose to aimlessly walk through the Glendale Galleria Mall was actually Christmas Eve. In my hazy perception of time, I thought it was the 23rd. I returned home that evening around 8:30 p.m. My answering machine was blinking like one little Christmas tree light in a dark room.

I didn't even check my messages right away, as I was hungry and made a box of Kraft macaroni and cheese. About an hour later, I played back my messages and sat there stunned listening to four separate messages from Jayne Meadows! Oh my God, it's Christmas Eve tonight! I had stood up the Allen family. I had obviously left the entire family waiting too. In one message, Jayne said that she hoped I was on my way, and that she was going to keep the turkey in the oven a little longer. Jeez, did I ever feel like an ass. I returned Jayne's call and sheepishly apologized, saying that I got caught in all the holiday traffic and just got home. She was so sweet and was just relieved that I was okay. That Christmas Eve, I wallowed in self-pity, taking two Restorils instead of one. Not only did I have the talent to do stand-up comedy, but I also had the talent to stand up one of the most brilliant men in the history of television! How many people can say that? I know I didn't say a word about it the next day to Mom and Dad. In fact, I lied, telling them what a wonderful dinner it was. Not having any money to buy gifts, the small gift of joy I gave them in describing the story of a dinner that never happened was worth the lie. Why ruin their Christmas too?

I was so tired of keeping up the appearance of being successful and not knowing how I was going to survive from one week to the next. Yet I was experiencing the world from a sneak peek perspective. Every so often I was asked to be a part of a celebrity charity event, whether it be Easter Seals, United Way, or United Cerebral Palsy (to name a few). There were formal dinners, where I was asked to either perform or just to be there to meet and greet, and celebrity sports events. At one such event at the Waldorf Astoria in New York, I actually got to perform for Bob Hope and Helen Hayes.

Even though I was rarely paid to do these, I usually said yes whenever I was asked. It felt strange, though — I was one of the celebrities but I felt like a person with a disability in need of assistance. I couldn't donate anything to an auction like the other celebrities, and whenever I was asked to, I felt embarrassed.

I remember when I was in Lake Tahoe doing a fundraiser for United Cerebral Palsy. It was a big weekend event, so I brought a new girlfriend of mine, Kelli, to enjoy the weekend. I had met Kelli in an acting class I took with Estelle Harmon. We were not a couple for very long — I just couldn't be who I really wanted to be, and Kelli couldn't convince me to out myself. We broke up, but remained friends.

When we got to our room, we got a call asking if I had remembered to bring something for the silent auction. I told the woman on the line that

I would be right down with my auction item. Kelli was aghast, knowing that I had nothing to give them.

"What are you going to do, steal one of the pillows from the bed and autograph it?"

"No, I'll give them this!" I removed one of my favorite lavender blouses from my suitcase.

"What makes you think anyone would *want* that?"

"But I don't have anything else to give them."

"Why didn't you just bring an autographed copy of your book?"

"Yeah, right . . . they asked for something of *value*, Kelli."

"Well, it would have been better than that blouse!"

Annoyed with myself, I ignored her and went down to give them my blouse. When I saw autographed tennis racquets, Gucci luggage, autographed paintings, and even an autographed golf cart, I knew I was not in this league. When the woman walked over to me, I slipped my blouse under the table behind me and apologized profusely for forgetting my auction item. She told me not to worry about it, that they had plenty. I walked back to my room, never returning to get my favorite blouse. It wasn't worth it. Besides, I had other things to obsess over.

I mentioned to Kelli how awkward it felt just sitting around watching all the other celebrities having fun playing sports. "Well, listen Jewelhead, I don't notice you doing anything about it. Tell them you want to be more active. Stop being such a wimp. Nobody knows what you can actually do unless you tell them."

Kelli was right, and being the good friend that she was, there was no way she was going to allow me to be a victim. I had to be proactive. I approached one of the producers and told him that I was grateful to be a part of this wonderful weekend in Tahoe, but that it's kind of boring to just sit around having cerebral palsy for two days. I know I do that well, I said, but I would like to participate in some of the celebrity sports events.

Quite perplexed, yet open, he asked me what I thought I could do. Similar to the *Sesame Street* scenario, I told him I would like to play tennis.

"Tennis? Are you any good?"

"Yeah, kinda."

I noticed that Kelli was laughing and rolling her eyes. I also added that I could ride a bike really well too. So, for a couple of hours that afternoon I went bike riding with several other celebrities, completely forgetting about the tennis. I wasn't worried about it either, because I honestly thought if they were going to arrange a tennis game the following day that they'd prob-ably have me play someone really easy like Emmanuel Lewis or ALF.

That evening when Kelli and I returned to our room, we were informed that I had to be out at a specified court at 10 a.m. because I was playing a doubles match with John McEnroe, Arthur Ashe, and Wayne Cook. It was going to be a live telecast on ABC's *Wide World of Sports*! Kelli couldn't stop laughing. I told her it wasn't funny, because I didn't know how to play tennis!

"Well, you'd better start practicing tonight, because there's no way you're going to get out of this now. This is your own doing, Jewelhead!"

"Yeah, I know. But I thought they were just going to let me be a part of a little game, nothing major! John McEnroe, Arthur Ashe . . . who's Wayne Cook?"

"Remember earlier today, we passed that really cute guy with cerebral palsy?"

"You've got to be kidding. Kelli, he may have CP, but he plays tennis like a pro!"

The next morning, Kelli and I made our way to the court, and I was introduced to my teammate, John McEnroe. Before the game started, I noticed something was missing. All the other players had racquets, but Jewelhead did not. Then I noticed a lone racquet leaning against the umpire's chair. Looking up, I asked our umpire, professional tennis player Vitas Gerulaitis, if I could "borrow" his racquet. It would be equivalent to a 16-year-old kid asking professional race car driver Jeff Gordon if he could "borrow" his Lamborghini for a couple of hours. I could tell Vitas was torn. He wanted to say, "Hell no! Are you nuts?" But seeing that this was a fundraiser for United Cerebral Palsy and I had CP, he felt a little put on the spot. "Okay, but whatever you do, do not drag it on the ground!" While he had to keep his eye on the game, I'm sure he kept an extra-focused eye on his racquet.

It ended up being an amazing game, even though McEnroe played both sides of the court from time to time. The producers actually gave me some really wonderful television exposure, showing some footage of me talking to several young people with cerebral palsy. And . . . John and I won! I even scored! It was a real fluke, but the fans gave me tremendous applause for doing so. I was embarrassed, but once again, I proved to myself how grati-fying life can be if you don't run away. Believe me, I could have just called the producer the night before and told him that I hurt my knee or something, but I didn't. After our match was over, Howard Cosell interviewed Angie Dickinson and asked her why she wasn't playing tennis. She said, "I didn't think I could play that well, but after watching Geri Jewell play, I really have no excuse!"

Even though I had a spectacular weekend in Tahoe and claimed victory in my first game of tennis, I came home to my little apartment on Courtney to find that my beloved Lady had disappeared. I had left her in the care of a friend of mine, Mac P. Rowell. He had forgotten to bring her in the evening before, and unfortunately she became a part of the food chain for the starving coyotes that roamed my street late at night. I was heartbroken. Lady being gone fed into my deep sense of loneliness, and not having her to care for any longer made it easier for me not to care about my own survival either.

I halfheartedly continued to go through the motions of living, but I was growing so tired of the struggle. I was angry about so many things, but as usual, I only knew how to understand it inwardly rather than unleash it outwardly and allow myself to work through it. I was angry with Mac, but knew I had to forgive him. Mostly though, I was angry with my first manager and Hollywood for not allowing me to afford the help and security that I needed. I was afraid to go back on disability after having to pay the government $9,999.99 from the first time around.

Two weeks before I had left to perform at Lake Tahoe, I had actually given my 30-day notice to move from Courtney Avenue. It was not the wisest thing I could have done. First, I only had a little over $500 in the bank, and second, I really had nowhere to move. Realistically, the *only* thing that would have been sensible would have been to move back home to Fullerton with my parents. However, to me, that would have been harder than what I was trying to do. As long as I was *trying* to accomplish something in Hollywood, it meant it wasn't over yet. To move back to the house where I grew up would have been a stark reminder that I was a failure.

When I returned from Tahoe, I had two weeks to find a place to live. I aimlessly looked at apartments that I had no money for while not packing one box. It was as if I were playing a game with the universe. "Okay God, Jesus, angels, higher power, Buddha, Pope John Paul . . . I need help here, or I'm calling it quits." Two days before I had to be gone, I still hadn't packed one damned thing, nor did I have anywhere else to live.

My whole existence reflected a lack of faith and my despair. Even in my teeny little bathroom, there was startling proof that I was lost. On my bathroom wall hung an advertisement for Restoril I had torn out of a medical magazine I'd perused in a doctor's office. It showed a news reporter holding a microphone, covering an important story. The caption read, "I got plenty of sleep last night, and today I can handle all the pressures of my demanding job because I'm having a Restoril day!" Because I was a comedian, the dark humor aspect of it didn't really alarm anyone. However, in my typical passive-aggressive fashion, it was a cry for help, even though I didn't really believe that anyone or anything could save me.

With that defeatist mindset, I placed a call to Liza Minnelli at her home. We had reconnected a couple of times after our first encounter, but never to the point of becoming friends. Instead, we would just run into each other at different events and catch up briefly. I was surprised when she answered the phone that day. She was pleased to hear from me, but the conversation quickly became awkward because I couldn't be honest about why I had called her in the first place. More important, I couldn't even be honest with myself. Out of all the people that I was much closer to, why would I call Liza Minnelli, who was 3,000 miles away? Perhaps I was flirting with the fantasy of Liza rescuing me. There wasn't even a shred of possibility to it. Maybe because my life had always been surreal in so many ways, a part of me actually believed that maybe Liza would offer to help me. When she asked me how I was doing, I told her I was doing great, that I'd just performed at the White House and was in the process of moving. The only thing that seemed blatantly dishonest was the "great" part. She asked me how soon I was moving, and if I were moving to New York. I laughed, saying no, I wasn't moving that far. We continued this meaningless conversation, and I hung up feeling like I had played my "trump card." I mean, who was I going to call next, Nancy Reagan?

I felt like an idiot. I again fought with the idea of calling Mom, but I couldn't. Instead, I called someone who I knew would tell me the truth I needed to hear. I called Ed Simmons, who had worked with me on the failed Sid Caesar pilot. Throughout my adult life I've developed relationships with surrogate dads. I've had at least five of them. My own dad was much harder to talk to. It wasn't just me; everyone had a difficult time understanding my dad. He was a very complex man, and it was very difficult to go to him. He battled low self-esteem his entire life, and sometimes he allowed that to affect how he related to his children. He could be extremely critical and hurtful when he wanted to, so it was hard for any of us kids to feel secure in his presence.

When I called Ed that afternoon, I wasn't afraid of him judging me or rejecting me; I only knew that he always had the ability to bring me back to the center. I told him all about my predicament, and that I stupidly called Liza Minnelli. He laughed and said, "Well, at least you didn't call David Cassidy!" God, he knew me well. I was sobbing, asking him what I was supposed to do. He calmly stated that I got myself into this mess by giving notice when I knew damn well I had nowhere to go. He went on to say that I should tell my landlord the truth, and see if I could keep the apartment for at least another month. He told me that I had to start believing in myself again, because if I didn't believe in myself, no one else will either. "Now hang up this phone, and start *realistically* helping yourself. God only helps those who help themselves."

I hung up, and did as he told me to. As it turned out, the building manager called the guy who was going to move in, and he was willing to take another apartment; I could keep mine. I wrote a rent check for $400, called Ed back, and told him that things were looking up, and that God does help those who help themselves. I was actually starting to believe in myself a little, and did a good show that night at the Improv. On the way home, I played my cassette tape of Robert Goulet singing "The Impossible Dream" over and over again, believing that I had turned a corner. However, when I turned the corner onto my street, I was in for a very rude awakening.

When I opened the front door of my apartment, I felt that I had stepped into the wrong apartment, or possibly right into an episode of *The Twilight Zone*. I flipped on the light switch, but my lamp didn't turn on. That was odd. I walked through the one room into the kitchen to turn on a light. When I did, I almost wished I hadn't. Once again my apartment had been robbed, only this time, whoever did it got away with a lot more. Upon inspection, I could see that the screen had been cut, and because it was such an old building, the windows never did shut properly. I had to go to a gas station to call the police, because my phone had been stolen too. While I was at the gas station, I also called Kelli, who arrived within minutes, right after the police.

I was totally inconsolable, basically having a mini nervous breakdown. The two officers tried to calm me down, but I was in a state of shock. The thieves had taken both my televisions, even a little one I kept in the closet. They took my stereo, two lamps, videotapes, a jar of quarters that I kept for laundry, a leather jacket, and even my blankets off the sofa bed. While the officers were patiently itemizing and dusting for fingerprints, I grabbed a copy of my autobiography (I had a stack of about 12 copies in the corner) and began reading the cover of the book to the poor officers.

"Let me read something to you: *Geri*, a warm, funny moving account of a courageous young woman's rise to stardom and her triumph over cerebral palsy! Does this look like triumph to you, officers? You notice they didn't steal any of these books. I couldn't sell them, and nobody will steal them either!" They both looked at me as if I had lost mind, and, in a way, I had. Tears were streaming down my face. The officers left with the itemized list of things that were missing, an autographed copy of my book, and probably felt horribly for me. Especially when I told them that God only helps those who help themselves, and that apparently the thieves — who had helped themselves to my stuff — were being helped by God, too!

I was losing my grip.

My friend Tony came and got me, taking me to his apartment for the night. The next morning, I hardly knew what to think or to say. Tony made a pot of coffee, and even put a bag of M&Ms in front of me to garner a smile. Instead of smiling, I opened the bag of candy and dumped it into my coffee. Tony gave me an extra phone that he had and drove me back to Hollywood. The following Monday afternoon, the phone rang. I was surprised to hear Detective Bob Piper's voice on the line. He was so sweet. He told me that he heard the news of my break-in and promised that they would try to get my things back. However, he warned me the chances would be slim. "I am so sorry, Geri. I wish you didn't have to live in such a seedy neighborhood."

"Oh, don't worry Bob, I might just give up this charade and move back to Fullerton with my mom and dad." He could tell that my spirit was temporarily broken, but he also knew how strong I was and made me promise him that I wouldn't give up no matter what. I never gave up: I didn't move to Fullerton, and through sheer perseverance, I kept on keeping on.

CHAPTER NINETEEN

An Amazing Decade of Making Lemonade

When I think of my life, especially in the '80s, I think of that familiar phrase, "When life gives you lemons, make lemonade." If cerebral palsy is, in fact, a lemon, then I have successfully made the best-tasting pitcher of lemonade possible. You simply can't have lemonade without lemons. Well, okay, possibly with imitation flavoring, but who likes imitation? If I had to live the '80s over again, truthfully I would not change a thing. I can never be accused of living an imitation of life — I've lived it fully, through the ups and downs, and thorns and crowns.

After my Hollywood apartment was broken into, I moved in with my friends Mac and J.T. They had a duplex in West Hollywood with a small spare bedroom. The few things that I did have left I either sold for extra money or gave away to someone who needed them more than I did. Although I didn't live with Mac and J.T. that long, this period allowed me to regroup, save some money, and get another apartment of my own. Tony and I decided to become roommates again. Neither of us fared well on our own, but with our combined income, we were both able to live a little better.

I was still able to get comedy and motivational speaking gigs from time to time, and occasionally received residual checks from past television work. I was also hired to do a stand-up comedy gig for the 1986 Victory Awards at the Kennedy Center. That year they were honoring Ted Kennedy Jr. This was a huge event, and President Reagan was in the audience that night. This time, I was dressed to the nines, with no embarrassing black boots. However, I was still very nervous, maybe even more nervous than I had been at the White House.

This was a grand gathering of entertainment and political figures. That night, I had the pleasure of meeting John F. Kennedy Jr. and have since met many members of the Kennedy family. Because the president was in attendance, secret service was everywhere. Wherever I looked, someone had an earpiece or was whispering something to someone. Celebrities who were performing or speaking that evening were each assigned an escort to make sure they were taken care of. I cannot tell you how many times my escort repeated to me, "Remember, don't tell that orgasm joke," like I was some kind of moron who wouldn't understand the advice the first time.

I did fantasize about walking out onstage, telling only the orgasm joke, taking a bow, and walking off again. However, I knew I would never really do that. Especially when someone with an earpiece took me aside *again* right before I was introduced and whispered to me, "Now, don't tell that orgasm joke." I was so tempted to ask him who exactly told him to tell me that, just so I could find the person later at the dinner and walk up to him or her and say, "Orgasm, orgasm, orgasm!"

When I walked onstage, I was more scared than usual, and I could feel my throat tightening. I wasn't sick or anything, but about four jokes into my routine, my voice started to squeak and then I had no voice at all. It was as though fear had knocked my voice right out of me. I wasn't onstage any longer than about three minutes. I said thank you and walked off the stage and into the empty greenroom. I was so angry and upset with myself. The only other time I had had that kind of fear onstage was back at the Improv when I was afraid of Jack being in the audience. What was I so afraid of this time?

Before I had too much time to think about it, Ted Kennedy Jr. walked in and sat down next to me. This was a show honoring *him*, and he had taken the time to see if I was okay. Truthfully, I was expecting my assigned escort, not him. He was even kind of laughing. He asked me what happened. "In all the years that I've ever seen you, I don't think I've ever known you to be speechless!"

I had tears in my eyes and told him that I got scared and now felt like an idiot. "I lost my voice in front of the President of the United States!"

Ted was so sweet. He told me not to ever worry about something I didn't say, it's always worse worrying about something you *did* say. Besides, he said, most of those people just thought losing your voice was a CP thing, and probably thought, "Isn't she adorable!" He got me to smile and walked me back to where everyone else was gathered. His sweetness that evening made up for any inadequacy that I was feeling. Yes, he definitely had that Kennedy charm about him.

Just when you might think you're either at the end of your rope or at the end of a magnificent dream, someone can walk into your life and show you how to restore your hope and renew the dream that you came into the world to experience. There were several such people who influenced me in that way time and again, and toward the end of the '80s one such person was Kathy Buckley. Kathy and I are soul sisters, and we have always looked out for one another throughout our lives. When I met Kathy in 1986, I had already lived a lifetime, and she was just about to embark on a similar road as mine, only minus some of the pain and pitfalls I'd had.

Kathy and I met at a Media Access Awards event, only now, instead of me meeting Norman Lear, it was Kathy Buckley meeting me. Kathy and I had a lot in common, but the most obvious thing was hearing loss. She sought me out that evening and spoke to me as if I already knew her. I was a little embarrassed that I didn't remember her, so I just acted as if I did, not realizing that the reason she was so familiar to me was because we knew each other in spirit. We exchanged numbers that evening and got together shortly afterward.

At the time, she was employed as a professional masseuse and, knowing intuitively how much pain I was in, offered to give me a massage where she worked. After having dinner at her home, we became fast friends. She wanted to be a stand-up comic and was told by many people she had to meet me. Very quickly, we both discovered how much we were alike, and we became very protective of one another. I wanted to protect her from the wolves in sheep's clothing that lurked in Hollywood and she wanted to protect me from them as well, like we were guardian angels for one another.

Not only was Kathy hearing impaired, but like me, she was molested as a child and grew up facing ridicule and humiliation. She overcame colon cancer and was run over by a Jeep while sunbathing. All of these things occurred before she even turned 30! Whenever I have felt badly about my own circumstances, I think of Kathy and am reminded of the perseverance and spirit that is inherent in both of us. For me, anyway, Kathy is living proof of what the human spirit can overcome. I also know it was no accident that we came together when we did.

As fate would have it with Kathy, there was a comedy competition being offered as a fundraiser for United Cerebral Palsy. I convinced Kathy to enter the competition, and she did so with the genuine belief that she'd be helping to find a cure for me! Together, we worked on Kathy's very first comedy routine. The competition was primarily offered to comedians just starting out.

Kathy had never done stand-up comedy before, but she had a professional stand-up comedian — me — as a coach! We worked on her routine for a couple of weeks. Unfortunately, we never got a chance to break it in, and Kathy's very first performance *ever* was in the first round of the competition.

She also had to write a short letter about herself: why she felt she should be accepted into the contest, and what she planned to do if she actually won the competition. Even though I was willing to help her with the comedy material, I did not help her with the letter. That was something that had to be written in her own words, and although writing was not one of her strengths, she did it anyway. She didn't even show me the letter before she mailed it. I just had to trust that she would be one of the few chosen from hundreds of comics who were fighting to compete.

About two weeks before the competition, Kathy was feeling a little blue; she hadn't been notified by UCP that she was accepted into the competition. She was beginning to think it wasn't going to happen. As fate would have it, I was asked at the end of that week to come into the local UCP office for something totally unrelated to the comedy competition. On my way out of the office I noticed all these letters and headshots spread all over someone's desk. There were hundreds of comedic hopefuls, and only a handful would be chosen to compete (similar to *American Idol*).

I sat down at the empty desk, perusing the pictures and letters. When the talent scout asked me if I knew any of the faces, I truthfully said that I didn't. That is, until I glanced down at the wastepaper basket and noticed Kathy's face smiling back at me. I couldn't believe it, out of all the pictures that were lying everywhere, hers was in full view to me from the trash. I retrieved it and read with tears in my eyes the letter that Kathy had written about herself.

I then asked the talent scout why he had thrown Kathy's headshot and letter in the trash. He laughed and said, "Whoever wrote that obviously doesn't know how to write that well. How can anyone do stand-up comedy if they don't know how to write?"

I simply stated that was an unfair judgment, that one has nothing to do with the other. "I'm sure there are brilliant writers who can't do two minutes of stand-up. That is very prejudiced."

"Why are you so defensive of this comic? Have you seen her perform?"

"Yes, as a matter of fact I have, and she's very funny!" He never asked me *where* I'd seen her perform, only *if* I'd seen her perform, so I wasn't lying — I mean, her living room counts as a venue, right?

"Okay, Geri, if you think she's good, we'll give her a shot."

The next day Kathy called me with the good news that she had been chosen as one of the contestants in the Stand-up Comics Take a Stand competition. She was so excited, and I acted as if I was hearing it for the first time. I did not tell her about discovering her picture until years later. There was no sense in her knowing that I had something to do with her getting in because then she wouldn't have believed that she had done it on her own merit. And she had . . . because she won that contest! She then went on to win several more prestigious awards, including best female comedian three years in a row. She became known as America's first hearing impaired female comedian and went on to do her award-winning one-woman show, *Don't Buck with Me.*

I am so proud of her for all of her accomplishments, including writing her own autobiography, *If You Could Hear What I See.* There was a brief time in the early '90s when I was a bit envious and felt I was being "replaced" as the new disabled comic, but I got over it quickly, and I don't think there is anything that could ever hurt our friendship. Even though Kathy and I have stark differences (she's six foot one, I'm five foot three; she walks straight, and I never have) it has always felt as if we were separated at birth. Our energies are so much alike that, even with our differences, people often believe we are the same person.

I continued to make new friends in the late '80s and have been more blessed by these relationships than I ever thought possible. Even before the actual signing of the Americans with Disabilities Act on July 26, 1990, there was a huge push in the United States to increase awareness of issues affecting the disability population, like the need for more employment opportunities. I was hired by a few Fortune 500 companies in the '80s to do disability sensitivity training, but the bulk of this kind of work did not happen until after 1990.

One disability event I will always remember happened as a result of a young woman with muscular dystrophy who had a big dream and followed through with it. In 1986, Lorraine Berry pulled off a spectacular event in Washington, D.C., called Barrier Awareness Day. It was a huge national event. There were people involved from all over the country: politicians, celebrities, CEOs, and even those representing religious organizations. We all came together in Washington for an entire day of disability awareness, observation, and simulation.

High-profile people with actual disabilities were each assigned a volunteer without a disability to travel to different locations in D.C. The catch was that the volunteer without a disability had to experience the day simulating one. Their escorts (who did have disabilities) were there to help them, guide them, and make sure they didn't cheat. For example, if volunteers were to simulate being blind, under no circumstances were they allowed to take their blindfold off. The goal was to create empathy, compassion, and respect for a person with a disability who has to live with these challenges every day, not just one.

I was a celebrity escort, and I had to laugh when I found out who my "non-disabled" partner was: Monsignor Thomas Keys — it seemed that no matter where I went, I'd see a nun or a priest. Father Tom had to simulate being a wheelchair user, and I was his escort. Here I was, pushing a priest around all day in Washington, D.C. We probably had more fun than most because, between the two of us, we couldn't stop laughing. Even though Father Tom was a priest, he was very laid back. In fact, he had enormous compassion about disability issues, because he himself had diabetes. Even long after Barrier Awareness Day, our friendship continued. One of our stops was an art museum. We had to take a very long trek to the back of the building because it was the only entrance without stairs. It was also very difficult to maneuver his wheelchair where there was carpet. But what I remember the most was entering a room with huge painting of a nude woman. I panicked, remembering that I was with a priest. I spun his chair around so fast, he almost fell out of it!

"What are you doing?"

"Father, trust me, you do not want to go any further into that room. We'll look somewhere else."

"Geri, if you do not want to look at those paintings, I understand. You can sit here and rest if you'd like, but I would like to see these paintings."

"You can't . . . you're a priest!"

"Geri. . . ."

"Honest, I saw a nude woman!"

Father Tom laughed, saying that we were in an art museum, not the Playboy Mansion. When I realized how I had overreacted, I lightened up and allowed him to view the paintings.

Another time, we had to hail a cab. It took a long time to get one to stop, though; I looked like I was either drunk or on drugs, and adding a disabled priest was quite an eyeful for any cabbie to consider stopping for. That, of course, was precisely why we had to get a cab, to learn the lesson that most cabs would not stop for us even though they were empty. Our driver kept looking around for a hidden camera, because when he took the wheelchair out of the trunk after we'd arrived at our destination, he was surprised that the priest could walk now, and I had gotten in the wheelchair. Yes, we cheated, but the only reason was because Father Tom felt so bad that I was getting winded and wanted to push me for at least 30 minutes to give me a break. Then he got in the chair again, and I continued to push him. But the look on our driver's face was priceless.

Besides Father Tom, I met a lot of wonderful people at the Barrier Awareness Day Celebration: Kelsey Marshall, Tony O'Dell, Lonnie Burr, Deborah McKeithan, Mary Doremus, Billy Barty, and Tom Farrell, to name just a few. Tony O'Dell starred in the sitcom *Head of the Class*, and although both of us were actors, we may not have ever met had it not been for Barrier Awareness Day. The same goes for Lonnie Burr, who was one of the original Disney Mouseketeers. Lonnie even mentioned Barrier Awareness Day in his own autobiography, *Confessions of an Accidental Mouseketeer*. Kelsey, Mary, and Deborah all are women with disabilities who have devoted their lives to increasing awareness of people with disabilities. Like me, Billy Barty, who had a form of dwarfism, was an actor, truly a trailblazer in Hollywood, and also started a nonprofit foundation, the Little People of America. He was a Hollywood veteran and was featured in hundreds of movies and television shows. More than anyone, Billy understood what it was like to have a disability in Hollywood, and even though he was much shorter than me, I could only look up to him with complete admiration and respect.

Tom Farrell became one of my surrogate dads. He and his wife, Evelyn, lived in Santa Rosa, California. Tom's link to Barrier Awareness Day was through his daughter, Susan. Susan was severely affected by multiple disabilities, including autism and mental retardation. She would always be nonverbal, and Tom's life had dramatically changed when his daughter came into it. To honor her life, Tom became a "voice" for her, becoming involved in bettering the quality of life for all people with disabilities.

Tom is a mover and a shaker and a tremendous organizer in bringing people together for a common cause. Through Tom, I became a member of the Rotary Club of Santa Rosa and developed a special relationship with the people of that wonderful city. It was as if we were a little "rat pack." Tom knew Charles Schulz (creator of the *Peanuts* comic strip) who knew Lorraine Berry, who knew Billy Barty, who knew William Christopher (from the television series *M*A*S*H*). What linked all of us was our passion for the lives of people with disabilities. Disability had touched each one of us in one way or another. Even though "disability" is often perceived as a negative, when people come together with passion, determination, and a higher power, the negativity disappears and is replaced by a positive commitment to bettering the quality of life for all people.

Tom Farrell accepted me into his family and has been my "rock" for good sound advice over the years. On one occasion, he and Evelyn even took me to meet their daughter, Susan. Susan has lived in a private care facility for most of her life, but Tom and Evelyn visit her frequently. They have fervently fought for her civil rights and well-being. Susan has never developed any type of connection that we typically look for in bonding. It is always so painful for parents of children with severe mental and cognitive disabilities who have to believe they are connecting with their child whether they see signs of it or not. They don't always have the proof or the feedback that their efforts are being felt. This is one of the most powerful forms of faith there can be.

When Tom and Evelyn invited me to meet Susan and to take her to McDonald's for lunch, I was quite honored. Both told me ahead of time what Susan's condition was so that I would be prepared. However, no one is ever fully prepared, even if you have been around "disability" for your entire life. Each person is different, so you can never know how each person will affect you emotionally. I felt uneasy at first, because there was no such thing as shaking hands, saying hello, or making small talk. Like everyone else, I was met with silence and had no ability to connect.

However, as we were sitting in McDonald's, it felt weird to me to just talk to Tom and Evelyn, ignoring Susan's presence, so I touched Susan's hand and told her that I was honored to have been able to meet her. I told her how much her parents loved her, and that I loved them as well. She looked at me for at least five minutes or so. As our eyes met, I caught a glimpse of this wonderful woman's spirit. Soon lunch was over, and Susan returned home.

It was later that Tom and Evelyn told me of the miracle that had taken place. In her entire life, Susan had never made eye contact with anyone until me. I was stunned. This only goes to show us how many small miracles are missed by all of us from one day to the next. We all take so much for granted, and Susan's beautiful spirit reminded me that there is so much more going on in life than meets the eye.

Even though Hollywood was still not working out for me in the way that I wanted it to, I began to realize through all my connections in the "disability realm" that there was a definite reason for all of my pain and struggles. I believe that had I continued to ride the crest of the wave of success from my initial springboard of *The Facts of Life* fame, I would not have become the deeply compassionate human being that I am. I may have never fully developed the spiritual tools needed to have a greater understanding, maturity, and yearning for spiritual enlightenment. I may have become spoiled, shallow, and egotistical, never embarking on my spiritual quest.

As it is, I became a seeker of truth. In spite of my pain and suffering all through the '80s, I also formed beautiful relationships that I may not have had otherwise. Another one of those relationships was with Mary Gilligan Wong. Because of my obsession with the Catholic Church and nuns, I read every book I could find about them. Karen Armstrong became one of my favorite authors after I read her first book, *Through the Narrow Gate*, which was about her years as a nun before she left the church and entered the world at large. Mary Gilligan Wong wrote her own memoir called *Nun*, later re-titled *Shattered Vows* when it was made into a television movie starring Valerie Bertinelli.

After reading Mary's book in 1984, I was determined to meet her. She had since become a clinical psychologist, was married to El Wong, and living in Encinitas, California, with their two sons, Ram and Aaron. Maybe my motivation was threefold: as a nun wannabe, I wanted to live vicariously through her; I realized that I was still in great need of psychological help in dealing with my own demons, pain, and suffering; and I had also coauthored a screenplay with my dear friend, Lotus Weinstock, called *God Loves Me Anyway* about a young postulant with cerebral palsy, and I needed some technical input about what life is like as a nun.

What I gained out of connecting with Mary was another surrogate family. From 1984 through 1988, I frequently drove to Encinitas to spend time with them. I never saw Mary as a therapist, but I did see her brother Patrick Gilligan, who was also a clinical psychologist and lived two streets over from Mary. Patrick even came to one of my last tapings of *The Facts of Life*, making the three-hour trek from Encinitas.

I truly thank God for every humbling experience that has helped to shape me over the years, and for the sense of humor that has allowed me to laugh when things didn't always turn out the way I had hoped they would. I remember once, in 1986, when my friend Lyle Gregory called me at the last minute saying that he had an extra ticket to the American Music Awards, and would I like to go. I only had an hour to get ready, and when Lyle picked me up, I was dressed up and ready for a walk on the red carpet. This was a chance to be seen — what ended up happening was quite humbling and humorous, to say the least.

We were extremely late, and upon arriving, we realized there was absolutely no place to park. Unless you were arriving in a limousine, you couldn't get close to the red carpet. We ended up parking about six long blocks away, with Lyle and I practically running to the event, huffing and puffing. We had exactly five minutes to get to the door before it was shut and locked for filming. I honestly didn't think we were going to make it and was quite irritated.

I was out of breath and just wanted to go back to the car, but Lyle was never one to give up on anything. We passed a biker, and Lyle ran up to him and asked him if he would kindly give me a lift to the red carpet, handing him a $20 bill. The guy took the money, and I hopped on. It was like a scene right out of *Easy Rider*, but with a more glamorous outfit. My tattooed friend roared past all the cars that weren't moving and took me directly to the red carpet. I could hear people screaming, "It's Cousin Geri on a motorcycle!" Even the announcer acknowledged my arrival. Over the loudspeaker, we heard, "It's Geri Jewell from *The Facts of Life*, and she just arrived on a motorcycle in the nick of time!" The whole thing was such a rush.

By appearances, it always looked as though I was on top of everything. The hardships that I endured were never news, so the assumption was always that I was successful and doing great. What people forget is that success is not a tangible object, but something that is fluid and ever changing. The face of success is constantly in motion. The '80s was a decade of successes and setbacks that had the pace of a vortex. Even something that was horrifically tragic ended up being spiritually successful for me. This occurred around the Liberty Celebration at Giants Stadium in New Jersey in 1986.

The entire weekend was one misstep after another. I was spending the weekend with my friend, Kelsey Marshall, at her parents' home in Summit, New Jersey. Her brother Tom surprised us with tickets to the huge Liberty Celebration Gala. I was stunned to find out that Liza Minnelli was performing that night, and before the show started, I went backstage to say hello to her. Afterward, I tried to get back to my seat in the stands. It was dark now, and I truly underestimated how difficult it was going to be to rejoin my friends. I was terrified of heights, and each step up toward where they were sitting was making me unsteady. I was also trying to stay crouched low because so many people were screaming for me to get out of the way! I almost lost my balance a couple of times and finally gave up and left the stadium, never seeing the show, instead waiting for my friends on the hood of my friend's car in the parking lot.

The next day, I took the train from Summit, New Jersey, to New York City. I was upset about missing the show and thought perhaps if I went into the city, it would cheer me up. It was blistering hot, and I only wore shorts and a T-shirt. I met up with my publicist, Penny Landau, mostly spending the day shoveling quarters into a Ms. Pac-Man machine in one of the small cabarets. At about 8:30 p.m., Penny saw to it that I got back to Times Square safely and made sure I boarded the right train to Summit. Had I stayed on the train, I would have been in Summit by 10 p.m. What I wasn't prepared for were all the stops before then. When I rode the train early that morning, I was oblivious to all the stops, but I recognized Times Square instantly, so I knew when to get off. However, late at night, I couldn't see anything out the windows, and I could not hear the location called each time the train stopped.

I got off the train when I did because I thought I heard "Summit" and saw several other people in my car get off as well. When I walked outside, there was only one cab sitting at the curb. I had my friend's address written inside of a book that I was carrying and showed it to the cabbie, asking him if he could take me there. He looked at me perplexed, wondering why I had gotten off the train. He told me it would cost me at least $200 to get me to Summit from where I was. I only had about ten quarters left and a $20 bill in my shoe, in case of an emergency. I had to go back into the train station and get back on the train.

I lucked out when a kind gentleman helped me find the right train to board. He even told me how many stops it would make before I got off again. The only problem was that it was only going to Hoboken this time, and I would have to wait in Hoboken for a couple of hours before the next train left for Summit. When I got off the train in Hoboken, it was already 11:30, and there were no people anywhere! I was terrified and tried to think of the safest place I could wait for two hours. I was able to find someone who worked there and asked him to show me to the train to Summit. I wondered if he could unlock the door and let me board, because it was too scary to wait anywhere else. He unlocked the door, but told me that there would be no air conditioning until the train was moving. I said that was fine.

As I sat there, I quickly I realized that on a hot night in July, any train that wasn't moving was like an oven, but I didn't care if I perspired to death;

I was not going to walk around anywhere by myself at that hour. About 25 minutes later, the employee returned to check on me, or so I thought. I thought he was going to open my window to let some air in, but instead he sat down next to me. Within seconds, his hand was inside my shorts and underwear. I couldn't believe it. I searched my mind as to why this was happening to me again. What made me so vulnerable? I wanted to scream, but was afraid that he would hurt me.

Then a miracle happened, and to this day I have never forgotten it. The book that I was carrying that night with my friend's parents' address on it was called *Jesus and Forgiveness*. In looking away from the ugliness of the man sitting next to me, I saw the reflection of the book in the window. Jesus was looking right at me as tears came to my eyes. I thought perhaps because there were so many people that I hadn't forgiven in my heart that the same pain kept happening in different ways. I still believe that was indeed a part of the message, but there was even a greater miracle that happened in the next second that even shocked the perpetrator.

I turned around and looked directly into his eyes and said in a very calm voice, "Jesus doesn't like what you're doing to me, so will you please stop?"

He stopped instantly, and the look in his face was of absolute shame. He got on his hands and knees, pleading for forgiveness. I didn't really have to grant it, as it was obvious that Jesus already had. When he got off the train, I cried softly and had no doubt that divine intervention had taken place. I kicked myself later for not reporting the crime, but I didn't want that kind of publicity. When I thought about it, I realized that all the prison time in the world could not change this man's behavior as much as my words probably affected him for life. I do forgive him and hope that I was the last person he molested. It was the last time I was ever taken advantage of sexually.

Looking back on these years, I realize that I was truly blessed with a lot of support from many corners of life, even through divine intervention in Hoboken. I continued to make new friends and was growing and evolving, working through so much inner pain. Had I not had all the support I did, I do not know that I would have been able to survive. The pain and disappointments would have been insurmountable on my own. That is one reason I encourage people to reach out for help, not to try to handle everything on their own. There should be no shame in asking for help, but rather shame in *not* asking for it and, instead, giving up.

Richard, My Ex-Husband

Honesty Within

In 2005, a movie was released about disability advocate Richard Pimentel called *Music Within*. It was a film based on his life . . . yet I was not even mentioned. Considering that I was his wife and we were together for over 12 years, being erased from his story hurt me deeply, as if I'd held no value in it at all. Although the previous chapter may seem a little short, it was composed with much contemplation. Symbolically, the blank pages say nothing but reveal everything.

I was aware of the film being in development, and Richard even gave me the heads up about the exclusion, explaining that because he was with someone else, and he and I were estranged, he felt uncomfortable including me. I understood, even if I felt like Richard had stepped on my heart, whether consciously or unconsciously. Quite truthfully, I felt that the executive producer, Steven Sawalich, did an excellent job with what Richard was willing to give him to work with. It actually is a very good movie, revealing many truths even while omitting others. Nevertheless, I was not prepared for the anguish of being discounted in such a public venue.

Over time, as I healed, I realized the most important lesson I could take from Richard's movie was to find the value within myself. Richard was an important part of my life, and a part of me will always love him. So, I will tell my story about him as honestly as I possibly can.

In 1987, Richard Pimentel walked into my life and changed it forever. Even though we had never been friends before we began our relationship, we had met years before and had run into each other periodically over the years. My first encounter with Richard in 1982 isn't a memory that I hold dearly and is even a recollection that I mentally blocked for a period of time. Richard and I were both speaking to NASA in Washington, D.C. After we were introduced, the organizers were apologetic about not specifying who was to present first in the program. "We'll leave it to you two." Richard was a big guy, arrogant and quite intimidating, and I was young, naive, and a little cocky with my newfound fame.

Richard asked me if I minded who presented first. I told him quite innocently, "I'm a professional comedienne, so you might not want to follow me." I had no idea the challenge I had just presented to him. I was only coming from a protective standpoint. I knew him as a writer, and I didn't want to "steal" his presentation with my *performing* ability. That was about the stupidest thing I could have said to him, or anyone with a male ego.

Richard was eight years older than me and knew that my remark had no malicious intent, but he chose to teach me a humbling lesson anyway. He laughed and said, "I am very familiar with your act, Geri. I am *not* a professional comedian, yet I'm funnier than you. But since you offered me the position, I will gladly go on first." I still didn't understand what I was up against with Richard. He took the stage and was clearly aware of the nature of my motivational speeches and what I talked about in them. He hit every cornerstone of my own speech, and left me with virtually nothing to say, without sounding like I was merely repeating what he had just said himself.

Afterward, I asked him why he did that. He said he did it to teach me a lesson: just because I was famous didn't mean that I really knew any of the issues surrounding employment and disability. "You were only hired because you're on a television show, you're cute and have CP, not because you are educated and understand the real issues of employment and disability." He asked me if I had ever had a "real" job and I truthfully answered no. He then handed me his business card and told me that he could teach me Windmills, which is an attitudinal program designed to provide a clearer understanding and empathy for people with disabilities and employment issues. Richard wrote this phenomenal program, which has been used worldwide to shatter barriers that people with disabilities are faced with in the workforce. By preparing me to become a Windmills trainer, he gave me a second skill, allowing me to work in the field of disability far longer than fickle Hollywood would keep me employed.

It was so odd: on the one hand, he cut me down, and on the other hand, he offered to help me. A part of me wanted to toss his card just because of his arrogance, but then another part of me hung onto it, in case his perception was correct about Hollywood. I attempted to call him a couple of times in 1984, but hung up when he answered the phone. Then I called him again in 1985 and actually agreed to meet him at the Disneyland Hotel in Anaheim.

However, I stood him up at the last minute, turning around and driving home. By this time, I faced unemployment and was no longer wanted in Hollywood, but I just didn't want to give him the satisfaction of having been right. And then . . . I erased him from my memory bank altogether.

I fell into the trap that a lot of child stars fall into where our public identities become so powerful that unless we make a complete break from those images, we spend our lives chasing after it. My identity as a disability icon was very powerful, and spiritually I felt a responsibility to honor it while I simultaneously wanted to walk away from it. I was locked in a vicious cycle of self-affirmation mixed with self-loathing for not being able to live up to an image. If it weren't for my "successful person with a disability" label, I would have left Hollywood many years earlier. My cerebral palsy became a noose around my neck because it was the one solitary identifying trait of everything that Hollywood and the public believed about me.

In 1987, I was invited to a Halloween party by Lyle Gregory. That night, dressed as Pee-wee Herman (but covered with blood with a plastic ax glued to my head) I met a woman named Lynda Jean Groh. She was dressed as a psychic medium. She told me that I needed to call Richard, and that he was doing wonderful work in the field of disability. "In fact, he's always asking about you," she added. I asked her to repeat his last name. Strangely, I had no immediate recollection of who she was talking about, although the memory was stored somewhere in the archives of my mind.

A week later, I took Lynda Jean's advice and called Richard's business partner. He said Richard would be happy to see me again. Wow, this Richard guy seems to know me quite well, I thought. Maybe when I finally see him, I'll be able to place him. I went to one of his seminars for the U.S. Army. I sat in the front row, listening and watching him intently, but at no point during Richard's talk did I put two and two together. It was as if the hard drive in my mind concerning Richard had been completely erased.

Afterward, I joined him for dinner. He was so intelligent and funny, and I enjoyed his company. We talked and laughed until the restaurant closed. He brought up the subject of NASA and actually apologized for doing what he did. All of a sudden it was as if the mental blindfold had been removed. I recognized him and my brain tried to wrap itself around the mystery of my memory lapse. After we clarified everything, I was exhausted and too tired to drive home. He said that I was welcome to stay with him for the night. I said okay, but I am sleeping in my clothes; I only want to share the bed, nothing else. He was a perfect gentleman and gained my trust by sleeping in his clothes also. After all my years of struggling with sex and sexuality, I met Richard's actions that night with complete awe.

We discovered that the following weekend he and I were booked at the same conference in Tahoe. The odds of that happening when we had not presented together since 1982 were amazing. A part of me believed it was an omen, signaling to me that somehow Richard and I were destined to come together. He asked me when I was flying in. I told him Friday afternoon, and that I'd be flying back to L.A. that evening. He was working Friday and Saturday and suggested that I change my ticket and stay in Tahoe for the weekend. I explained that I had a cheap nonrefundable ticket, so it wasn't possible. He then wrote me a check to purchase a whole new ticket altogether. Wow, this mystical, wonderful, funny, exciting man with the wing-tipped shoes was definitely bringing new energy into my life! I didn't understand it, but I was already infatuated with him.

I stopped at the Burbank airport on Thursday to pick up my new ticket, thus voiding the first one. I then stopped at the store to pick up a few things for the trip. I got home, packed my bags, and slept on a sleeping bag in front of the warm fire glowing from the fireplace, fantasizing with every flickering flame about my upcoming weekend in Tahoe with Richard. I then bolted up at three in the morning, suddenly aware that I had not seen my airline ticket since I had been in my car. After retracing my steps, I realized that I had placed the ticket in the paper bag from the store. I went into a full-on panic, knowing that I had used the bag to start the fire.

I called Richard at the hotel in Tahoe. I could tell that I had woken him, but didn't have the courage to tell him what I had done and hung up. I called the airline, explaining that I had accidentally burned my ticket to Tahoe, asking if they could issue me another ticket. No, they said. Burning an airline ticket was equivalent to burning money. I moved on to plan C: the next morning, I went to the airport and told someone at the ticket counter my story, hoping they might recognize me from *Facts of Life* and issue me another ticket. To my relief, plan C worked. When I arrived, there was Richard with a big box of candy and a big white fluffy teddy bear! I was so moved by such sentiment, as it was the first time anyone had done anything so special for me like that. I was absolutely swept off my feet by him.

I laughed when he told me he was a little tired, because he had been up since 3:30 in the morning when the phone had woken him. He thought it was his 6:30 wake-up call, so he'd gotten up, showered, dressed, and went downstairs to the conference room only to discover that it was only 4:30.

"Some drunk must have called my room by mistake." I asked him how he knew the person was drunk, that maybe she had CP. I confessed it was me who woke him up. We both laughed. Our sense of humor was the glue in our union on many levels. We laughed often, and we both *needed* to laugh.

Not long after Tahoe, Richard was booked in Hawaii and took me with him for five days. The allure of this journey had a dreamlike quality. I had never been to Hawaii before, so it was a very big deal! Hawaii was wonderful, and when we returned we were a bona fide couple.

Did Richard really love me? I believed that he did, but there were other times when it was confusing because Richard had a lot of anger issues and his rage frightened me. However, these times were "hopscotched" with times of extreme sweetness and kindness. Subconsciously, I was looking to Richard to rescue me from Hollywood, especially when we became engaged in Hawaii. Shortly after returning, I moved to Vancouver, Washington, to live with him. I enjoyed the feeling of being romanced and fell madly in love.

Leaving Hollywood and the state of California in 1988 was difficult, but also a relief. I would have preferred him moving to L.A., but he had a 10-year-old son in Oregon and wanted to be able to be with him on the weekends. I knew how important that was, so it was me who had to move. But I was still leery about leaving my career. Dramatically, Richard darted his eyes all around, as if searching for something that wasn't there. "What career? I don't see a career, do you?" I had to admit, I had not worked in Hollywood since 1984, so he had a valid point. Then he added, "You will have a career again, but only if you have the courage to walk away from the illusion of having one now. Hollywood will want you again when you stop wanting Hollywood." These kinds of statements made me idolize him.

However, there were two issues that I felt I had to address before I went anywhere with this man. I have always felt that honesty is the best policy, and I told him that I was still addicted to Restoril, explaining to him what it was. He agreed that if I continued taking Restoril that I would lose him. Knowing also that I wanted to have children, he explained that I had to choose between the drug and a future with him and a child. That was all the "rehab" I needed to stop. I promised I would never take Restoril again, and I was true to my word.

The other issue was that I had previously been sexually involved with women. I told him that I was willing to try being straight, but I wasn't sure what to expect. Between Restoril and women, I risked losing him before we even began. I believed I was strong enough to say no to both drugs and women for the sake of having a supportive relationship: quite truthfully, it was more of a sacrifice to leave California than leaving the idea of being with a woman. The fact that he had no problem going to the next level *after* I had dropped that bombshell only reinforced my love for him.

He also put up with CP-related issues, which, in my mind, I didn't believe any other man would in a million years. Early on, while his son was staying with us for the weekend, I had a CP accident and didn't make it to the bathroom. I was mortified. I ran and stood in the shower and bawled under the running water. Richard got in the shower with me fully clothed, holding me in his arms, telling me that it was okay and insisting that I get dressed so we could go to a movie together. No matter how you slice it, it was love.

What some people have difficulty understanding is how I could possibly be with a man when I was attracted to women. Since I know I am not bisexual, the only way I can describe it is to say that so many sexual traumas had happened to me that my sexuality had basically shut down. I had *zero* sex drive, and no lusting for anyone. All I really wanted was to be held. It was affection that I longed for, and Richard gave me that. What I was not capable of doing was sharing sexual intimacy. With so many walls that I had built up over the years, this level of intimacy was not within my grasp. To Richard's credit, he had a lot of patience, but possibly unrealistic expectations of changing that part of me any time soon.

The first five years of more than a decade together were good for the most part. In my heart, I felt so blessed that someone wanted me even though I was "broken." My life had become stable, and the momentary glimpses of Richard's anger were overshadowed by an idealistic window of normalcy in my mind. We did family things like taking many trips with his son, going to Hawaii and visiting the Kah-Nee-Ta Resort in Oregon, where we splashed in the natural hot springs and spent three nights in a teepee. We visited Seaside and enjoyed the beautiful Oregon Coast.

But it wasn't just physical suitcases we were hauling with us: I had brought a lot of baggage into the relationship, and he loved me anyway. What I didn't fully understand until years later was that Richard probably had even more baggage than I did, but because I idolized him I didn't really pay close attention to all of *his* bags that kept going around and around on the carousel. I think we spent so much time on the road that it prevented us from having to deal with normal day-to-day things. We felt like Lucy and Desi, and often jokingly called each other by those names. And our union was just as complicated as the Arnaz marriage.

Vancouver could be very isolating much of the time, and I missed my friends and family. Like his son, I often only saw Richard on weekends because he was booked on the road so much of the time. A part of me wanted to jump ship and move back to California, but at the same time, Richard provided me with a certain stability that I had not experienced on my own.

Eventually, Richard's company was booking me on more speaking gigs than at any other time in my career. I grew leaps and bounds as a speaker. With our shared income, we were able to move to a nicer apartment, and live a little easier. We bought bicycles and rode together on weekends. We ate out, went to movies, played Scrabble and video games. I felt loved, and I had completely fallen in love with Richard. I had a real family now, but *only* if I continued to work, perpetuating the "Geri Jewell" image. Richard and I both wanted to get off the road, but the road was our bread and butter. I believed that we would be financially secure enough at some point so that we could try to have a child, maybe even adopt, and I could hang up my "Super Disabled Person" cloak in the closet forever.

He already had a grown daughter and a son from previous marriages and did not share my enthusiasm of having more children, *but* he reassured me that if it would make me happy, he would do that for me. He agreed on *many* occasions to have a reverse vasectomy when we were in a better financial position. I absolutely wanted to have a baby. In my mind, having a baby would shift the focus off "Geri Jewell," allowing me to have a normal life, to experience loving a child, and to leave my career in the dust where I half-heartedly believed it already was.

However, because of my success as a speaker and the money we were making from it, that never happened. Richard and I began working together as a team, creating another image of the "Super Disabled Couple." In a way, I validated Richard within the disability community. He told me many times how frustrated he was over the reverse prejudice issue from people with disabilities themselves, believing someone who wasn't disabled had no right speaking on their behalf. Besides that, he felt that he really did have a disability — a hearing loss and tinnitus, which he acquired when he was in Vietnam. Because it was hidden, it wasn't taken seriously by people with visible disabilities. I sympathized with him and always carried a torch for Richard, telling everyone how brilliant and wonderful he was.

I tried to make Vancouver work, but I felt too isolated much of the time. Some of my friends flew up to see me, and even my mom and dad drove up for a weekend, but most of my friends didn't have the money or the time to do that. I also missed working in Hollywood and hadn't given up on that dream completely. In 1990, I flew up my friend Mac to help me write a treatment for the television series *21 Jump Street*. The reason I chose *Jump Street* and not another show was because I wanted to focus on producer Stephen J. Cannell, whom I had met years before at a party. He was so sweet to me then and told me how proud he was of me. He also told me that he had overcome his own disability of dyslexia.

The story idea I had was of my being an undercover cop, trying to nail a guy who repeatedly raped women with disabilities. Mac was a good writer, and he knew all the characters of *Jump Street* far better than I did. Together, we built on my original premise. Richard even added his two cents, writing with Mac late into the night one evening after I had gone to bed. When I awoke the next morning, the treatment was totally different, but flowed better. My basic inspiration and idea was still there, but the story had been changed by Richard and Mac overnight. In a way, it felt like my autobiography again, with someone else taking over the writing duties on my story, but I put my ego aside and realized that Richard's input actually improved the flow of the story a great deal.

Richard didn't want any credit, explaining that Hollywood was my world, not his. "Sweetie, this is your baby, not mine," he said. To our excitement and amazement, we sold the treatment, but the producers wanted to hire one of their own writers to write the actual script. So the script changed yet again.

The only change that was really disappointing to me was the absence of Johnny Depp's character from the storyline. He was filming *Cry-Baby* at the time, so I never did get to meet him. I was paired with Peter DeLuise instead. Peter was an absolute sweetheart, and I am so grateful to have had the opportunity to work with him. He had a wonderful sense of humor, and we laughed a lot. I remember once we were filming a scene over and over again one morning, but something kept bothering everyone except me. Finally, Peter stopped in mid-sentence and said, "And where is that damn teapot whistling?" The whistling teapot ended up being my hearing aids. I had shoved them in my pocket, but failed to hear that they were still on!

Richard and I expected *Jump Street* to jump-start my career, but Hollywood has always been a crapshoot. You never know what will be a hit or a miss. Although it didn't send any ripples through Hollywood that I was still here, it did get me more motivational speaking gigs throughout the United States and Canada. Even though Richard loathed Hollywood and

Los Angeles in general, he wanted me to have the exposure I did, because he knew the more visible I was in Hollywood, the more speaking gigs I would get. There was no more serious talk about having a child, so I put the baby idea on the back burner.

We were on the road more than anything else. When we weren't, we spent time with his son. I loved his son deeply, and I always will, although I had a difficult time in the role of stepmom. He lived with his mom in Oregon, and I could never take her place, nor would I have wanted to. However, psychologically it was difficult for him to know exactly how to relate to me. He loved me, and for the most part, we got along. I think in some ways, because there was such an age gap between Richard and myself, he viewed me more like a stepsibling than as a parent. I didn't blame him either, as I had no experience in parenting and was thrown right into the gig of suddenly parenting an 11-year-old child. It is always a difficult thing for anyone to do, much less someone with my background.

While I was trying to learn how to be a mom, I was suddenly faced with the possibility of losing my own. My mom had retired from the post office, and with Gloria's knowledge of real estate, and her offer of financial help to my parents, my mother was able to at least fulfill her dream of living by the ocean. Gloria sold my parents' home in Fullerton and moved them to a beautiful home in Laguna Niguel, which was high on a hill, overlooking the sea. We all thought that my mom would finally get to rest after working so hard for the postal service for so many years. However, it was only a little more than a year later that she was diagnosed with cancer. I was devastated.

In 1990, I was making frequent trips to L.A., mostly driving, so I wouldn't have to rent a car when I arrived. My time in California was spent looking for a new agent or manager, trying to find work, and visiting Mom when I could. I even temporarily moved in with my friend Tony and his partner, Charles, while looking for a more permanent place to live. Richard's son was now 15 and I thought perhaps Richard would be more willing to give L.A. a try, since I had given Vancouver a try. He was, but with resentment. I should have seen his reluctance to support me as a major red flag, even if I hadn't paid attention to any previously. Looking back, we were drifting apart even at that point, but I kept thinking that things would get better. We still enjoyed each other's wit, which became a diversion from facing the real issues at hand.

I think that because I could not be an equal partner in bed, Richard did eventually grow tired of trying. By the same token, I couldn't even come to embrace him as I once did, because I increasingly witnessed a side of Richard that could be abusive and cruel. For example, one evening I had prepared dinner and asked him to remove the chicken from the oven. But it was hardly cooked, even after several hours. He noticed I had set the heat at only 120 degrees and became furious. He threw the half-frozen bird on the floor, screaming at my stupidity, as I cowered with my hands over my ears.

Over time, I realized that he became angry and demeaning with others as well. He once told me that I was one of the few people in his life who wasn't afraid of him, but whether he realized it or not, I *did* become fearful of making him angry. He had anger issues that went back before me, and I was just the next person in his path. I tried so hard to get him to harness his anger, especially when it was directed at someone else. I came to understand his temper as being his disability in a way. I felt that if he was able to accept my disability, I couldn't turn my back on his.

Richard and I both agreed that I needed to be in L.A. I managed to find an inexpensive studio apartment that I rented temporarily until Richard was willing to join me from Vancouver. However, understandably, he resented it at the same time. I would fly up north to see him or he would fly to L.A. to meet me. After several months of commuting, we found a two-bedroom condo in Burbank and he left Vancouver. As fate would have it, the very week that Richard moved into our condo, I was booked on the road and couldn't be there. He called me, saying that L.A. was like a war zone, that there was a curfew, and there were military tanks going down Hollywood Way, which was the street we lived on. Richard's first experience of living in L.A. happened during the 1992 riots that broke out after the unpopular Rodney King verdict. Richard had already hated L.A., and this dire vision only intensified his anger.

If there had been a place to plant flowers outside our building, it would have been more appropriate to have planted tiny red flags at this time and watch them grow into bigger red flags. It was during this period in our relationship that we should have called it quits, but, instead, we both tried to force it to work. Even though the verbal abuse could be intense, and our unhappiness was palpable, we decided to get married on June 27, 1992. Why? Perhaps because I was still clinging to the hope that something would change, that we would buy a home together and have a baby. My mom was dying of cancer, and I believe that Richard had promised her that he would always look after me. It was quite noble of him, but hardly realistic when you consider all the problems we were having.

Both of us got married for the wrong reasons, stubbornly denying the truth that we had grown dangerously apart and were clinging to a fantasy rather than reality. We chose to get married at the Little Church of the West in Las Vegas, Nevada. Richard and I laughed as we browsed through the brochure, discovering how many famous people had been married there, including David Cassidy and Judy Garland.

My mom was too sick to come to our wedding, but it was probably better that she didn't, as it was overbooked, and it was 120 degrees outside (hot enough to cook us, but not a chicken, as I'd learned). My dad gave me away, and Gloria and her boyfriend, Brian, came as well. My brothers were both out of state, but several cousins on my mom's side of the family came, including my mom's brother, Uncle Ed, who filmed the whole thing so that my mom could watch it at home. It was a small wedding, with a very short guest list. I believe, underneath it all, Richard and I both knew that we were making a big mistake, but neither of us was willing to admit it.

At one point, everyone in the church started laughing because I was having a hard time hearing the minister. Because of the loud air conditioner, I wasn't able to hear the words that I was supposed to repeat. He said something about "enjoining our lives," and I got flustered, asking without thinking, "I'm supposed to enjoy him?" The minister smiled and said I could do that too. Then he said something else, but again I couldn't hear him. I patted the minister on his shoulder, and asked, "Excuse me, what's my line again?" Richard smiled and said, "Sweetie, this is our wedding, not a movie!" The thing is, in a strange way, it didn't feel as though it was real. It felt more like filming a scene for a movie, and we were just a couple of actors mimicking the emotions without actually feeling them.

After our film wrapped . . . I mean, our wedding ended, we threw a small reception and, the following day, Richard and I both spoke at a Society for Human Resource Management (SHRM) conference. We had actually picked June 27 because we were both booked at that conference in Vegas. We went to bed early, but we were awakened in the wee hours of the morning. We were on the thirtieth floor of the Flamingo Hilton, and the whole building was swaying from side to side. People were jamming the stairwells, sounding like a herd of elephants. Yep, on our wedding night, it wasn't our love-making that made the earth move, but a 6.4 earthquake! If that wasn't a red flag, I don't know what is.

CHAPTER TWENTY-TWO

Building on a Shaky Foundation

Richard and I lived in Burbank for only one year, but it was a very pivotal one because of all the changes that it brought about. I was so happy that I was living in California as opposed to Washington. My mom was dying, and what little time I had left with her meant everything in the world to me. Richard was not happy about being in California, but he knew how important it was for me to be near Mom. The problem with Richard was that he still harbored a lot of anger, even though it had more to do with his past than what angered him in the present. Because he still had not worked through his own demons and pain from the abuse he endured as a child, he continued his own "anger dance," reacting disproportionately to the frustrations that were facing him in the present.

My failure to secure work in Hollywood was a constant disappointment for both of us. I battled depression once again because of everything that was going on around me, and also because the physical pain that I endured was getting progressively worse. X-rays were taken of my neck, and due to all the abnormal movement from CP, my neck looked like a truck had ridden over it. I suffered from bone spurs, bone loss, bulging discs, and arthritis. Even though I had long ago given up my use of Restoril, I was now taking pain meds and a muscle relaxant called Soma to help alleviate my severe neck and back pain, not even realizing that this fed into my previous addiction.

Quickly, I became addicted all over again. The problem was that I was taking them not only to numb my physical pain, but also to dull the pain of both my mother's terminal illness and of being in a marriage that was deteriorating. Maybe on some level Richard was feeling the same way, since we both let our union go on far longer than it should have. I remember looking at other couples who appeared so happy, holding hands and gazing at each other lovingly, and wishing that Richard and I could be the same way. However, we were in the throes of a dysfunctional relationship, only briefly sharing moments of real joy.

Richard and I were breaking a cardinal spiritual law: chasing happiness outside of ourselves instead of realizing that true happiness can only come from within. One of the most important aspects of a relationship was missing as well. Richard and I could never see eye to eye when it came to God and spirituality. I think I wanted to believe that we were on the same page spiritually, because at times he did seem to be. But then, as quickly as one could blink an eye, he would laugh at my own concept of spirituality. This was a dangerous aspect of our union; I still believe today that if partners do not share the same beliefs or at least respect each other's opposing viewpoints, it can cause a sort of fault line that will eventually give way.

My mother having cancer may have been our meeting point of compassion. Mom was so brave, and what stands out in my mind was that in spite of her own pain and suffering, she greeted everyone who came to see her with a smile that always radiated with love and a passion for life. She fought ovarian cancer with every fiber of her being and was always thrilled when Richard and I would visit her. Richard may have fallen out of love with me, but he did respect and love my mother. Richard's own mom suffered from mental illness, and she abused him horribly as a child, so in a way Richard could receive the motherly love from my mom that he had never received from his own.

Dad was there for Mom the best that he was able to be, but he could only be supportive up to a point. I think that to truly understand my father at that point in his life you'd have to walk a mile in his shoes. Not to say he was a poor father, because we loved him deeply, but all of us kids walked on eggshells at one time or another while growing up, and Mom became the one who always made everything "okay" again. There was a part of him that was so broken from his own abuse as a child and lack of self-esteem that he was incapable of having unconditional love for his children. We just accepted that as Dad being Dad and went to Mom when we were upset about something he'd said or done.

I believe that when my mother got sick with cancer, she lost her job of harnessing my father's selfish behavior. Mom wasn't well enough to say "Jack!" So, Dad became more fearful and unsure of himself, retreating into certain traits that had *always* been there, but had previously been tempered by my mother's influence. While Mom was battling cancer, Gloria and I were constantly reminding Dad that this was not about him, but about Mom. I know that he loved my mother deeply and was terrified of losing her, but "baby Jack" was actually jealous of the attention that she was getting.

There are so *many* examples I could use to illustrate this, but the one that first comes to mind happened during one of Mom's hospital stays. Gloria, Dad, and I were doing shifts every day, sitting by my mom's bedside, praying and willing her to live. One evening, it was just me and Dad, and Mom had fallen asleep. Dad suggested that we go down to the hospital cafeteria to have dinner. During our meal, Dad told me to prepare myself, saying, "She may not make it this time." I started crying into my crappy hospital food.

It wasn't an odd thing for him to say, given the fact the doctors weren't giving us much hope. But then he went on to say that he was not going to live much longer either. I said, "What?" He explained that he only had two years to live. My mom was dying of cancer, and now my dad was telling me that he was dying too. I shifted gears to try to understand what he was really telling me. I asked him how he knew he only had two years left. He told me an angel had come to him and told him so. I just looked at him incredulously and asked him what the angel looked like. He told me he looked like Michael Landon!

I didn't know whether to laugh, cry, be angry, or be sympathetic. He then went on to explain that "Archangel Landon" told him that he made a lot of mistakes in his life, but that he was going to be given two years to do better. Looking back, I believe that my father was terrified at the thought of losing Mom, his anchor, but was not able to fully express his fear and vulnerability. In not being able to embrace those emotions, he was unable to be there for anyone except himself.

Like all of us, he was angry, watching hopelessly as my mom's body became more and more ravaged by cancer. He was working as a security guard at one of the private hillside communities, but Gloria had to help out Mom and Dad financially as the medical bills became insurmountable. Of all of us kids, Gloria was the one who was there for Mom and Dad when they needed help. She was living in Laguna Beach, so she was physically close as well. I was extremely grateful for Gloria, as there was no way I could have offered the same kind of support, and both of my brothers lived out of state. When I wasn't on the road, I drove from L.A. to see Mom and called her daily, but as far as being there day in and day out, the bulk of that fell on my sister's shoulders. Gloria became the mother, the father, the daughter, the sister, and the caretaker all at the same time.

Even though there is not a lot of humor associated with anyone having cancer, there were funny things that happened during this time. Once, I used Mom's private bathroom in the hospital to pee instead of walking down the hall and using the public one. I stepped on a floor lever, thinking I was flushing the toilet, but it ended up being the emergency sprinkler system in case of a fire. I panicked, unable to turn the damned thing off. I opened the door with my pants around my ankles and began screaming for a nurse. My mom, who was on morphine, yelled to me, "Geri, why aren't you wearing any pants in the rain?" I couldn't stop laughing.

During my mom's plight, there were some moments that offered her tremendous joy, like being able to live long enough to celebrate her fiftieth wedding anniversary. She was determined to do this, and the cancer was not going to keep her from achieving that goal. The one thing that I loved most about my mom was that it never took much for her to feel joy. What would seem like no big deal to most meant the world to her. We all went to my mom's favorite restaurant in Newport Beach to celebrate my parents' life together. They didn't accept reservations, but Mom didn't care. She waited in line like everyone else in her wheelchair with her little bald head covered with a scarf. When I look at the vhs video of the evening, my mom looked the happiest of all of us at the table as her spirit radiated from her small victory.

In 1993, I called Robert Goulet, asking him if he could call my mom on Valentine's Day as a surprise. Mom had always loved him, and I was just trying to think of something special to do for her. I told him that she was battling cancer, and I just wanted to make her smile. Robert was happy to do it, but the gift kind of backfired.

Mom was on a lot of different meds, so sometimes she was confused. When she picked up the phone that morning, Robert Goulet would have been the last person she would have expected to be calling her. From what I gathered, this is the way is the way it went:

"Olga?"

"Yes?"

"This is Robert Goulet!"

"Oh, you don't have to try and humor me, but that's very funny."

"Excuse me?"

My mom laughed. "Oh, I'd recognize your voice anywhere. How sweet of you to call me, doctor."

"Olga, your daughter Geri asked me to call you."

"Oh, that was silly of her, she doesn't know how busy you are! She just worries. But honestly, I am doing everything you told me to do. But I have to tell you though . . . I have not had a bowel movement in two days! Is that normal?"

"I'm . . . not a doctor, so I don't know if it's normal or not. However, I'd like to sing to you." Mom laughed again at the thought of her physician singing to her. Then Robert serenaded my mom with the song "My Funny Valentine."

My mom's response was "You do have a beautiful voice, but I don't think you're as good as Robert Goulet!"

Robert had a wonderful sense of humor and called me to tell me that talking to my mom was a humbling experience. When my mom found out later that she really *was* talking to Robert Goulet, and not her doctor, she couldn't stop laughing. Laughter is a wonderful, natural healing tonic, and we all inherited our sense of humor from Mom.

In early 1993, Mom was back in the hospital again, this time at Scripps in Orange County. As Gloria looked out my mom's window, she noticed a large crowd of people gathered below, holding a vigil. They were holding candles, rosaries, and several poster boards that read WE ARE PRAYING FOR YOU and WE LOVE YOU MOTHER! Gloria said sweetly to my mom, "Oh look how many people love you, Mom!" Mom looked out the window and was in awe. Even though they were really there for Mother Teresa, who was con-valescing at Scripps at the time, Mom knew that prayer was prayer and felt blessed nevertheless.

Mom had been up and down with cancer for almost three years. She would do really well for a while, and we would all believe that she was going to get better, and then she would take a sudden turn for the worse. There was always anxiety around holidays as well, because most of my mom's family had died on holidays, and Mom told us that she would also. Every time a holiday would pass, we would all breathe a sigh of relief . . . but there was always another one around the corner. She made it through Christmas, but then we had to get through New Year's. She made it through Good Friday, but Easter was still ahead.

At the end of June 1993, when my mom was back at home, I had a long talk with her about dying. I knew it was important to let her know that it was okay to let go. She was so tiny, weighing under 80 pounds, and we knew she did not have long to live. The only holiday that was on the horizon was Independence Day, so again I had mentally prepared myself for her possible death on the Fourth of July. I had asked Mom if she was afraid of dying. She answered, "No, I already died when I was three years old." She told me the story of how her sisters Gerry and Mary were giving her a bath. A traveling salesman had come to the door, selling a little electrical device that would make a cup of coffee or cocoa hot. Having very little heated water, my Aunt Gerry put the device in my mom's bathwater *with my mom in it*! The three-year-old was electrocuted.

Mom told me that she went through a long tunnel and into the most magnificent white light, that it was the most beautiful feeling in the entire world. She told me that she was greeted by total unconditional love bestowed upon her by angels of light and relatives. But she was also told that she had to return to Earth, that it was not her time yet. I asked her, "If it was so beautiful, didn't it piss you off that you had to leave so quickly?" She laughed and said yes, but she knew she had a lot of work to do first. I asked her, "If you're not afraid of dying, then what's keeping you here in so much pain?" She had tears in her eyes and said that she didn't want me to be angry with her for abandoning me. I hugged her for the longest time and told her that that would be impossible, because she was in my heart and mind forever, and that one day we would be together again after I finished all *my* work on Earth. "But what *will* piss me off though is if you do not give me a sign from the other side, letting me know that you are okay. What sign will you give me, Mom?"

Mom told me it would be an orca. I laughed. "Mom, can't you make it a little simpler, like perhaps an orchid? I mean, what are the odds of seeing a killer whale?" I laughed with her as I joked, "Yeah, I'm going to look up in the sky and there will be a killer whale flying by!" Mom winked at me and told me that I would indeed see a killer whale in the sky.

The following week, Richard and I went to see Mom together on the morning of July 2, after we returned from a gig. We arrived early and spent the whole day with her. Mom knew that I had tickets to see Carol Burnett in Long Beach. I told her I wanted to stay with her instead. She then took her wedding band off her finger and slipped it on mine. Holding my face with both of her hands (which I have never forgotten because Mom was never very demonstrative), she looked into my eyes. When I looked back into hers, it was as though we became one. She kissed me on my forehead and told me to go see Carol. "With this ring, know that I am there with you. I will see you tomorrow. I love you, Geri."

"I love you too, Mom!"

It was around 5:30, and although I had mixed feelings about leaving her, I felt that it would be okay because she would wait until the Fourth of July, and I would return first thing on the third and spend all day with her. On my way out the door, my dad saw the ring and demanded that I take it off.

"What?"

"Take it off! It is not your ring!"

"Dad, she put it on my finger. I am not going to remove it!" He then went on to tell me that it was *his* ring, as he had paid for it. Although his reaction upset me, I realized that the ring being on my finger told him that his wife was leaving for real this time.

I was upset when I left my parents' house, but Richard was no more supportive of me than my dad had been. I think everyone was upset that my mom was dying, and because our nerves were all on edge, no one was acting normally. At this time, though, Richard being angry was the norm. The ride to Long Beach was mostly an awkward, angry silence. Richard did not want to see the play, and maybe we should have just gone home to Burbank, but we continued the journey to Long Beach. The happy evening that I had anticipated two months earlier when I ordered the tickets was gone, and the play hadn't even started.

Once we got there, it got worse. I gave a note to a theater employee letting Carol know that I was there, asking if I could say hello after the show. When I did that, Richard exploded. "I can't believe you just did that. Like she's really going to see *you!*" I begged him to stop, telling him that we could have a good evening if he would allow it. But he would not stop. He went on to tell me that my belief in God, and all my little fantasies about Hollywood were equivalent to those of a child of seven. "There are people dying all over the world, there's starvation and injustice, yet you believe that there's a God answering prayers. If there was really a God, Geri, your *dad* would be dying, not your mom!"

I longed to be loved and supported in this difficult time, but Richard was incapable of shifting gears. As he continued to berate me, the theater door opened and the woman whom I had given the note to excitedly said, "Boy, do you have a fan in Carol. She is so thrilled that you're here and would *love* to see you after the show." Richard was speechless. After the show, I didn't say everything that I wanted to say to Carol, because I was so emotionally derailed, but the look on Richard's face when he met her was priceless.

The next morning, Richard and I drove back to Laguna from Burbank. We hit a lot of traffic on Interstate 405, and with my mom's life slipping away, every minute seemed like an eternity. We got to Mom and Dad's around 11:30 in the morning. My dad was sound asleep and Gloria was watching over my mom. She mentioned that she thanked God that I was not there the night before, as she and Dad had been up all night with Mom, and it had been awful. Mom had been hallucinating and they'd had to hold her down to keep her calm. Dad had finally fallen asleep about an hour earlier. Mom was sleeping too, and Gloria was starving. I didn't want to leave again, but Richard and I went to get food for Gloria and my dad when he awakened.

We returned about an hour later with pizza. As we were setting up paper plates and opening the pizza box in the kitchen, Gloria came in with tears in her eyes. She said that Mom's breathing was very shallow, and she wasn't sure if Mom was breathing at all. Rich and I joined Gloria at my mom's bedside. All three of us were whispering, primarily so we wouldn't wake up my dad, but all three of us couldn't decide if Mom was alive or not. Gloria's heart was breaking, "I think she's dead, but I'm not sure."

Richard told me to go find a mirror. "A mirror? What for?" Richard explained, "I saw this on the television show *Quincy*. We'll put the mirror up to her face; if it fogs up, she's alive; if it doesn't, then she isn't." I watched as Richard held the mirror to my mom's face. As he kept checking it for fog, I started to laugh and couldn't stop, because the whole moment just seemed too absurd. Just then, my mom jumped. We all jumped actually, and we were still standing there like the Three Stooges, wondering if she was alive or not. Finally Gloria went next door to get our dear friend, Dr. Jeff Brandon. Although he didn't ask for a mirror, he did get a lamp and put the light in my mom's open eyes. Dr. Jeff closed her eyes, and we understood that Mom was finally free from the disease that had tormented her. I woke up my dad and held him in my arms as he wept.

The next evening, Richard and I stood on the balcony of the nearby hotel where we were staying. To his credit, he *was* supportive on this day, and I was grateful that I had him by my side. When Richard *wanted* to, he had the ability to be "there," and his large frame felt protective. We watched the fireworks, and I wondered why my mom chose to die on the third instead of the fourth. I looked for an orca in the sky, but only saw one isolated red balloon that I thought perhaps could have been a sign from Mom. But I knew in my heart of hearts that it was simply a balloon that had gotten away from a small child. It wasn't Mom.

We ended up having her funeral with the Neptune Society, which is an awesome service that allows families to have burials at sea. Private boat owners donate their boats for the services. Our whole family gathered at the dock. The boat was called *Orca*! The entire boat was decorated with killer whales. There was a killer whale flag, killer whale coffee mugs, and even the curtains on the windows were all decorated with killer whales! It was a small miracle and I knew my mom was smiling at the vision herself.

Not long after we left the dock, we noticed three dolphins swimming along-side us. We all thought it was the perfect time to put her ashes at sea along with flowers. As we stood on the top deck, we shared our memories of Mom, and then, with beautiful flowers, we sprinkled her ashes in the sea, honoring her wishes. At the same time, a small plane flew overhead trailing a huge banner of a killer whale, advertising the opening of the movie *Free Willy*. All of us were in such shock over the sight that none of us thought to take a picture of this miraculous vision. Mom was right — I had seen a killer whale in the sky.

After Mom's death, Richard didn't see the need to remain in L.A. He was ready to move again. He originally wanted to move to Reno, Nevada, but I didn't want to move to a place that far away. I compromised, saying that Las Vegas was still Nevada, but not as far away as Reno. There was no way that I was going to convince Richard to buy a home in L.A. especially when the homes were so much more affordable in Vegas. Besides, I told myself, maybe now with his son moving to Nevada and with the two of us having our first real home together, Richard would finally be happy, and we could concentrate on having a baby together.

As fate would have it, while we were in Vegas picking out blinds and carpeting for our brand new home, Los Angeles was hit with another major quake. When we returned to Burbank, the only thing that was broken was our television, which had flown across the room. The only reason nothing else was damaged was because all our things were pretty much packed in Bubble Wrap, ready for the move. I instantly recalled the earthquake the morning after our wedding in Vegas, and now, as we were returning to Vegas, the prelude was *another* quake. Could it have been mere coincidence that the only thing that had been damaged was symbolic of the career I was leaving behind?

CHAPTER TWENTY-THREE

Finding My Way
Back Home

When we moved to Vegas, we tried our best to make it work. We had a new home; Richard's son moved in with us; we held barbeques, swam in our pool, enjoyed wonderful buffets at the Golden Nugget, watched movies and NBA basketball (I was for the Lakers, Richard was for the Trail Blazers), played games, and even welcomed four kittens that were flown in from New Jersey. All this and more could really only mimic the happiness each of us was unable to attain from our music within. We had tried to breathe life back into a marriage that did not have any more lung capacity.

Las Vegas was difficult for both of us, and I share the responsibility for my unhappiness. My struggle with addiction to meds, as well as the grief and depression that seeped from my pores, played a part in the breakdown of our union. However, if Richard perceived that the failure of our marriage was my fault, then he is in denial about his lion's share of the collapse. Richard did no drugs per se, but I believe Richard's drug was his anger and sharp tongue. Neither one of us was a victim. We both made the choices we made, regardless of *why* we made them. My depression was borne of the unhappiness I felt as part of a marriage I *wanted* to work, but it suffered from Richard's outbursts. He got angry with me, which made me more depressed, which made him even angrier. It was a vicious cycle.

Looking back, I think that sometimes Richard's anger was justified. For example, about two weeks before we had gotten married, I got a call from my friend Mac asking me if I would meet him at Budget Rent-A-Car and rent him a car for three days. I had known Mac for a long time and remembered when he let me live with him for a while after my apartment was broken into in 1985. Although I was uncomfortable putting this expense on my credit card, I thought it was relatively harmless, as it was only renting a car for three days. Mac promised me that he would transfer the expense to another card he was getting from his father. However, unbeknownst to me, the only transfer that was made was Mac upgrading the car, which I also paid for with my card.

A friend of Mac's worked at Budget and arranged things so the entire time that I was renting Mac a car, the charges would not yet show up on my credit card statement. Soon after, Mac showed up at my wedding uninvited, having driven from Los Angeles to Vegas in the car I was still paying for (even though I didn't know it). I think the reason he chose to do that was to make it look like he was my friend, buying some time before he figured out what to do about getting the car onto another credit card.

About a month and a half later, I was notified by Budget that I had stolen a car, and that they were going to sue me for grand theft. This was the first time Richard had learned that I had even rented a car for Mac and was rightfully furious that I could have been so gullible. From the get-go, he hadn't liked Mac and couldn't understand how I didn't see his flawed character. I always want to see the good in people — including Richard — but I have learned that seeing the good in people shouldn't mean turning a blind eye to the "not so good" part.

The incident with Mac went to court, and it ended up being a huge victory for me in being able to stand up for myself. The car in question had been totaled by Mac, so now I was not only being sued for almost two months of car rental, but also for the entire cost of the car. Richard told me I didn't stand a chance in a court of law, and that I should just cut a deal with Budget, but I refused. I was so sick of being taken advantage of. As a matter of principle, I fought. I ended up winning in court, only having to pay Budget $100 for a three-day car rental. The judge agreed that because I had never been notified by Budget that the car had been upgraded after three days, any further financial liability was a moot issue. His exact words to Budget were, "Money is money, and business is business. My heart breaks for you, but go find Mac if you can." I don't know if Budget ever found Mac, but I gratefully never saw him again.

Although I'd been excited about having Richard's son living with us in Las Vegas, the new arrangement had its share of problems. He was a teenager and had issues with his dad that went way back, long before me. I was left with his son most of the time while we lived in Vegas because Richard was booked far more than I was, and my stepson dealt with his frustrations in much the same angry way that his father did. I loved him dearly, but it was so hard dealing with the anger from both of them. The eggshells I'd already been walking on were starting to crack.

Physically, I was also declining, going from neurosurgeon to neurosurgeon, begging for pain relief. No one wanted to operate, as such invasive surgery on top of cerebral palsy had to be an absolute last resort. BOTOX was not even considered an option for chronic pain in the early '90s, so the only thing that was available to me that I could afford with our health insurance was physical therapy (which I was doing) and the old-fashioned way of dealing with pain through muscle relaxants and painkillers. For the first time in my life, I owned a wheelchair to use for long distances and was feeling as though I was losing my fight to remain physically capable. The drugs and my faltering marriage didn't help me get a handle on my physical pain. In fact, they made it a lot worse.

I was also dealing with the grief of losing my mom, and as my dad began to reinvent himself after my mom's death, I felt like I was losing him, too. I was so looking forward to strengthening my bond with him, but unfortunately he was not able or willing to bond with his own kids. Sadly, I didn't really begin to have a relationship with him again until 1999. The years prior to that were wasted by my father's stubbornness in not being able to admit that he may have been wrong in the way he treated us. I felt mostly sad for my sister and my brothers, as I think they were hurt the most.

My father and every single one of his brothers were so abused as children by their own dad that their psyches were permanently damaged. All of my cousins on his side of the family have Jewell stories. The most hurtful incident that happened between my father and me was when he called me in Las Vegas in 1995 and told me that he wanted me to pick up all my childhood pictures. I told him to just hang onto them until I made a trip to California, but he said he would only hold onto them for a little while. I was told to come and get them or he would get rid of them. As insane as it sounds, I drove five hours to Laguna Nigel to pick up my pictures. When I rang his doorbell, he answered the door with a box of pictures in his arms marked, GERI. I smiled and said, "Aren't you even going to ask me in?"

In a nutshell, my father had a feud going on with Gloria, and if the rest of us didn't take his side, we were on his shit list. Of course, my father had always been this way, but after Mom died, he had no one to anchor him. He remarried and for the most part started over, with his new wife mostly unaware of his prior life.

We walked into his office where I forced him to sit down, as I sorted through the GERI box of pictures. True to the label, there were only Geri pictures in it.

"Dad, what about some family pictures of all of us?"

He was not willing to give me any of those. He said that after he died, he would give them to Fred (the golden child at that moment). Over the years, I had resized childhood photos and put them in nice frames as gifts to my parents. The pictures were all in the box, minus the frames. I pulled out a picture of me at the White House, shaking Nancy Reagan's hand. "You don't want this?"

"No, I don't. I am not a Republican." A part of my father's reinvention was denying that he ever was a Republican; his new wife was a diehard Democrat. Then I spotted a picture of me performing at the Comedy Store.

"Dad, this was a gift to you!"

"It was a long time ago, Geri. You don't want it?"

"No, Dad, I don't want it. I wanted you to have it." I handed it back to him, and right before my eyes, he put the picture through the electric shredder. The sight of my father shredding my photo as if it were a piece of junk mail broke my heart. I knew my father loved me, but his callous indifference — one that had been ingrained in him by his own father's similar dismissive attitude — was still painful.

There is a theory that women have a tendency to marry men like their fathers, and I believe that is exactly what I did in marrying Richard. Richard, like my father, endured so much pain as a child that he subconsciously relived it again and again through all three of his marriages, mine being his third. All three of us wives dealt with Richard's rage in one way or another. However, we all loved him as well. There is a part of Richard that is wonderful, otherwise I would have not fallen so deeply in love with him in the first place. The problem with both Richard and my father was that neither man loved himself. If we cannot truly love and respect ourselves, then we will never be able to fully love and respect a partner.

I was also clinging to a relationship with someone instead of fully healing my own pain and suffering. Relationships of this nature rarely last. It is only the diversions that keep them going. It seemed fitting that we lived in Vegas; our marriage was a gamble, and every now and then we'd hit three sevens and there'd be a momentary reward and happiness. One of our jackpots was the four Japanese bobtail kittens we adopted and had flown to Vegas from the breeder in New Jersey. I had always loved cats, but Richard was allergic to them. He'd heard that 90 percent of people who are allergic to cats in general are not allergic to Japanese bobs. Luckily, the gamble paid off.

We did not get all four of them at once, but rather two at time. Max and Eloise were the first. They were both born on Valentine's Day and lived up to the sweet nature that is typical of the breed. These two precious babies added so much joy to our household, buffering the tension. I also came to accept that having the kitties was about as close as I was ever going to come to having a child of my own. Richard didn't want to be a father again, and I realized I had been foolish to believe that it was ever going to happen.

I became friends with my next-door neighbor, Linda, and cherished her friendship and support. She had three small boys of her own, the youngest born shortly after we moved in. In fact, today I am friends with her oldest son, Nick, who was eight when I lived next door. He emailed me years later, telling me how much I had influenced him as a kid. Long after I had moved from Vegas, Nick was diagnosed with Tourrette's syndrome and went through tremendous pain and anxiety. From the time he was a boy, he wanted to be an actor and still wanted to pursue a career in film. Because of me, he was going on to college to major in film. I cried when I read his letter because I realized that even when I was in the grips of grief and despair that God was still working through me, inspiring Nick.

There was little inspiration in our own home; instead threere was mostly anger and a desire to escape. Richard was a big spender, and I was constantly trying to get him to spend less. One prime example of this was when we bought a pool for our small yard. We were sitting at the table with the pool salesman, and as the salesman pitched Richard on the advantages to upsizing the pool, ours got bigger by the minute. I took Richard aside and told him we didn't need *that big* of a pool! I wanted a little room for a yard too. But instead . . . we bought Lake Mead.

It was a sore spot, because I was home every day watching it being built, and Richard was on the road, oblivious. I remember him calling me one afternoon, asking me how the pool was coming, and I told him that when you open the sliding glass door in the dining room, you'd better watch your first step! The size of our pool was a big issue, because everything associated with it would cost more; symbolically it represented the size of our discontent.

I remember noticing when we went to pick out the tiles for our pool how expensive they were. I spotted these cute dolphin tiles that we could put at the bottom of the pool. I actually wanted an orca in honor of my mom, but they didn't have any. When I saw the price of each dolphin, however, I realized we could only afford one. It was kind of funny seeing this big pool that had one little dolphin swimming by itself at the bottom of the deep end. Sometimes I'd look at that little dolphin and see myself in the deep water, feeling alone too.

I came to loathe Vegas almost as much as Richard loathed L.A. Because Richard always worked more than I did, I battled the same loneliness that I had when I lived in Vancouver, Washington. I didn't have any social outlet, and believe it or not, I didn't have a computer either. Richard did, but I didn't dare touch it for fear of breaking it.

Instead, I spent hours zoning out with PlayStation video games and playing draw poker in the grocery store. (Even grocery stores were in on the gambling in Vegas — "Hmm, I need to buy groceries . . . but if I take my grocery money and put it on draw poker instead, I could buy even *more* groceries!") I worked when I could, even doing comedy at the Improv in Vegas. I did an episode of *New Adventures of Lassie*, and worked on the road through Richard's company, but most of the time I was at home in Vegas. This was my life, and as I became more and more depressed, I reached for the numbing meds.

In 1996, I got two more kitties from New Jersey, again for the same reason unhappy couples have children, thinking the new baby will make all the pain go away. In our case, it just added more cat shit. I was already thinking that our marriage was going to end, and in my desire to make it as painless as possible, I figured Richard could have two cats, and I could have two cats. Even though my thinking was really ridiculous, all four of our cats, Eloise, Max, Joey, and Norma Jean provided me with more love and healing than I ever thought possible.

In 1998, I finally separated from Richard and moved back to Los Angeles. The dysfunction had to stop somewhere. Even though I had considered leaving Richard long before 1998, I didn't because there was always something that occurred that I just couldn't walk away from. First, one of Richard's lungs collapsed, and I just couldn't leave him. Then he developed diabetes and was going through a lot of issues with his teenaged son. When I finally did leave Vegas in 1998, it was not a choice that I made, but rather a choice that Richard made. We had gotten in another heated argument, and at some point Richard snapped. He told me that the marriage was over, and that I had to leave. He was very emotional, explaining that no matter what I did or said, it would piss him off. He was afraid that he would actually physically hurt me, and he knew that I didn't deserve it. I was already intimidated by his bark; I didn't want to see what his bite was like. I left.

Truthfully, me leaving our home instead of him was the best case scenario, because I didn't feel attached to it in any way. I'd never wanted to leave Los Angeles in the first place, so it made sense that I would be the one to return. The only thing that really upset me later was when I discovered through the grapevine that Richard told people that I had abandoned him; to the contrary, the Richard I'd fallen in love with had abandoned the Richard he now was.

After we separated, he dated other women, and I encouraged it because I felt that I was never completely there for him sexually, that maybe it was better to allow him to find someone who would make him happy. I'm not sure what I expected to be accomplished from this. I still loved him deeply, but knew I couldn't live with him. Also, guilt and fear ruled my emotions, and I was beating myself up for everything that was wrong in our marriage. I know now that just as it is wrong to blame someone else for everything, it is also wrong to blame ourselves for everything. Nothing constructive comes out of it either way.

I moved into a one-bedroom in the Park La Brea Apartments, a famous old Hollywood landmark, with some of the apartments refurbished from the '30s and '40s. I moved into a twelfth-floor unit even though it was not the wisest thing to do. I had brought two of my kitties with me, Eloise and Joey, and so I didn't want the only other apartment they had available on the first floor. The thought of my babies accidentally getting out was a greater fear than being physically trapped by a fire or a broken elevator.

While I was living at Park La Brea, Blaine Moss, my dear friend and teacher from Troy High, called me to say a former student from Troy was looking for me and passed along his number. The student was Tim Prager from my drama classes. Tim was the one who shook me on the Jeep in *The Teahouse of the August Moon.*

Tim was now a successful film writer in London. He was working on a project in the U.K. with his friend and colleague, British actor and producer Anthony Andrews of *Brideshead Revisited* fame. Tim had received a script written by Alex Martinez. It was the fictional story of a young girl with cerebral palsy who rebels, leaves home, and becomes a stand-up comic. It was based on the story of his daughter Francesca, who was experiencing some fame as a young actress in the U.K. Francesca, who also has CP, shares a similar journey with me, as she was the first actress with a disability to star in a BBC television series. The series was *Grange Hill*, a popular teen show equivalent to *The Facts of Life* in the United States.

Tim was amazed by the similarities in Alex's script to my life and used me as an example when trying to sell the script to Anthony Andrews. Initially, Andrews had scoffed at the idea of someone with CP being a comic, and felt that Alex's story was unbelievable at best. Tim was determined to acquaint Anthony with me, and they both flew to Los Angeles to see me perform at the Ice House Comedy Club in Pasadena.

Even though I was not well, as usual, I was able to pull a rabbit out of a hat onstage. All good performers know that no matter what else is going on, it must all be put on the back burner when performing. I did a great show that night, and two months later, Anthony flew me to London to advise and consult on Alex's script. He also wanted me to meet Francesca and coach her on what it is like to really be a stand-up comic.

It was the first time I had ever been to the United Kingdom. Had it been any other point in my life, I would have had a great time. I even got to meet Tim's wife and his son, who also has cerebral palsy. I loved Francesca and her family and saw a very young version of myself in her. We all went to a comedy club together in London and had a blast. However, for whatever reason, the project never took off and there were no future trips to London. Alex's script was never produced, but Francesca was inspired by me and went on to be an incredibly successful stand-up comic in the U.K. To this day, she performs all over the world. Francesca was actually born the same year I stepped onto the stage at the Comedy Store for the first time, and 20 years later, in 1998, she met me, and the course of her life changed because of it. So, her father's script was actually the vehicle that took his daughter to the next level. I couldn't be more proud of her. Not only is she an incredibly talented performer and writer, but a beautiful, kind soul, and I feel blessed that our paths crossed.

I will always hold Tim Prager dear to my heart, not only for remembering me, but also for introducing me to Anthony Andrews. Anthony is a very sensitive person, and in 1998 he knew intuitively that I was in deep trouble. He put me up at the Kensington Palace Hotel, which overlooks Hyde Park and the Palace Gardens. Had I made the trip a few months earlier, the whole area would have been covered with flowers that were placed in memory of Princess Diana. I spent four days and five nights there. Usually, London is damp and cold, but the week I was there it was experiencing a rare heat wave, and as I walked in agonizing pain from my neck and back, my clothes became soaking wet with sweat. I carried just 103 pounds on my five-foot-three frame, and I was weak and easily became out of breath.

It was obvious to most people that my health was in serious need of intervention, but my new friends in London were hardly in a position to help me. I had one free day before I was to fly home, and I chose to walk through the streets of London by myself. I didn't have much money, but I wanted to get a souvenir. I walked into an athletic sports shop that sold rollerblades, skateboards, and roller skates. As I looked around, I suddenly saw this beautiful pair of black skates in front of me. I couldn't take my eyes off them. I looked at them with the eyes of a child, remembering when I could physically roller skate (even if it put a giant yellow bird in peril). Thoughts of my bicycle and my skateboard went through my mind, and I could remember every fiber of my being telling myself that I would learn how to do these things in spite of cerebral palsy. Then my eyes welled up with tears, knowing that I didn't have that ability any longer. I wondered if my life was ending.

I bought the skates to remind myself what I could accomplish if I set my mind to it. I had to somehow find that will and determination that I had lost. I had allowed myself to be beaten up by life. My sense of humor had even become stale, and I didn't know if I would be able to find my way back to that little girl who believed anything was possible. I also didn't believe that I could ever be out of physical pain, and the fear of living with it became great and daunting.

Anthony, Tim, Francesca, and everyone else was stunned that I had made such a purchase, joking that they'd hoped I bought a helmet, knee pads, and elbow pads. I laughed and said that I had no intention of trying them out in Hyde Park and might never try them out, but they were so beautiful I just had to buy them. To any outside observer, I acted insane, but I was only trying to hold onto something that at one time had empowered me.

The next morning, Anthony picked me up at the hotel to drive me to Heathrow Airport. When he saw me carrying the skates, he assumed that there had not been room for them in my luggage. He offered to ship them to me, but I told him I was holding onto them so I could place them in the overhead compartment. That is when Anthony realized how important the skates were to me. He stayed with me until I boarded the plane. He hugged me and told me never to give up my dreams. When the plane took off, I wept because I wasn't sure if I had any dreams left.

As I took the twelve-hour trip back to Los Angeles, I thought about all the blessings that I had experienced up to that point in my life. I fondly recalled a time in 1987 when I had the pleasure of meeting Flip Wilson. I was booked at a rehabilitation conference in Puerto Rico, and Gloria had come with me. He was invited to the show by my friend Michael Bainbridge, and to my surprise, Flip came! Afterward, I spent some time with him, enjoying many stories that he shared with me. He told me that he understood the battles I'd been through being the first disabled comic in Hollywood, since he'd been the first black star on television. He told me how difficult it is to be the first one, because our doors are the heaviest. I told him how Carol Burnett inspired me, and he removed a gold lighter from his pocket that was engraved with her name, a gift from *The Carol Burnett Show*. He told me he always carried it with him. On my way to the airport to fly home, I bumped into him one last time in front of the hotel. I reached in my pocket and gave Flip a simple crystal heart, which I carried with me for good luck, and thanked him for coming to my show and spending time with me.

Three weeks later, his son had knocked on my door and said that he had a gift for me from his father. When I opened it up, I was overwhelmed. It was a beautiful sapphire pendant with several smaller sapphires surrounding it in a heart shape. His son told me Flip was so touched by the little heart I had given him that he wanted to give me something special too. He said that it was originally a ring that he wore, but he had taken it to a jeweler and had it redesigned as a pendant so that I could wear it. The beauty of the gift and the sentiment had brought tears to my eyes, and now, as I flew back from London, my face was tear-stained once again as I remembered promising Flip that I would never give up.

CHAPTER TWENTY-FOUR

My Ground Zero

Returning home from London was not something that I really wanted to do. I can relate to people who just walk away from their lives and start over, disappearing completely from the lives they once knew. It is a fantasy many have had when faced with daunting circumstances. However, we can't really run away from our problems, no matter how much we'd like to. Our problems will catch up to us in one way or another, whether it is in this lifetime or another. It is best to face the music, no matter how difficult or painful the lyrics may be.

I came home to the reality that divorce was imminent, but I was not clear-minded or strong enough to know how to bring about that change in the healthiest way possible. I tried to talk to Richard, but my fear of his anger got in the way of being as strong as I needed to be to speak the truth. I was also wracked with enormous physical pain, which always clouded my judgment. I ended up in the hospital overnight when I thought that I had taken too many Somas and my therapist sent an ambulance to come and get me. However, I was actually suffering from acute anxiety. I was sent home the next day.

I did overmedicate, as I had done before when I lived in Vegas, but never to the point of passing out or having my stomach pumped. I did, however, on occasion take enough meds to scare the hell out of me and flirt with the possibility of not waking up once I fell asleep. I thank God that never happened, because I know that death is not the answer. The only answer is to have the courage to keep moving forward.

My kitties Joey and Eloise were a source of tremendous unconditional love upon my return from the U.K., but I still failed to get a handle on my emotions regarding Richard. We had one therapy session in Los Angeles, but it was a disaster; I had gone into the session with the intention of standing up to him, saying that I was afraid of his temper and his bullying, and that the only way for us to live together again was if he got some ongoing counseling himself. I thought that with my therapist in the same room, I would not be afraid to confront him.

However, the moment we were together in that room, I suddenly felt intimidated again. I remember feeling that it would be "easier" just to say the marriage was over because I was gay. My fear of making him angry by saying anything that made him look bad was greater than the pain I'd cause myself by sucking up all the blame. I knew it was cowardly and realized I was wasting my one therapeutic window.

My being gay wasn't the issue, as there was no other woman in the picture. I had simply wanted Richard to look at *himself* and accept his own part in the downfall of our relationship, so that we could begin to piece it back together again. But I blew it.

I was angry with my therapist, who didn't challenge me to go deeper while Richard sat right there. Couldn't she see how intimidated I was by him? Years later I recognized that she couldn't do the work for me — I had to stand up to him myself, and I simply couldn't. When Richard left that day and drove back to Vegas, I knew there would be no going back. What I didn't know, however, was that I was about to experience more physical pain than I ever had imagined possible.

As usual, my old friend Tony was there for me, often coming over to keep me company, and help me with the laundry and the cleaning. I was so weak and in so much physical pain that these things were difficult for me to do. He also went grocery shopping for me and forced me to eat some good food. I was eating very little; I had lost my appetite for life and was so depressed that all I wanted to do was sleep. Other friends came by and tried to help, but they knew that prayer was the most important help they could offer me. My family didn't know what had happened to me — Gloria was in Laguna and could not check up on me as frequently as she would have wished.

Then, one evening, I called Blaine Moss, my friend and teacher from high school. I was wailing, telling him that I didn't know how to survive anymore. I told him that all my dreams were gone, that my career was over, Mom was gone, Dad was no longer proud of me, and my marriage to Richard was totally fucked up. Blaine had always been a "matter of fact" kind of a friend who told me the truth as he saw it. He told me that my dreams were gone only because I'd stopped believing in myself.

I asked him how I could believe in myself again when my own dad didn't believe in me. He told me that my father's beliefs should have no bearing on my own, and that everything I was looking for in others had to come from within.

"But . . ."

"But nothing, Geri. You have got to get well and get off the prescription meds."

"How can I do that when I am in so much physical pain?" By now I was sobbing.

"Geri, I've known you since 1971, and you have time and again beaten all the odds against you. You are one of the strongest human beings I have ever met. I do not know what the answer is in regard to the physical pain that you're in, but whatever you are doing now obviously isn't working."

I stood up as the conversation was coming to a close. However, I was on so much medication that I lost my balance. On the floor behind me were my skates, where I had carelessly left them next to a large box. Somehow I had managed to flip backward over both items, landing on my head (with the phone still in my hand). Blaine was still talking to me, totally unaware that I had fallen so hard. I was really sobbing now, but not for the same reason. I felt my neck crunch under my own weight and realized that I may have broken my neck. I should have said something, but I didn't tell Blaine what had just happened. I figured, he was 65 miles away, what could he possibly do? Why worry him more than he was already worried about me?

I hung up the phone and continued to lie on the floor with Joey and Eloise staring at me. My head and neck hurt badly, and the fingers of my left hand were going numb. I didn't know it yet, but I also had a concussion. My thinking was definitely skewered, I didn't even realize the severity of what had just happened. I should have called an ambulance, but I didn't. I had been in so much pain before the fall, I just had the attitude that pain was pain, so I alleviated it in the same habitual way that I had for so long: I took more Somas and went to sleep.

I think every guardian angel must have tended to me while I slept, because it is a miracle that I even woke up, much less that I was able to get out of bed and walk. I fed my babies and casually called my doctor, requesting an appointment. She saw me the next day. She would have seen me immediately had I told her of my fall, but I didn't mention it until I saw her face to face. Maybe I was worried all my meds would come to a halt. That was just too much to bear at the time — it would mean that I had to admit to myself that I was a drug addict. I already loathed myself as it was.

To see myself in an even more pathetic light was too painful, especially if there was nothing to numb my vision.

However, I had no choice but to face the reality the next day. My doctor was alarmed by my stark weight loss and saw how weak I had become in only a three-month period. I told her the truth, and she was furious with me for not telling her earlier. I had an MRI immediately, and it was discovered that in that fall, I had not only cracked discs in my neck, but I had also bruised my spinal cord in four places. She then sent me to Dr. Leo Treciokas, who was doing marvelous work with BOTOX as a treatment for chronic pain. Between my doctor and Dr. Treciokas, I was able to be pushed up the ladder to get in to see one of the best neurosurgeons in the country, Dr. J. Patrick Johnson.

I did let Richard know what was going on, but I knew I needed more support than he was able or willing to provide. I called my sister Gloria and she went with me, as she had done before, when we had looked for a neuro-surgeon. Dr. Johnson let both of us know that he was willing to do the surgery on me and that he felt confident that he could save my spinal cord. He had seen my MRI and X-rays prior to our first meeting and remarked that he would have never guessed that the neck that he just looked at belonged to such a young person. From the looks of my prematurely aged bones, he said that he would have thought he was going to meet someone in her seventies.

Because of my cerebral palsy, the surgery would be a hundred times more complex. Although he had previously done other neck surgeries on people with CP, each one was different with its own set of circumstances. I was sur-prised at how many people with CP had neck surgery, but have discovered since that it is quite common because the neck is often worn down by all the involuntary movement associated with CP.

There is a wide range of severity with CP, but regardless of the range, pain is always a part of the CP experience. The only thing that varies is *when* it becomes painful and *how* painful it is. The pain can be debilitating for some, and, unfortunately, alternative medicine and therapies that could be viable solutions are not taken seriously and not covered by most healthcare providers. After all, pharmaceutical companies *love* people with disabilities. . . .

In any case, I was about to go under the knife and I was scared. Dr. Johnson was concerned about how weak I was, and wanted me to gain at least 10 pounds before I had surgery. He told me that because I had bruised my spinal cord, I could also become paralyzed. Without surgery, I would most definitely become paralyzed, and with surgery there was still a risk of paralysis. He was one of the best surgeons that I could have gotten, and I was blessed that I was able to find him.

Gloria helped me move out of Park La Brea and into her house, putting most of my belongings into storage. She kept enough of my things to make her guest bedroom homier for me. She also took me back to Dr. Leo Treciokas to get BOTOX injections in my neck and shoulders to alleviate some of my chronic pain. The most important thing to me at the time was to regain my strength so I could undergo invasive surgery. I had to drink tons of Ensure and eat, eat, eat. My sister even lovingly took in Eloise and Joey to live with her in Laguna. Gloria already had two cats of her own, Elliott and Bob, so her home was fast becoming an animal (and sister) rescue center.

My surgery was scheduled a week before Mother's Day in 1999. Gloria took me to UCLA for pre-op and surgery at about 6:30 in the morning. Before I went under, Gloria's smile was the last thing I saw. For whatever reason, Richard never conferred with any of the doctors and was in Vegas or on the road working when I had surgery. We were still married, but we had been separated for almost a year and there was so much tension still between us that maybe it was better that he wasn't there. During pre-op, they removed the only two pieces of jewelry that I was wearing — my mom's wedding band and my own — which made me sad.

I found it interesting to be back at UCLA. The first time I was there I was diagnosed with cerebral palsy at a symposium in 1958. Now, 41 years later, I was back at UCLA, diagnosed with a damaged neck and about to undergo surgery and then begin therapy to learn how to walk again. It was as if I was being given a second chance at life. I had absolutely reached my bottom and the climb back to health was one of the most challenging of my life.

The first person I saw when I woke up after over eight hours of surgery was Dr. Johnson. He was right there, welcoming me back. Normally after this kind of operation, I would have been in a halo with screws into my head, but I don't think I deserved a halo for anything, and another screw in my head really wasn't necessary. Seriously, however, Dr. Johnson opted against the halo because of my cerebral palsy. I had so much involuntary movement from CP that the halo would have been like Chinese torture. So, for at least a couple of days, I was only in a neck brace.

It was decided that I would be kept heavily sedated with muscle relaxants and strong pain meds, but my muscle spasms were so severe that my entire body felt agonizing pain. The doctors then custom-built me a brace that went from my chin to the bottom of my torso. I could not even move my left arm for months because of the pain. I had to be fed my meals. I could walk, but I was very unsteady, because I wasn't used to walking with my neck and head frozen in one position, not to mention how weak I was.

I had learned to walk as a child by using all my CP movement as a rhythm to develop balance. With that rhythm taken away, my brain had to learn a whole new way to compensate if I was ever going to balance myself well enough to walk again. I was so frustrated, angry, and impatient with the process of healing. Every time I went to sleep at night, I hoped that it was time to let go, but each morning I was awakened to another tray of disgusting hospital food and a can of Ensure. The nurse would put a straw in it and lift it to my lips. I sucked it in, but not without reciting the lines from the famous *I Love Lucy* episode, "Vitameatavegamin": "And it's so tasty too!"

I was at UCLA for two weeks before I was transferred to a rehabilitation hospital in Inglewood. The entire time I was there, Gloria drove up from Laguna every single day to visit and advocate for me. One of the funniest things she did was put a huge sign above my head that read: I AM HEARING IMPAIRED! IF YOU HAVE SOMETHING TO SAY TO ME, PLEASE MAKE SURE THAT I HEARD WHAT YOU SAID BEFORE YOU LEAVE THE ROOM! THANK YOU KINDLY.

No one could have done more for me than my sister, and from 1999 through 2003 her own life was basically put on hold while she cared for me. Friends came to see me when they could, including Fern Field Brooks, Kathy Buckley, Natoma Keir, and Lynda Jean Groh. Even Randy Bradley from grade school and my dear friend Chad Everett came to see me when I was transferred to Inglewood. Norman Lear called me when he found out through Fern Field what I was going through. My brother David flew in from Minneapolis to see me, and even my dad finally came to see me after my Aunt Mary gave him hell for not doing so. I will never forget one day when he was holding my hand at UCLA when Dr. Johnson walked in. He introduced himself as my dad and still holding my hand, with tears in his eyes, he said, "Thank you for saving my baby girl's life."

It was probably the sweetest thing I *ever* heard my dad say and even as I am writing this now, I have tears in my eyes. It is one memory that proved to me without a doubt, no matter how hurtful my father could be, he loved me. I felt his gratitude in that moment. I felt genuinely loved by my dad that day, and I didn't have to do anything but be alive.

If there was ever a time when I needed Richard the most, it was at this time, but in the two weeks that I was at UCLA and the following two weeks that

I was in Inglewood, I saw him only three times. The only support he gave me at the time was paying for my health insurance. Other than that, I just dealt with his angry outbursts over the phone. I was too fragile to fight to save our relationship, and Richard was too angry to want to save it himself.

I did make good progress at Inglewood, but the insurance company would not cover a longer stay. That was a huge obstacle because it was so obvious that at least two to four more weeks would have made a significant difference in my recovery. They gave me two options: enter a cheaper nursing care facility, or obtain outpatient therapy and live in a private home. Gloria ended up rescuing me again. My rehabilitation team took a van from Inglewood to Laguna to inspect the premises and make sure that it was suitable for further recovery. My sister's home was perfect, as it was one level and Gloria was willing to install handrails in the shower for me.

I moved back in with Gloria and used my wheelchair until I was better able to balance myself without falling. I took Access Transportation to physical therapy twice a week, and Gloria drove me to Santa Monica to get BOTOX and meet with Dr. Johnson for follow-ups. I tried to the best of my ability to get well, but at times it seemed like such an uphill battle. The muscle spasms were agonizing, and I was back on meds again because the pain was so severe. I was prescribed an antidepressant, but it merely took the edge off. I was still battling depression and didn't have any idea where my life was going. And on top of *everything* else, after surgery I never had another period . . . as if I wasn't dealing with enough, I had to endure the change of life too!

I had bills up the yin yang and no income to pay them. Gloria paid all my monthly bills after I moved out of Park La Brea. Before I went into the hospital, Richard filed his taxes separately. So, on top of everything else, I had not filed my 1998 taxes. My financial nightmare had only just begun. My insurance company would not cover BOTOX, so that was coming out of my pocket. I was finally able to be reimbursed $11,000 five years later, but during this time of financial stress I was paying for it up front. Richard gave me $3,800 at one point and continued to pay for my health insurance, but he claimed that he could not afford to do more, as he was struggling financially himself. I accepted that and went on Social Security/Disability. I dreaded this, but I really didn't have a choice. In hindsight, I should have just filed bankruptcy, but it didn't even occur to me as an option.

On December 1, 2000, only six months after the spinal cord surgery, I entered a 30-day drug rehab facility. I had called my dear friend Billy Barty, who, like his wife, had undergone multiple surgeries throughout his lifetime. They both suffered tremendous physical pain from the form of dwarfism they had. I told Billy that I wanted to get off all prescription drugs and asked him if he knew which rehab facility was the best. He was honest, saying that although my desire was admirable, he felt that because I had not yet completely healed from the surgery that I may be rushing things a bit. But, knowing how stubborn I was, he named a few facilities that he felt were good.

I called the Betty Ford Center first, but just as Billy told me, they felt that I was rushing things and would not accept me. Not only was I trying to get off pain medication while I was still in pain, but they also mentioned I was too much of a physical liability issue, and that they were not equipped to handle physical recovery from neck surgery combined with cerebral palsy. Even though I was warned twice, I would not abandon my quest for drug rehab. I finally found a facility that would accept me, but to this day I have mixed feelings about that experience.

I think one of the reasons I was so determined to enter rehab when I did was because in my mind it was an escape hatch. I felt horrible about being such a burden on Gloria and was at a complete loss with Richard. Christmas was around the corner, and I didn't want to celebrate it. In my childlike mind, I was looking at rehab as a sort of respite and I could just focus on being drug-free. However, as with any 12-step program, there is more than one step — I was kidding myself in thinking that one of those steps was running away from reality.

I believe in the 12-step program, but only if one of the steps does not include rushing the healing process of *very real* spinal cord surgery. Also, rehab facilities need to be in compliance with the Americans with Disabilities Act, allowing people with physical disabilities to have reasonable accommodation. I remember one night early on, when they had given me something before I went to bed: I was in my room alone with no ability to call for help. I was vomiting all over myself and got out of bed, trying to reach the bathroom. I lost my balance and fell, still vomiting, and did not have the upper body strength to pull myself up again. I lay there for roughly 15 minutes before someone noticed me and alerted a nurse.

I had to fight with them about allowing me the use of a computer or an electric typewriter to keep up with all the written work, as the 12-step program requires a lot of writing and assignments from the classes we attended in the day. Handwriting has always taken longer for me because of CP so I tend to type instead. But it was explained to me that this was against the rules, that the act of writing was part of the therapeutic process, and also a part of the process was to ask for help with the writing from another patient. They told me it would give someone the opportunity to think of someone other than themselves. I countered that it fed into co-dependency because I wasn't able to write my own homework. In reality, both perceptions held some truth. I lucked out with an especially wonderful counselor, who helped me win this particular battle. Once I was allowed the laptop, I was able to finish assignments along with everyone else.

It was often difficult to determine the difference between a CP issue and a drug addiction issue. There were both going on, and sometimes they overlapped. I remember one night around 10:30 p.m. I had gotten up, unable to sleep because my right arm was affected by severe CP spasms. Unless you have ever had them, you cannot know how horrible they feel. My arm was flying all over the place just as it had done when I was a baby. I tried lying on top of it and holding onto it with my other arm, but nothing was slowing the movement down, and it was wreaking havoc on my poor neck.

I was sitting alone in the common area after being denied anything for my arm. As I was flipping channels, I caught the tail end of a TV movie, *The David Cassidy Story*. It was so eerie watching this movie from drug rehab, but just as I thought it couldn't get any sadder for me, it did. The 11 o'clock news reported the death of Billy Barty. I sat there and wept for at least 15 minutes. Then I charged into the nurses' station and said that I was checking out. As if it were some kind of a hotel, I thought I would just go outside and find a cab. They reminded me that I had no money, and I told them that I would pay them when I got to Laguna with a check, that I had money at home. I told them that Billy Barty had died, and I wanted to go to his service, and my arm was going nuts, and I needed a real fucking doctor! They told me to calm down, that in the morning I could ask my head doctor if I could go to the service.

At that point, I was beside myself with anger and frustration. I yelled that no one had committed me, that I came in here by my own free will and that I could leave the same way! It seemed every ounce of anger that I had carried around my entire life just oozed out of me. I sarcastically said that their arts and crafts class was equivalent to special education, and that I was sick of all their stupid ass rules and that the only reason they loved people with disabilities was because we were their meal ticket! I then stormed through the facility, trying to find an open door. If there was one, and there probably was, I didn't take notice of it because I was too upset and angry. I remember yelling something like, "Why don't you just wrap me in cellophane?!" Why cellophane? I think it was an easier vision for my mind to accept, as opposed to being in a straitjacket.

I was going through a complete meltdown, and every injustice that I felt I had endured in my life rose to the surface. Above all else, I felt powerless. I couldn't even walk through a door if I wanted to. I was angry with Richard, George, Jack, Jaymie, Daria, Dr. Sleeper, and *The Facts of Life*. I was angry with the special education system that tried to keep me pigeon-holed rather than help me achieve my goals. But mostly, I was angry with myself for not having enough self-worth to stand up for myself when I needed to. As much as rehab was a step in the right direction, I did enter for the wrong reason, and therefore, emotionally, it felt as though I were right back in special education, and *that* was mortifying for me.

After storming through the halls, I quietly gave up and slipped back into my room. I took all my clothes out of my locker and shoved them in my duffel bag. I tried to open the window to no avail. Then, of course, I felt powerless again. This is when overlapping takes place, because what I did next was definitely druggie behavior.

I decided that I was not going to allow these stupid night shift nurses to win. I was going to trick them into thinking that I had indeed found an open door and had gotten out. I found an empty bed and locker across the hall. When no one was looking, I took my duffel bag over there and then tiptoed back into my room. I made my bed and then climbed into my locker and shut the door. (Remember, after three months in an incubator and six months in Schimmel's closet, this locker was almost comforting.)

About 15 minutes later, my bedroom light went on; there were two nurses searching my room. They looked under my bed, in the bathroom, and in the shower. I could see them through the metal slats of my locker, and it was quiet enough that I heard the dialogue.

"I could have sworn I saw her come in here. . . ."

"No, all her things are gone. I don't know how she did it, but she got out . . . I'd better call the doctor and let him know."

I was trying not to breathe too loudly and was enjoying my momentary sense of power, even if it was a bit warped. Then before I could take another stifled breath, my locker door flew open. The nurse was smiling and yelled to the other nurse that he'd found me. "Come on, get out of there."

"No, I don't have to!"

"Geri, come out of the locker!"

"No, and you can't make me! Jeez, I am not taking drugs, drinking, or harming myself or anyone else. So what is it to you whether I stay in here or not? Leave me alone!"

"Okay, have it your way." He walked out of my room, shaking his head, and I am sure I got written up again. I was not allowed to go to Billy Barty's service and was crushed.

However, other times I was *clearly* out of line. For example, we had to attend classes all day, signing in each time. This rule struck me as funny, because I reasoned, "Where else could we possibly be?" I attended every single class, but I signed a different name each time: Marilyn Monroe, Rock Hudson, Mae West, James Dean, Elizabeth Taylor, and Frances Farmer. Okay, I was a comedienne, but it was pointed out to me that drug rehab was not the Comedy Store, and that I was doing a disservice to myself by not taking my rehabilitation seriously. However, I *was* also taking my sanity seriously, and I completed the 30-day program. My "Little Rehab on the Prairie" experience taught me some valuable things about addiction that I didn't know before, and even though it was rushed, I returned to Laguna Beach on January 2, 2000, and I was drug-free. I still had a long way to go, and still more challenges to face, but with rehab I proved to myself one more time that I was a survivor.

CHAPTER TWENTY-FIVE

The Three Ds:
Divorce, *Deadwood*, and Determination

Months before I even entered drug rehab, I was contacted by *E! True Hollywood Story* to be interviewed for a new installment entitled *"Facts of Life* Girls." I was torn, because I had no business doing something like this when I hadn't even healed from spinal cord surgery. I was still in a body brace, on meds, and in excruciating pain. However, it was my career (or what was left of it) and I didn't want to miss an opportunity to let the public know that I was still around. I asked production how long the interview would last, and they told me it wouldn't be longer than 20 minutes. What I did not stop to consider was the time involved to set up the cameras, and that I had only gotten out of the hospital five weeks earlier. Gloria did not think it was a good idea, but I overruled her decision.

Gloria helped me get dressed for the interview, as this was a task that I still struggled with. Just lifting my arms caused severe muscle spasms. Against the doctor's orders, I also removed the body brace because I wanted to look good on camera. As the minutes crawled by while the crew was setting up, my body screamed in pain. With no body brace to help restrict the involuntary movement, I had no choice but to take a pain pill and muscle relaxant. When they were *finally* ready to interview me, I was high and wished that I had just said no in the first place. Of course, by this point I had to follow through with the poor choice that I had made. Overall, the interview went fairly well, and I managed to hide most of my physical pain.

I thought the interview would consist mostly of reminiscing about the series, until a question came out of left field that I was entirely unprepared for: "At one point, you were quoted as saying that Charlotte Rae was like a mother to you, can you elaborate on your relationship with Charlotte?" That question caused more involuntary movement in one minute than I had previously had in all of my 43 years.

My physical pain halted filming, and Gloria came to my side, trying to calm me down. She whispered for me to just tell the truth. However, at that time, I was so emotionally and physically fragile that I really didn't know what the "truth" was. Had I not been on meds and thinking clearly, I would have simply stated the obvious, which was that I had *never* said that, that it simply wasn't my quote. I never had a mother/daughter relationship with Charlotte and I hadn't yet come to terms with any of the issues regarding *The Facts of Life*. I certainly did not want to bad-mouth Charlotte in any way and was trying to explain a very complex set of circumstances in a 30-second sound bite. I thought that by mentioning that she had difficulty relating to me because of having a son with a disability, that I was speaking an obvious truth for most parents, without going into the whole drama about Jaymie and the many individual misunderstandings I had with Charlotte as a result of Jaymie's manipulations. That one sentence ended up being a statement that Charlotte resented and caused even more issues with her than I had previously.

When another television tabloid show, *Truth Behind the Sitcoms: The Facts of Life*, interviewed me, again I felt ambushed, and my statement from the previous interview in 1999 came back to haunt me. It was brought up again, only this time Charlotte was allowed to react. The hurt feelings perpetuated a ridiculous dance of denial over what had really occurred during those years in question.

In 2009, I was approached again, this time by A&E's *Biography: The Facts of Life*. I foolishly tried to tell my story within the context of a television show that could use, or not use, whatever I said in any way they wanted to. I have nothing but respect for the producers of A&E's *Biography*, and based on what they had to work with, they were extremely fair. I was not on any drugs and I was clear-headed, but I still struggled with the pain of not being validated by what I had been through regarding *The Facts of Life*. My words were like lava, flowing from my mouth and seeming unstoppable. To be discounted and greatly misunderstood carries with it an overwhelming desire to be counted and respected.

Right before my interview was over, the producer informed me that Charlotte Rae was on her way up to the room and asked me if I would like to leave before her arrival. I told them that it wasn't necessary, and that I would love to see her, as I had not seen her since 1984. Truthfully, I welcomed the moment and was hoping that we could put our differences behind us. It was a bit awkward, with only greetings and small talk. Neither one of us quite knew what to say to the other. Things probably would have remained tense and awkward between us, except that something inside of me didn't want to leave things unspoken.

Before I left, I stepped into the bathroom where Charlotte was getting makeup. Sensing that we needed to be alone, the makeup artist left the room. Charlotte must have felt the same way I did, wanting to clear the air. She expressed how hurt she was by my comment on *E! Hollywood True Story*. I apologized for hurting her, as it was unintentional. She handed me an olive branch by expressing her desire for peace, forgiveness, and to move forward.

I wholeheartedly wanted the same thing and sincerely hope that by detailing all the pain that I had endured over the years regarding the chronicles of *The Facts of Life*, Charlotte can begin to understand my hurt feelings as well. For many years, I was angry and felt railroaded by the producers. I no longer harbor any anger. I only wish to be validated in that what happened to me was *very real*, and not the product of being a drama queen as Charlotte suggested in *Truth Behind the Sitcoms: The Facts of Life*. (Admittedly, I was a little bit of a drama queen at the time, so her perception wasn't *entirely* wrong.) I am sorry for the pain that we both endured and am grateful for the peace and forgiveness we have shared together.

But back in 2000, I was still reeling, healing, and feeling my way back into a world that had spun 180 degrees. I was living on disability, going to physical and psychological therapy, and getting BOTOX injections in my neck every three months for chronic pain. Until the middle of 2001, I was still wobbly and was horribly afraid of falling, so I was still using Access Transportation and my wheelchair. My upper body and arm strength were not what they used to be, and when I did fall (frequently) my head always went down first with nothing to brace the impact. Falling will always be a risk because I will *always* have cerebral palsy. However, I am a lot stronger now and have discovered ways to compensate and only use a wheelchair for long distances.

My new friend George Boley (whom I had met through a friend of Gloria's) was a godsend at this time in my life. His friendship absolutely helped me to get stronger, and he drove me to Las Vegas to retrieve my other two kitties, Max and Norma Jean. I admit I felt as though I was a cat burglar because I got them when Richard was out of town. It was not to be mean or selfish, but rather because the communication had so broken down by this time that I was fearful of derailment when facing him. Richard was furious that I had taken them, but he had also reamed me out when I had left them with him in the first place. I was damned if I did, and damned if I didn't.

I dragged my feet in filing for divorce, though, in part because I just wasn't strong enough emotionally to go through with it, but also because Richard had talked to me about how he had changed — that he no longer had a temper. Without me even bringing it up, he apologized for his angry outburst in Long Beach the night before my mother died. He said that he was willing to give our relationship another chance.

However, I didn't trust that he really had changed, and the last thing I wanted to do was to move back to Las Vegas. At no point did he mention that he would be willing to move to Los Angeles so he was still looking out for what was best for him. Also, I *finally* knew for sure that I never wanted to be with another man, that I was gay, and even in the best-case scenario, we could only be friends. I still loved him, but recognized the truth: we absolutely could not live together ever again.

When we went through the divorce proceedings, I asked only for the bare minimum, believing that he would understand that I wasn't trying to hurt him in any way, and only wanted what I believed was spiritually the right thing to do. When my attorney pointed out that by California law, I was entitled to half Richard's business, and that attorney fees were to be paid by Richard, I looked at Richard and felt guilty as he reminded me, "I told you, Jewell, that I would have to pay for the whole divorce!"

My attorney sensed that I was being manipulated and told me not to be intimidated, that it was the law and in my best interest, as I wasn't asking for much else. But, to me, it seemed only fair that everything be divided fifty-fifty regardless of the law. Even though I was legally entitled to half of his company and other things, all I wanted was: half the value of our home, giving him a huge window of time to sell it or buy me out (his choice), and to keep my health insurance active for at least two years after the divorce was finalized.

I've learned many lessons in life, but one of the most important is to truly forgive and move forward. Because there was so little emotional healing that occurred between my separation from Richard and my spinal cord surgery, there were many unresolved issues between Richard and myself. By the time *Music Within* was in the works, our ability to communicate was so broken down that there was no closure for me. There were so many unanswered questions in my heart and mind, and I felt as though I was forced into an unsettling silence that vacillated between grief, anger, unrequited love, and a feeling that Richard was ashamed about my being his ex-wife.

I can only hope that one day Richard will realize that I had always tried to do the right thing with him. I really never stopped loving him. And I will never forget what he said to me right before I moved out of our home in Las Vegas: "I tried to instill in you the ability to stop allowing people to walk all over you, to have self respect, and to stand up for yourself. I just never thought you'd be using those skills with me." But that was just the beginning; I have continued to stand up for myself ever since.

I lived with my sister, but I strived to live independently. Before going into rehab, I had had my driver's license renewed and had passed the road test. That was a small victory for me, because with a titanium neck, I hadn't been sure that I would be able to drive again. When I passed my test at the DMV, I was overjoyed. For me, it was very symbolic: one more step toward regaining my independence. I was soon becoming more confident to make the drive to Los Angeles from Laguna Beach, driving to my doctor appointments without Gloria, and staying with friends on some weekends, welcoming and appreciating the times spent socializing again.

On one memorable weekend, I was visiting my friend Lynda Jean, and traveled from her home in North Hills to Santa Monica for my 10:30 a.m. appointment with Dr. Leo Treciokas. As much as BOTOX is a tremendous relief from chronic pain, I dreaded going because the initial shots are always painful. I am usually right on time, or a little late, but I am *never* early. I took my time getting ready that morning, and thought about not even going at all. I was overwhelmed by physical pain, and was tired of my financial struggle.

Lynda Jean had left very early that morning, but left a pot of hot coffee for me and a sweet note, telling me to have a beautiful day. As I enjoyed my morning cup of coffee, I perused a book that Lynda had in her bathroom. It was a book of angels and saints, which explained how to pray to the right angel for specific needs. As I read about each angel, Archangel Michael caught my eye. He was the angel of *big* miracles. I knew I needed something big to happen to get me out of my current struggles. Even though I have always prayed daily, this time, I specifically asked Archangel Michael for his guidance.

I finally got in my car and headed toward Santa Monica on Interstate 405. Traffic was bumper to bumper, but I thought that by leaving Lynda's by 9:20 I would have enough time to pick up the BOTOX at the pharmacy, and get to Leo's office by 10:30. As I was standing in line at the pharmacy, an imposing gentleman in front of me turned around and told me that I could go ahead of him. Taking a second glance at me, he smiled and asked me if I was Geri Jewell. I answered that I was, but I was embarrassed because I was in so much pain and didn't look good.

He said that he was a huge fan of mine and told me how much he loved my comedy and that I had inspired him many times over the years. I thanked him for the compliment, but felt a little sad thinking of how long it had been since I'd last performed. I have had cerebral palsy all my life — I don't know what it would be like *not* to have it — and for years I hadn't felt like I had a disability at all because I'd proven that I could do anything I wanted. But now, with a titanium neck, I felt like I had a disability again, and I had lost a lot of my confidence. I didn't believe that I would ever be able to work in television again; I no longer felt strong enough to open the heavy doors of Hollywood. But it turned out that those doors weren't as heavy as I thought because that gentleman I was speaking with was none other than David Milch — creator, writer, and producer of *NYPD Blue*. I was stunned, knowing how many actors and writers would pay to have a meeting with him. David is a genius, and he was talking to *me*!

After he told me who he was, he added that he hadn't seen me on television in many years and asked what I was currently doing.

"You mean besides BOTOX?"

David laughed. Without going into great detail, I simply said that I was just getting back on my feet, recovering from spinal cord surgery. He smiled and asked me if I would like to be in a television series on HBO. At first I thought I had heard him wrong, but he went on to explain that he had been contracted to develop a new Western series called *Deadwood*. He handed me his phone number, written on an antidepressant advertisement the pharmacist handed to him. I was so excited I almost forgot to get the BOTOX! Worried that I had lost track of time, I glanced up at the clock on the wall. Oddly, it was only 9:45 a.m. I mentioned that their clock was an hour off, that it had to be 10:45, but the pharmacist assured me that the time was correct.

To this day, I don't understand how it happened. Every clock that I looked at that morning registered an hour later in my mind, including the one on my cell phone. It was as if Archangel Michael had gotten me to the pharmacy early enough to cross paths with David Milch. When I went up to Leo's office, not only was I early, but I was also thrilled. I told Leo the whole story and showed him the antidepressant ad with David's phone number on it. I got my six painful shots of BOTOX and was walking on air as I left the doctor's office.

I drove home to Laguna Beach and told Gloria about my amazing morning! I felt like Lana Turner being discovered in Schwab's, only I was Geri Jewell, being rediscovered in Horton & Converse Pharmacy.

I didn't call David Milch immediately, so as not to appear desperate. I waited about a week before I placed the call. I did feel a little apprehensive and fought fears that he would not remember me when I called him. I had been played so many times over the years that I half expected him not even to take my call. To my delight, he took my call. He invited me to his office at Paramount Studios to have lunch with him and his team of writers to discuss the character development of a role that would be created for me on *Deadwood*. The lunch was another surreal experience, instilling a sense of hope for reigniting the flame of my career.

April 16, 2002, was a magical day that made up for the day before, when I paid my taxes and found myself financially back at square one again. Being back on the Paramount lot brought back all the fond memories I had of when I met Anson Williams and had lunch with him in the commissary. I had come full circle and was about to embark on a new beginning. My greatest challenge was letting go of my fear of the past. Old fears *can* sabotage new opportunities. Even faced with the miraculous presence of David Milch holding my hand and promising me a gift, I still had to believe that I was worthy of receiving it.

After lunch, David walked me to my car. I was excited and couldn't even find the words to express my gratitude. Before seeing me off the lot, he told me that he wanted me to forget all that was discussed at lunch in reference to my character. He paused, giving me a brief moment of guarded disappointment. Smiling, he continued that he instead wanted me to create my character as I imagined her. He asked me to write out her life story so he could understand my perception of who this character was meant to be. In the past, my own publisher had no confidence that I was capable of writing my autobiography, and now David was asking me to write my character's autobiography. David's desire to understand the depth of my ability was a level of respect that meant more to me than he could ever know.

He gave me $1,500 in cash, telling me to consider it an advance, and that he was serious about working with me. He also gave me a book to read — *Deadwood: The Golden Years* by Watson Parker — about the black hills of Deadwood in 1876. I drove back to Laguna and read the book in one sitting. I then scoured the internet for anything about the history of Deadwood, South Dakota. I read stories about Calamity Jane, Wild Bill

Hickok, Buffalo Bill Cody, and many other stories about the Civil War and the years that followed. I also discovered that cerebral palsy was not even officially diagnosed until 1921. I realized that whatever I wrote was going to be strictly from my imagination about how someone like me could have existed and survived in such a brutally harsh time in history.

It took me about a week to finish all of my research and write a backstory about the character I helped to create, and initially named Crazy Kate. I faxed it to David's office at Paramount and was shocked when he called me an hour later, telling me how much he loved my writing. There were only a few minor details that he felt would be problematic, but overall he was very impressed with my own vision of the character. However, he wasn't completely crazy about the name Crazy Kate and wanted my character's name to be Jewel. Although it was eerily like "Cousin Geri" on *The Facts of Life*, I accepted it as an omen that I was indeed beginning a new cycle in life, playing another role that was linked to my real name.

When I received the script for the pilot episode of *Deadwood*, I was shocked again. I honestly thought it was going to be a warm, fuzzy Western like *Gunsmoke*, and that my character was going to be along the lines of Miss Kitty. I had been out of the loop with the entertainment industry for so long that I was out of touch with how much it had changed and what kind of entertainment HBO was now producing. Had I done my homework in exploring the programming HBO was famous for, I would have known that *Deadwood* was not going to have a "Happy Trails" kind of appeal, but more like, "Get off your cocksucking high horse, or I'll cut your fuckin' balls off!" This wasn't network TV, it was HBO . . . and David Milch was a brilliant combination of network and cable, creating a once-in-a-lifetime kind of series that I am truly honored to have been a part of.

I was still living with my sister and collecting disability when we filmed the pilot. There was no need to rush back to L.A. or get off disability until we all knew for sure that the pilot was going to be picked up as an ongoing series by HBO. As with most pilots, it was a long, arduous process for everyone, but when it was finally in the can, ready for airing, David couldn't have been happier. He called me to invite me to have lunch with him at his office so we could watch the pilot together. "You remember where my office is, right?" I said I did, but was confused when he added it was really close to "our pharmacy." He gave me the address, which did not match the address of Paramount Studios, the only office that I had ever been to. Instead of clarifying my confusion on the phone, I said nothing, for fear of appearing stupid. It turned out he was mistaken about me ever being at the office in question.

Letting old fears interfere with new opportunities is a dangerous formula and can result in situations that could have been avoided in the first place. To make sure I wouldn't get lost trying to find his "other" office, I relied on MapQuest. I got an early head start from Laguna and was so excited about seeing the pilot with David. I followed the MapQuest directions, but they ended up taking me to a rundown mini-mall, where no one spoke English. I was already 15 minutes late, so I called David from my cell phone, asking him where his office was. I told him that I was in the parking lot, but that everyone I tried to speak to didn't know English. "Geri, don't tell me you went to East L.A."

"Okay, I won't tell you that . . . but I think I did."

"I told you it was near our pharmacy." Then his secretary came on the line, telling me not to be upset, that I wasn't the first person to have done that, especially if I used MapQuest. She told me to make sure my windows were closed, my doors locked, and to return to Olympic Boulevard heading toward Santa Monica. I arrived at David's office almost an hour and a half late. I felt like a complete moron, never had lunch, didn't view the pilot, and wanted to cry.

It ended up being a very short meeting, and it was awkward for everyone. David introduced me to the other executive producer, Gregg Fienberg, and one of the directors, Davis Guggenheim. I had wandered in almost 90 minutes late after he'd told them how wonderful I was, which probably didn't make him look very good. When he offered me bottled water, I was so flustered and frustrated that I had an involuntary movement and drenched him with it. On the way out the door he asked me for my parking stub, saying that at least he could validate my parking. When it was stamped with the cartoon character, Wile E. Coyote, David smiled and said, "You are indeed, the Wile E. Coyote." I knew my cartoons, and I knew what he was implying, but all things considered, I couldn't really argue the perception in my own mind.

He held my hand as he had done before and walked me to my car. Then he took notice of my left foot. "What's the matter with your foot?" I was walking very poorly, and in tremendous pain because I had fallen the day before and broken my baby toe. I was absolutely paranoid of telling him that I fell and broke my toe! I mean he already thought I was Wile E. Coyote's cousin . . . how much more could David tolerate? I just laughed and reminded him that I had CP, that I have always kind of dragged my left leg, and it was strange that he hadn't noticed it until that afternoon. When I drove back to Laguna, I cried all the way home and hoped against all odds that I had not ruined the opportunity of a lifetime.

I was ecstatic when David agreed to rent an apartment for me at the Oakwood in 2003. I welcomed being back in L.A. and living on my own as a working actress. He paid for my moving costs, and by all appearances, it looked as though I was going to finally be able to be independent again based on how successful *Deadwood* could be. However, he did stress to me at this point that my character was going to develop slowly. I only understood that to mean that I would be on contract longer.

I had halted all disability payments, and eventually even told Richard that he didn't have to pay my health insurance any longer, that by working on a Screen Actors Guild show, I qualified for the Producer's Healthcare Plan. It may have been a case of counting my chickens before they hatched, but I hated being on disability and feared getting in trouble again like I did in 1984 when I got the bill for $9,999.99. I also wanted to be free of any ties to or guilt about Richard.

As it was, because *Deadwood* was such a huge show, there were only a few primary actors who were on contract with HBO. I was not one of them. I was a day player, and therefore every day that I did not film, I was not paid. But Milch was paying for my apartment and utilities, so I was still being compensated on an ongoing basis. I was grateful that I did enough episodes of *Deadwood* to keep my health insurance active. I was fine with the conditions and hoped that as the series continued, I would be able to prove my value to HBO and be offered more security down the road.

Interestingly, in the next episode that I filmed of *Deadwood*, "Deep Water," Milch had incorporated dragging my left leg into the script. In the scene, I carry a pot of coffee over to Al Swearengen (Ian McShane) and dutifully pour him a cup. Swearengen takes notice of my leg and comments, "When are you going to stop draggin' that fuckin' left leg!" I knew immediately why the line was written and so I walked into the scene as if I still had a broken toe. I refused to clarify the issue with Milch, and just continued dragging my leg for the next several episodes. However, it dawned on me that if I didn't think of something really creative, and if *Deadwood* was a huge success, then I could possibly find myself dragging my fuckin' left leg for a long time.

Even though I was now working on *Deadwood*, I felt intuitively that something had changed between David and me for whatever reason. Maybe I was projecting my own insecurities about being perceived as "not able," but I felt like David didn't see me the same way after I was 90 minutes late for our lunch that day. The last thing I wanted was to be perceived as problematic. Also, because my character was only used sporadically, I couldn't help but remember what had happened with *Facts* and worried that I might find myself dragging my leg all the way to the unemployment line. Whether my fears were real or not, I wanted to work and felt intuitively I had to do something to keep Jewel interesting. I had to take a risk in order to bring about change and growth to my character. I told him I had a brilliant idea, and would he be open to it?

Between scenes, we sat down on the stairs in the Gem Saloon. I gingerly explained that dragging my leg might not be in my best interest or in the best interest of the character. "So what is your brilliant idea?" I told him that I thought Doc Cochran (played by Brad Dourif) should build Jewel a leg brace like the kind some soldiers wore after being injured in the Civil War. I thought it would be a powerful storyline, and then I wouldn't have to drag the leg anymore. David's face lit up, and it was as though I'd rekindled his initial reaction to me in the pharmacy.

David graced me with a script that was written just for me and was called "Jewel's Boot Is Made for Walking." In this episode, he had incorporated my leg brace idea. There was a very powerful scene when Jewel walks through the muddy main street of Deadwood to show Doc Cochran a book that illustrates different leg braces. Jewel is met with the ridicule that I remembered from when I was a kid. She then slips in the mud and realizes that no one is going to help her up. My favorite part of that scene is when Jewel gets up by herself and wipes her brow with dignity. Director Steve Shill was the one who suggested I do that, and it was so powerful on many levels.

The next episode, "Sold Under Sin," continued the story of Doc bringing Jewel her new leg brace. A part of the season finale was a tear-jerking dance scene that will always have a special place in my heart. At that time, in 2004, I still had not completely healed from the neck surgery. Even BOTOX couldn't take away the excruciating muscle spasms I was still experiencing from time to time. I wasn't prescribed anything additional for pain for the obvious reason of addiction. I was on my way back up, but I was not quite out of the woods yet.

When we filmed that dance scene, it was around 1:30 in the morning. I had been on set since 10 a.m. With most shoots, the majority of the time is spent waiting. That scene kept being pushed back. By the time they were ready to shoot, I was in extreme pain. At that hour in Santa Clarita, the high desert of southern California, it was freezing. I was exhausted, and the muscle spasms would not quit. Everyone on the set was concerned and supportive. They even suggested that we do the scene the following day. However, I stubbornly refused because I didn't want to send the message that I was a wimp. The crew set up heat lamps to keep me warm, covered me with warm blankets between takes, and gave me hot tea and vitamins.

Brad Dourif couldn't have been more patient and wonderful. He knew I was in agonizing pain, and the only way we could make that scene work was if he literally carried me through it. Even though the scene was played as Jewel teaching the Doc to dance, Brad actually lifted me and moved me, knowing I couldn't do the steps myself. I've had several die-hard *Deadwood* fans tell me that the dance scene between Doc Cochran and Jewel was their favorite *Deadwood* scene of all time. It was the last scene of the first season finale, and I always felt that when the character Al Swearengen gazed down at me from the top of the stairs, symbolically, it was Milch looking at me, wondering what this Wile E. Coyote was going to do next. I never did tell him about my broken toe — he won't know about it until he reads this book.

Working on *Deadwood* was an amazing experience, and there was not one cast or crew member who I didn't have respect for. Of course, I was closer to those I actually had scenes with, like Ian McShane, W. Earl Brown, Brad Dourif, and Paula Malcomson. Everyone was so supportive of me. I even opened for Earl's rock band one evening. McShane was a sweetheart, and we shared much laughter when we weren't on the set. Keone Young, Leon Rippy, Gerald McRaney, and Jim Beaver were like my extended family. Every single one of us felt passionately about *Deadwood* and really cared about each other.

I will never forget what David Milch did for me during a period in my life when my self-esteem was at an all-time low. He put me back on the map and challenged me to continue to fight and go after my dreams. I also had the chance to rebuild my perseverance and determination, which had taken a beating. Other people would have shown me the door when I was an hour and a half late for lunch, but even though David probably second-guessed himself, he still believed in me, allowing me to be a part of a groundbreaking series, and to collaborate alongside one of the most talented ensemble casts I have ever worked with.

So many wonderful things came out of *Deadwood*. I appeared on *The Young and the Restless* and got the role of Lolly in the independent film *Night of the White Pants*, where I got to work with Tom Wilkinson, Nick Stahl, and Selma Blair. I also had a wonderful guest star role on the Lifetime series *Strong Medicine*. None of these roles would have come along had David not cast me on *Deadwood*. David even paid for me to attend the Emmys one year, which I had never been to before.

I miss *Deadwood*, and like everyone else, I was heartbroken when it was canceled. In the final season, my name was put forth to be considered for nomination for Best Guest Actress in a Dramatic Series. I didn't get enough votes to get an actual nomination, but the fact that I was even submitted was an amazing victory in itself.

I will never forget David Milch and A. C. Lyles, another *Deadwood* producer, flying up to Santa Rosa to attend a fundraising dinner in my honor. I was presented with the 2005 Independent Living Legacy Award. Not only did David Milch speak on my behalf, but he generously raffled off a walk-on role on *Deadwood*. Blaine Moss and his wife, Sandy, were also there for the event, as well as my old friend Kathy Buckley, who Milch offered to fly home with him and A.C. in his private plane. I think Kathy still has a one-way ticket left from Santa Rosa to L.A.

John Rizzo, who did my makeup on *Deadwood*, had remained a good friend of mine. He never made Jewel glamorous like Alma Garrett, but he did make my teeth look rotten and my skin look filthy (gee thanks, John). Even though Jewel was the "fuckin' gimp," she had a lot of moxie and a spirit about her that even inspired me. On more than one occasion, when faced with a challenge, I've asked myself, "What would Jewel do?" She put up with a lot of bullshit and scrubbed a lot of blood off the floors, but no one was ever going to tell her she couldn't dance! She danced as if she were as nimble as a forest creature.

Unfortunately, not everything was rosy during my time on *Deadwood*. Knowing how my dad's idol was John Wayne, I wanted to invite him to the set of *Deadwood* and introduce him to David Milch and the rest of the cast and crew, but sadly my dad was dying of cancer during that time, and it never happened. My dad died on Good Friday in 2006. Unfortunately, by that point in time, he had also alienated all of us kids, but I still took him out to dinner for his birthday two weeks earlier, and we had a wonderful time together. We both knew that he didn't have long to live, and he had finally realized all the time that had been wasted by his false pride.

I will always have memories of Dad that make me smile. I laugh recalling that Dad always had "sticky fingers." As I was paying for our dinner that day, I saw him pick up the bowl of mints on the counter and dump the entire contents into his jacket pocket. When he realized that I had seen him do it, he rolled his eyes and put two mints back in the bowl. Long after my father's death, I found some of those mints lying on the floor of my car; they had fallen out of his pocket. It was a sweet reminder of my dad and the follies of his life.

I was still able to give him one last gift that day by telling him from the bottom of my heart how much I loved him. I reminded him of all the good things that he did, like all the times he would take Gloria and me to the beach, and bike riding, always stopping for ice cream. Or the time in high school when I was so depressed because I never got to go on a real date like Gloria. Dad tried to cheer me up by playfully asking me to go on a date with him. He took me to see *Billy Jack*, and afterward took me to the local bar and actually played a game of shuffleboard with me.

I also recalled the few times he took the train from Fullerton to Los Angeles just to spend the day with me. I'd pick him up in downtown L.A. and we'd go to lunch together, come back to my apartment, play a couple games of Scrabble, and then I'd take him back to the train station in the evening. They were special days with my dad that I loved and cherished, even if he did kick my ass in Scrabble from time to time.

Even though later in life my dad made it difficult to get close to him, he was a good father. When you look at the high statistics of how many fathers leave when they have a child with a disability, I am grateful my dad didn't. He loved me and accepted me. When I was in drug rehab in 1999, Gloria brought him to see me on Christmas Eve. He brought a basket full of cookies and told me to share them with the other patients who didn't have family. Even though I was lost and didn't feel loved by my husband, my dad came to see me, and I knew he loved me enough just to be there when I felt so utterly alone.

The last time I saw my dad was the day before he died. I think for the first time I saw something different when I looked at him. I had spent so many years trying to be close to him, playing his games, trying to make him proud, and for the first time as I stood over him, it wasn't me looking for his approval — instead he was seeking mine. His speech was garbled as the cancer had spread to his mouth. He tried to say "I love you" several times, until I finally understood what he was saying. If he hadn't been so sick, I am sure he would have rolled his eyes after the third time I asked him to repeat himself.

The year 2006 marked the end of *Deadwood*, the passing of my father, and the beginning of new challenges as well as the continuation of old ones. Persons with disabilities account for two percent of employees in the entertainment industry. That is why the Tri-Union I AM PWD (Inclusion in the Arts & Media of People With Disabilities) Campaign was created in 2008, led by Robert David Hall of the television series *CSI*. All the unions, including AFTRA, SAG, and Equity, came onboard to support the movement of equal opportunity for employment of qualified people with disabilities in front of the camera as well as behind it. Has Hollywood made progress? Well, there is a new awareness that a huge problem exists today, and that Hollywood really needs to continue to step up to the plate and hire more *qualified* people with disabilities.

When you look at all that I have accomplished as an actress, it would be shocking to know that since 2006 I have had a total of two auditions. When *Deadwood* ended, so did my ability to get work in Hollywood. The only difference between my experience in 2006 and the similar one in 1984, when I was out of a job and faced with the same prejudices and lack of opportunity, is that now I am more mature and my faith is solid.

I think that what life has taught me is the utmost importance of self-respect. I am not ashamed of being who I really am. Perhaps if I had not been so afraid of being gay early on, and had not associated so much trauma with my sexuality, I could have avoided a lot of unnecessary pain. For my entire life, I have tried to walk "straight," in one way or another, so that I would be embraced by society. I missed the mark time and again.

I have since come to understand that the real disabilities in life are those that feed into hypocrisy, false pride, prejudice, and hatred. The challenge for all of us is to overcome the negativity that can destroy our dreams and belittle our faith. We need to believe in ourselves even when others don't believe in us, because, ultimately, what we believe about ourselves is what is reflected back to us and everyone else.

I have also learned that no matter how bad things are, they will get better. I refuse to undermine my own journey by buying a ticket to ride the "I Can't" train to Defeat. Each morning, I wake up knowing that with each effort I make toward moving forward, I will.

I am so blessed with all the wonderful friends I have, and also for having my sister who has always been there for me no matter what. I am grateful for every opportunity I've been given to live life to its fullest. Each breath we take is a celebration. I believe that all of us are the sum total of what we value. For me, that is love, forgiveness, and honesty. I also value taking risks in life — it is the risk takers who realize their dreams.

Years ago, when I was 12, Carol Burnett wrote in one of her letters to me, "There is no guarantee that you will become a professional comedienne, but you will never know unless you try." I *have* tried, I have achieved more than most people could ever dream of. My legacy is that anything is possible if there is enough will behind it.

My mom used to tell me, "Be careful what you wish for, because you just might get it." She couldn't have been more right.

The thing I value above all else is my sense of humor, and I always urge people to never lose theirs. Mine has gotten me through so much in my life and allowed me to get past many obstacles. If you've lost your sense of humor, keep looking for it until you find it. After all, you must have left it somewhere. Laughter is a wonderful, healing tonic that prevents us from becoming spiritually brittle and broken from the hardships we endure.

Go after your dreams, and never underestimate the power of the human spirit.

THANK YOU

A special thank-you to each of you who contributed to helping us to stay on course to finish this book. Without your unwavering encouragement or the lending of your services, we couldn't have made the book what it is.

Sunny Bak
Elayne Boosler
Crissy Boylan
Lynne Braiman
Kathy Buckley
David Caron
Erin Creasey
Ruth Cobb
James Cummins
Anna Marie Patty Duke
Suzanne Ensch
Tom Lacy
Norman Lear
Jen Hale
Gloria Jewell
Penny Landau
Mary Latini
Kathy Fields Lander

Ian McShane
Rev. James Mellon
David Milch
Lynn Nichelson
Sharon O'Hara
Susan Olsen
Emily Schultz
Cynthia Sharvelle
Denise Silberman
L. Jane Thomley
Lily Tomlin
Josie Varga
Simon Ware
Rev. Diane Wolcott Watson
Anson Williams
Steve Wishnoff
Jeff Wisot
David Zimmerman

One of the most difficult aspects of writing a memoir is to pick and choose what stories to tell. I didn't have enough pages to include everyone who has touched my life and gave me love and support along the way. I am grateful for each and every one of you, and if I somehow missed you below, know that there is an even longer list in my heart eternally. Love to you all.

Corey Allen
Loreen Arbus
Andy Arias
Bill Austin
Sue Babin
Sue Beekman
Steve Bennett
Cheryl Booth
Dr. Jeff Brandon
Kaleta Brown
Rich Brown
Al Burton
Rory Carmody
Lisa Whelchel Cauble
Joseph Disante
Bonny Dore
Christina Engelhardt
Emily Ennis
Jeanne Elfant Festa
Fern Field
Bud Friedman
Tobias Forrest
S.A.G. Foundation
Linda Fulton
The Actors Fund
Lindsey Gatt
Ann Gibbs
Michael Lee Gogin
Marc Goldman
Lynda Jean Groh
Dr. Jerry Hershey
Michael Jacobs
Laurie Jacobson
Keith Jennings

David Jewell
Fred Jewell
Tony Benge Johnson
Annie Keating
Natoma Keir
Joel Kimmel
Kelli McDowell
Jo Ann Maher
Bobby Marchesso
Joe Everett Michaels
Danny Mora
Jeffrey Morgan
Jamie Morris
Frank Nelson Fund
Susan Ortolano
Barbara Pearl
Dr. Ann L. Peters
Diana Polsky
Charlotte Rae
Julie Ann Ream
Tom Ritter
Randy Rogers
Mitzi Shore
Tari Hartman Squire
Michael Steiner
Stanzi Stokes
Jason Stuart
Amy Talkington
Bud Thune
Jim Troesh
Alex Valdez
Christopher Voelker
Stuart Wolpart

GERI JEWELL has enjoyed a thriving career now spanning over three decades. She has been the recipient of many awards, including the 2005 Independent Living Legacy Award and the 2006 Victory Award. She lives in Los Angeles, California.

TED NICHELSON, a native of Normal, Illinois, is also the author of *Love to Love You Bradys* with Susan Olsen and Lisa Sutton. He earned degrees in harp performance from Ball State University (DA), University of Michigan (MM), Illinois Wesleyan University (BA), and a degree in musicology from Illinois State University. Dr. Nichelson works full-time as a freelance harpist in Hollywood, California, where he serves Los Angeles County and surrounding areas. He is also employed as a property manager, and as a teacher for the Beverly Hills Unified School District. In 2007, Dr. Nichelson was presented the "Pioneer Hall of Fame" award from his alma mater, University High School.